Front cover photograph of Captain Walter Jackinsky Jr., May 2004, by J.R.B. Pels.

Back cover photograph of the M/V *E.L. Bartlett*
from the Jackinsky family collection.

As noted within, *Any Tonnage, Any Ocean* is drawn primarily from Walter
Jackinsky's recollections of events in his long and active life. Any factual errors
in the book are more likely to be misinterpretations by the compiler than lapses in
the captain's encyclopedic memory. One matter of mutual concern is the spelling
of people's names. In some cases we have found no records to check against;
in other cases the records disagree among themselves. Hardscratch Press takes
responsibility for any such errors and would appreciate hearing about them.

Printed in the United States of America.

First printed September 2004.
Hardscratch Press, 2358 Banbury Place, Walnut Creek, California 94598.
Library of Congress Control Number: 2004107640
ISBN: 0-9678989-5-1

Cataloging-In-Publication Data

Any tonnage, any ocean : conversations with a resolute Alaskan : Captain Walter
Jackinsky of Ninilchik, 34-year veteran of the Alaska Marine Highway System /
compiled by Jacquelin Benson Pels.

p. cm.

ISBN 0-9678989-5-1
   1. Jackinsky, Walter, 1916- . 2. Jackinsky family. 3. Ship captains – Alaska
– Biography. 4. Ninilchik (Alaska) – Biography. 5. Ninilchik (Alaska) – Social
life and customs. 6. Alaska Marine Highway System. I. Pels, Jacquelin Ruth
Benson, 1937- . II. Jackinsky, Walter, 1916-

F910.7.J23A69 2004
979.8/3—dc20

9 8 7 6 5 4 3 2 1

In loving memory of my father, who named me,
and my stepfather, who urged me on.

—J.B.P.

For my children.

—W.W.J.

ANY TONNAGE, ANY OCEAN

CONVERSATIONS *with a* RESOLUTE ALASKAN

COMPILED BY

Jacquelin Benson Pels

A HARDSCRATCH PRESS BOOK

C O N

...TENTS

INTRODUCTION
THE SALMON TSAR

Via e-mail, May 25, 2003: By the way, Dad would like to meet you. Do you have time to stop on your way to Homer?

In the expectant light of a late spring evening in Alaska, McKibben Jackinsky and I threaded our way through stands of gray-green birch trees to her father's homestead cabin near Ninilchik. Most of the original evergreens are gone now, she told me, killed by a spruce bark beetle that is devastating the Kenai Peninsula. At one turn we yielded the path to a contemplative cow moose and twin calves.

McKibben knocked at the screen door, a voice with a smile in it called, "Come in!" and we were enfolded in the fragrance of frying potatoes and onions.

The next few minutes are a blur. Somehow, even as introductions proceeded, I found myself in charge of the potato pan while another cast-iron skillet went on the gas stove and four thick salmon steaks appeared from nowhere. "You're staying," said the smiling voice in what I took to be a question. My attempt at "Oh, I couldn't . . ." impressed no one. "You're staying," he said again. He drizzled olive oil into the second skillet, covered the browned potato and onion slices with a lid after adding a little water from a coffee mug, lowered the steaks into the hot oil, and a three-way, two-hour conversation began.

My first impression, after the warm welcome, was that even beyond the ready smile 87-year-old Walter Jackinsky bore a great resemblance to my late stepfather, Ralph Soberg, the man who raised my sister and me: Narrowed blue gaze of a northern latitude seafarer. Stubborn jaw. Strong hands and forearms that had spent more time outdoors than in. Trace of a European accent (Walter's first language was Russian, Ralph's Norwegian). And a direct manner

9

of speaking that nevertheless seemed to be holding in reserve as much as it offered.

With the potatoes and the salmon, which Walter had caught that afternoon at Deep Creek, five miles to the south, we had a salad of the season's first fiddleheads, also harvested by the chef. Much of the conversation was about mutual acquaintances. Walter had known my mother and stepfather in the 1940s and '50s, when Ralph was overseeing construction of the highway that runs past the Jackinsky place to its end in Homer. Along with the familiar affability I sensed more than a little of Ralph's singlemindedness in Walter. I knew something of Ninilchik's rich history and hoped to hear about Walter's own life. But he deflected my few questions with "Has McKibben told you about the time she . . . ," and eventually I had to finish my long day's drive.

A glance at a plaque on the wall as I left told me a little more. "So, your dad served aboard Alaska ferries," I said to McKibben the next time we happened to talk. "Yes," she said, "for 34 years. He's proud of his master mariner's license—any tonnage, any ocean."

"Any tonnage, any ocean," I repeated. "That's a book title, McKibben!"

Walter Jackinsky's writer daughter and I first met when she reviewed an earlier memoir from Hardscratch Press. She had since seen me through two more such projects, so she recognized the signs. With her encouragement, Walter agreed to take a couple of weeks off during my next trip to the Kenai, September 2003, to chat with a homesick Alaskan. I left there with 22 audiotapes and a case of Ninilchik salmon. Thanks to all the helpful people listed herein, I'll be going back with a book.

Jackie Pels
Hardscratch Press
Walnut Creek, Calif.
May 2004

Note: As its subtitle indicates, *Any Tonnage, Any Ocean* is a personal account of the long and active life (thus far) of Captain Walter Jackinsky Jr. It is by no means a definitive history of Ninilchik, or the Alaska Marine Highway System, or even the

Jackinsky family. Those have been well served in various of the books listed as Resources. Most of the stories here are drawn from Walter's recollections of 20 or 30 or 70 years ago and are told from his perspective. Several members of his crew lined up to reminisce about the captain for Chapter 4, "Tales of the 'Blue Canoes.'" The Introduction and the final chapter, "Ninilchik, 2003," are based on my own impressions. And threaded throughout are pieces by other writers generously lent for this book, some previously published, some not.

For my own love affair with the Alaska Marine Highway System I have my parents to thank. They lived from the mid-1960s in Seattle but took the Alaska ferry "home" at least once a year. As a child I had traveled Outside, as Alaskans say, by ship, but all my trips since had been by plane.

Toward the end of Ralph's life, when he was writing the books that launched Hardscratch Press, he arranged for me to make the trip to Skagway and back with my mother, Ruth, just to give her a week in the Alaskan surroundings she craved. Although he reserved a four-berth stateroom, so neither of us would have to clamber into an upper bunk, I had read Ellen Searby's *Alaska's Inside Passage Traveler* and wanted to try my sleeping bag on the solarium deck. The first dawn I woke to a crackling sound and thought drowsily, my eyes still closed, "Oh, good—Jill has started the fire," imagining that a friend and I were on one of our group camping trips in Northern California. I opened my eyes to see the huge U.S. flag that the purser had just raised for the day, snapping in a brisk wind over the blue and white wake of the ship. And I *was* on a camping trip. A magical seven-day campout with kindred spirits and occasional homemade music and an ever-changing vista, more glorious than I could have remembered. (And, except for Jill's sourdough specialties baked over the fire, better food!)

The ferries are coastal Alaska's bus line, and every stop was an adventure. I'm sure there's much to be said for travel by luxury liner, but like Walter I'll take the ferry ride. I commend it to you, along with Captain Jackinsky's story.

11

Aerial view of the M/V Malaspina *in Southeast Alaska,* © *Charles (Buddy) Ferguson,* *www.crfimages.com. Used by permission.*

THE EXHIBITION RUN
1

When the sleek new ferry M/V Malaspina tied up at Anchorage on the rainy morning of June 14, 1963, able-bodied seaman Walter Jackinsky threw the first line ashore and then scanned the welcoming crowd for his family. Alice Jackinsky had driven 200 miles from their home village of Ninilchik with daughters Autumn and Risa and son Shawn, who clutched Father's Day gifts for the man they hadn't seen in five months.

A couple of honorary seamen were along for the ride. The state public works commissioner, Dick Downing, and Walt Welch, a radio station executive from Juneau, had obtained crewman's working papers so they could make at least part of the voyage—no passengers were permitted on that exhibition run. But 47-year-old AB Walter Jackinsky was signed on in earnest. More than three decades later he retired as senior captain of the Alaska Marine Highway System with an honorary title of his own: Commodore of the Fleet.

"I heard about that [seaman's] job, and I *wanted* it," Walter Jackinsky says in 2003. His smile is genial and his blue eyes retain their usual bright hint of mischief, but there is no mistaking the intensity in his voice even after 40 years.

"In a year I got my mate's license. I became a mate. In another year I got my inland master's license. But they had quite a few masters. I had to wait a while. I went for another license, for 'unlimited'—an ocean license. High as you can go. I got that, and they said, 'OK, you'll get a ship.' But it took a while, close to 10 years, to get a master's job. . . .

"Some of the mates didn't want to go any higher than being a mate. They didn't want the responsibility. I wanted it all! I sent letters to the main office: 'When is my turn going to come? Look at

13

the letters of recommendation I have!' I sent at least six different letters from different captains and finally they said, 'OK, your turn's coming up.'"

His first assignment as master was alternating with Captain Richard Hofstad on the *LeConte* (Alaskans call it the LeCon'tee), a brand new ship. "The run was all Southeast—Juneau or Auke Bay, Haines, Skagway, Hoonah, Sitka, Angoon, Kake, Petersburg. I made the original run into Pelican. The governor's wife, Bella Hammond, was on that run, and the state commissioner's wife, Alice Harris. Pelican had been waiting for that run. We had a special trip there once a month. I don't know whether they're doing it now, but that's what we did.

"That was my ship till they sent me to Prince William Sound. They said, 'The captain on the *Bartlett* wants to be relieved for about six weeks. Can you go up there and relieve him?' I said sure. So they put someone else in my place on the *LeConte* and I went up there for six weeks. Then they said, 'Can you stay a year?' [laughing] Yeah! And the crew wanted me bad—they said, 'That guy is so mean with us. Why don't you get to stay here? Let's make a petition.' They made a petition and they all signed it asking that I stay on the *Bartlett*. So I stayed the year and that was it. They forgot all about us and I ended up staying 17 years.

"I liked it. I liked the *Bartlett*. It was away from home, from Juneau, but it was closer to my country here."

NINILCHIK, 1851
2

*There are signs that this beautiful spot on Alaska's
Kenai Peninsula was favored by early inhabitants who built their*
barabaras *among the forests. However, by the time the Russian American
Company was attracted to the area in the early 1800s, those earlier settlers
had moved on, leaving little in their wake except for the scattered indenta-
tions in the ground that were once their homes.*

*In the 1820s, the administrators of the Russian American Company
. . . decided to establish retirement settlements. The requirements to gain
permission to live in these communities included:*

*— Marriage to a Creole or Native American woman and a desire to
stay in Alaska because of ill health or old age, having become accustomed to
the climate or lifestyle, or because the employee had been away from Russia
so long that no close relatives remained there;*

— Submission of a formal petition for colonial citizenship; and

*— The removal of the employee from the census rolls of his home area
in Russia.*

In return, the Russian American Company would:

*— Construct houses for these settlers and provide them with necessary
tools, livestock, seeds and provisions for the first year;*

*— Consider the settlers' children Creoles and acceptable to work for the
company;*

*— Permit the settlers to sell any surplus produce to the company at
free-market prices;*

*— Ensure that the residents of these retirement settlements did not
burden Natives living in the area; and*

*— Extend the rights of colonial citizenship to Creoles who had chosen
an occupation and desired to stay in Alaska. . . .*

From "The Settling of Ninilchik," in Chainik Keepeet: The
Teakettle Is Boiling, *a collection of oral histories published by
Ninilchik Native Descendants, Vol. I, Issue 1, Winter 2003.*

Ninilchik village, looking west across Cook Inlet to Mount Redoubt on the Alaska Peninsula, winter 1949. Photo courtesy of Earl Simonds.

When Walter Wallace Jackinsky says "my country here" he means the Kenai Peninsula in Southcentral Alaska and in particular Ninilchik, established more than 150 years ago at the mouth of the river of the same name, which winds through the village on its way to Cook Inlet.

His great-grandmother Anna Oskolkov Astrogin was one of Ninilchik's original "Creole" colonists, Creole being the term for families of Russian and Alaska Native lineage. Accompanied by four sons from her first marriage, Anna arrived in the settlement in 1851 from Sitka with her second husband, Leontii Astrogin. The youngest son, Grigorii Oskolkov, married Matrona Balashoff from English Bay, now called Nanwalek, at the tip of the Kenai Peninsula. (Nowadays the Russian names are more often Anglicized: Leonty, Gregory, Oskolkoff. Some records spell the family name Ostrogin.) Family history has it that as a girl Matrona made the perilous voyage to English Bay from her family's home in Kodiak in a *baidarka*, a skin-covered craft similar to a kayak. She and Gregorii had 17 children; Walter's mother, Mary Oskolkoff, the third eldest, was born April 13, 1897.

Walter counts himself "five-eighths Russian and three-eighths Alutiiq," as the proud Native strand in Ninilchik's history is known. Alutiiq, plural Alutiit, has become the accepted designation for the Native people of Southcentral Alaska misnamed "Aleut" by early Russian arrivals. His father, Walter Jackinsky Sr., was born in 1892 in present-day Lithuania, then part of the Russian empire. Walter Sr. and Mary Oskolkoff both spoke Russian as their first language. Walter Jr., born May 19, 1916, and his brother Edward, 16 months older, spoke only Russian until they started school as first-graders.

"That's all we knew at home, and that's all my mother or my dad knew, was Russian. School was strictly in English. You couldn't say a word in Russian, or you got punished. It was hard. But it was harder for some. What made a difference in our family was, as we learned English we started speaking it more at home, and our parents were picking it up pretty fast from us. My dad got himself a dictionary, a Russian-American dictionary, and it didn't take him very long. My mother was picking it up, too. That made it easier for the younger kids."

Walter Jackinsky Sr. would have had some acquaintance with English before settling in Ninilchik. He had emigrated from Russia to the United States when he was a young teenager and lived for several years with relatives in Portland, Maine—"the Kamilavich family, a Polish family. I was there in 1969 to see some of them, and by gosh, they had grown up and some had gotten pretty old by then. I went across to visit them for a while, to know who they were. Good family."

Walter Sr. headed west with a friend and ended up in Alaska around 1910. "Alaska had some jobs—he was interested in Alaska—so he came here. After working for a while around Cordova, he came to Hope, Alaska. I think he spent the summer working at some of the gold mines there. My Uncle Alex was there, my mother's oldest brother, and some of the other Ninilchik men were there. They talked him into coming to Ninilchik. He came here, met my mother, and settled here. Ninilchik finally suited him."

Walter's mother, Mary, might still have been in school when Walter Sr. arrived. She was one of eight Oskolkoffs among the 20 students enrolled for the year 1911–12 in the old Russian school in the village. She and Walter Sr. were married Nov. 10, 1913. She was 16; he was 21. "My mother was born and raised and died in Ninilchik," Walter Jr. says. "She made one trip with Dad and that was to Seward—took a boat from Ninilchik to Seldovia, then Alaska Steam to Seward. Visited there for about a week and returned the same way. That was their honeymoon, and that was the extent of her travels."

Mary and Walter Sr.'s children attended Ninilchik's "new school." Built in 1913, it overlooked the village from the top of the steep hill where the Russian Orthodox Church of the Transfiguration of Our Lord still stands. Classes went to eighth grade when Walter began in 1922 and to ninth when he finished in 1931. By then two teachers were assigned to the school each year.

He recalls some of his teachers: Elizabeth Forker was "really strict—she'd slap your hands with a ruler." Bertha Stryker was "good—only a little strict." He recalls that Arnold Granville ("from Portland, Oregon, I believe") was teaching the year he graduated. For "Mrs. Nonini," L.L. Nonini, "we had a nickname—*Rapchik*, spruce hen. We liked her. And there was a Norwegian

Mary Oskolkoff Jackinsky, c. 1914. Jackinsky family photo.

Walter Jackinsky Sr. with Bertha Kvasnikoff and her son Dean.
Photo courtesy of Ninilchik Native Descendants.

lady, Inga Tornsvold. . . . She was easy to get along with, very gentle. She said, 'You boys should have some home ec.' She taught us a little about cooking and sewing, things like that. We were then in seventh or eighth grade. She and Mrs. Nonini shared the school quarters, and they had trouble keeping the place warm. We'd go over there after school sometimes, clean out their stove, you know, and she'd treat us to toasted cheese sandwiches and hot chocolate. We thought that was just the best."

We?

"My uncles Jack and Joe [Oskolkoff] were pretty close to my age. Jack was a little older, Joe was younger, maybe a year or so. Sargus Kvasnikoff was about my age. Bob Resoff. Charlie Resoff. Quite a few were in that same age group—we got along pretty good together. Nick Leman. He was in my class. There were four of us in the same class for seven, eight years: Nick Leman, Bob Resoff, myself and Claudia Kelly. We stayed in the same class until we finished ninth grade. The four of us graduated together."

Walter's impression is that the young teacher at the earlier turn-of-the-century school down in the village hadn't had much education himself, although he did his best. "My mother learned to read and write in Russian, and that's about it," Walter says. A generation later Mary Oskolkoff's daughters Margaret and Cora, Walter's next younger sisters, were the first in the family to graduate from college. Margaret, who was born in 1919, attended Seward High School across the peninsula, and Cora, born in 1921, went to a high school in Snohomish, Wash. Both graduated with degrees in education from the University of Alaska. Mary and Walter Sr.'s first daughter, Mauria, died as an infant in 1918.

Of the youngest siblings, Adolph Jackinsky died on his 16th birthday in 1940, when a small plane in which he was a passenger crashed not far from the village. George Jackinsky, born in 1927, returned to the Kenai Peninsula after attending college Outside (Alaskans' term for the "lower 48" states) and still lives on his Kasilof homestead. Barbara Jaklin was a toddler and Clara Linstrang only 19 days old when their mother died in 1932. By then Mary and Walter Sr. had divorced and Mary was remarried. Barbara and Clara both grew up elsewhere, and after Mary died George was

Ninilchik Territorial School, 1923-24. **Back row**, *from left: Maurice Panshin, George Cooper, Fred Kvasnikoff, Polly Crawford, Ollie Oskolkoff, Groonya Kvasnikoff, Martha Kelly, Juanita Leman, John Kelly, Bill Kvasnikoff.*

Middle row, *from left: Dora Kvasnikoff, Sargus Kvasnikoff, Nadia Kvasnikoff, Paraskovya Kvasnikoff, Isaac Cooper, Minnie Crawford.*

Front row, *from left: Alex Kvasnikoff, Ralph Cooper, Walter Jackinsky, Luba Matson, Claudia Kelly, Mary Kvasnikoff, Jack Oskolkoff, Edward Jackinsky.*
Photo courtesy of Ninilchik Native Descendants, with thanks to Mike Steik.

22

Alaska Public Schools

MONTHLY REPORT OF

(Pupil) *Walter Jackinsky*

School Year 19 25 and 19 26

Grade 3 _____ *Ninilchic* School

Studies, Etc.	1st Mo	2nd Mo	3rd Mo	4th Mo	5th Mo	6th Mo	7th Mo	8th Mo	9th Mo	Term Aver'ge
Reading										
Writing										
Spelling				E	E				E	
Arithmetic			E	E E		E E	E	E		
Grammar or Language										
Geography										
History										
Physiology										
Drawing										
General Av										
Deportment										
½ Days Abs.	0	0	0	0	0	0				
Times Tardy										

MARKING Scale: 100—Denotes Perfect; 95 to
99 Excellent; 90 to 94—Very Good; 80 to 89—
Medium; 70 to 79—Low; Under 70—Unsatis-
factory.

Promoted to
Grade _____

Elizabeth Forker

Teacher.

reared by Mary's mother. In age and circumstance Walter has been closest to brother Edward.

Chainik Keepeet, the Ninilchik oral history series, notes that with few exceptions the brothers' generation was the last to be delivered by "skilled and respected village midwives," and goes on to count other changes in Ninilchik over the years since the sale of Alaska to the United States in 1867: "Land that was shared became land that was owned. Catching of salmon for food became catching of salmon for sale. Rowing, sledding and walking were replaced by outboard engines, automobiles and airplanes. Garden vegetables stored in root cellars gave way to store-bought vegetables stored in refrigerators." But at least one tradition thrives. As in many other Alaskan communities, the Russian Orthodox Church has remained a focal point of life in Ninilchik. The current church on the hill was built around 1900. There the old ways continue. Walter and his daughter McKibben Autumn both were baptized as infants in the wooden baptismal tub made by Gregory Oskolkoff before the turn of the 19th century.

As is still the case, a visiting priest officiated at weddings, baptisms and funerals, Walter recalls. For regular services, "there wasn't usually a priest, but they had elders that did pretty good. My grandfather Gregory Oskolkoff was a *starosta* [the equivalent of a deacon, or church warden]. He was a very devout church person. And he was a sort of undertaker when there was a miscarriage. No one even knew where he buried them.

"My Uncle Alex went to Sitka to become a priest. He didn't finish his studies there but he was good at all that. My uncle next to him, Uncle Simeon [Walter pronounces the names the Russian way: Grigo'ry, Simyo'n], was good, too. They called him Little Simeon. Big Simeon was Simeon Kvasnikoff. He was related, maybe a cousin. A little younger than my grandfather. . . ."

Simeon Oskolkoff's son Simeon Jr., Walter Jr.'s first cousin, is a Russian Orthodox priest now retired from a parish in Anchorage but still active in the ministry.

A Mixed Bequest

Over the course of 142 years . . . until Russia sold Alaska in 1867, chart-makers, navigators, physicists, astronomers, artists and naturalists sailing for Russia worked to achieve [Empress] Catherine's order to "bring to perfection . . . knowledge" of the North Pacific.

It must not be forgotten, however, that their writings, their collections, their maps and illustrations, their scientific data all were conducted within the context of a colonial empire, whose principal interest was commercial and geopolitical. Great social dislocation and cultural losses occurred within the regions of America colonized by Russia. Disease and hard labor devastated the population of the Aleutian Islands and Kodiak in the 18th century.

In the next century, Russian policymakers tried to mitigate the effects of an imposed economy and western culture. Russians encouraged the use and preservation of Native languages, founded schools with bilingual education, and they did not forcibly prohibit traditional customs, blending many of them with the new Orthodox Christian religion from Russia. They introduced public health programs, including vaccinations for smallpox. For the declining population of marine mammals, Russian officials introduced conservation practices as early as 1803. . . .

From Science Under Sail: Russia's Great Voyages to America, *1728-1867, by Barbara Sweetland Smith. Published in conjunction with an exhibition at the Anchorage Museum of History and Art, May-October 2000.*

Turn-of-the-19th-century Russian school in Ninilchik village, 2003. Photo by J.R.B. Pels.

Easter is *the* church holiday in Walter's memory. "Christmas is big, but I think Easter is the biggest holiday for Russians. I think every place in Alaska where there are Russians has a big church service at midnight. . . .

"Before the service there's a guy up in the belfry ringing the bells. People walk around the church carrying candles. One time I carried the cross. And in Ninilchik we had this old Russian cannon —*pooshka*, in Russian—that they'd shoot every Easter, up on the hill right close to the church.

"Big Simeon was the guy who knew how to shoot this cannon. A couple of young guys—Fred Kvasnikoff and Ted Crawford—had been with him and learned how to shoot it, but one Easter when I was 9, 10 years old they were really going to show everybody how the cannon worked. Instead of putting half a can of black powder in there they put a whole can. They said, 'All right! That will make a loud noise!' They lit the fuse and ran into the graveyard to hide. When they ran out after the explosion there was a big flame that lit up just about the whole village. Pieces of cannon were flying all over. That was it for the *pooshka*."

Easter season meant Easter foods: *pirok* (savory salmon and rice pie), for instance, and *kulich*, yeasty Russian Easter bread baked in a coffee can to give a tall, domed shape to the dried-fruit-filled loaf and call to mind the domed steeples of the church. Easter eggs, colored mostly red, blue or orange in Walter's recollection, with dyes made by soaking colored paper in water, weren't for eating but for greeting. "You'd carry your egg with you as you walked around. If I saw Babushka, I'd say, '*Khristos Voskrece* [Christ is risen],' and she would say back, '*Voistinu Voskrece* [Yes, He is risen],' and then we'd [motion of touching cheek to cheek on alternating sides] and give a kiss and trade eggs. Then to the next person you see. . . ."

Of course, food memories span the year. The first king salmon of the spring, a phrase that usually carries an exclamation point. Razor clams fresh from the beach. "Salt fish, we ate a lot of salt fish. That's the only way they could preserve it. Or smoked salmon. My dad was good at making that. Every family had their own smokehouse, and everybody's was a little different. But it was all good, we thought." Moose meat. "We killed lots of moose—sometimes

*Transfiguration of Our Lord Russian Orthodox Church on the hill above Ninilchik village,
September 2004. Photo by J.R.B. Pels.*

for feeding the dogs or the foxes [on the family fox farm north of Ninilchik], but that was our main meat, too." Wild northern blueberries. "I have some of those near my place now. And highbush cranberries. They made good jelly." Sourdough hotcakes. Doughnuts fried in rendered bear fat. His father's sourdough bread—"what we call Russian rye. He made a lot of it. My mother—all the mothers—made *pirok*. Fix a crust first, then rice and fish and onions. It's pretty easy. [laughing] Now I can do it better than they did! And my mother made fishhead chowder. Babushka was the one who really liked that." Matrona Balashoff Oskolkoff and her peers were known to all as "Babushka," an affectionate Russian term for grandmother.

"Moose meat was good. We were raised on it—hamburgers, roasts—and it was healthy. Healthy meat. Of course, everybody wanted fat, loved the fat meat, you know. Moose meat is leaner than beef, but in certain areas it's fat. The brisket, they call it, there's a lot of fat on that. Some of the ribs have fat on them. The insides, the kidneys and heart—plenty of fat there.

"The liver's great. Everything: tongue, liver, heart, kidneys, we ate all of them. They made sausages with the intestines. And moose nose head-cheese is delicious.

"Moose were plentiful. Gosh, no one hunted any farther than maybe a mile off the beach because there was no need to. A mile off the beach would be about as far as anyone went to get their moose."

Porcupine meat was mostly for fox and dog feed. "But you know, porcupines are vegetarian, so their meat is good. They have thick hindquarters with a little fat on them. We would boil them, mostly. . . . Boy, it was so easy. Slice it up a little bit. It has a good bone in it, you know." Would he compare the flavor of porcupine to some more familiar meat? "Groundhog. That's similar." Thank you, Walter.

Water for all village uses came from the river, carried in twin buckets with a shoulder yoke. That daily chore was an adventure in winter, as the river ice mounted and the water level dropped. "You'd have steps [in the ice] that went down four, five feet, just to get enough water," recalled Ninilchik elder Leo Steik for the first issue of *Chainik Keepeet*. The shallowness of the river meant using a

Matrona Balashoff Oskolkoff ("Babushka") and daughter Ollie, Ninilchik village.
Photo courtesy of Ninilchik Native Descendants.

dipper to fill the five-gallon buckets. "By the time you got two cans filled, you would put your yoke on and [the water] would be frozen," Leo Steik said. Walter seconds that recollection, having carried his share of winter water. On the fox farm where the Jackinsky family spent part of each year, he says, "we had a nice spring about 400 feet from the house, artesian water," where a yoke and buckets were also put to good use.

Walter and his brother Ed helped dig razor clams on the beach at Ninilchik for the family, but they also had jobs digging clams at Polly Creek, directly across Cook Inlet. "Two years my brother and I went there, at the very peak of the summer, clam-digging time. I was just 14 years old the first time. He was 15. And we worked like anything, digging razor clams commercially for a cannery in Seldovia. We were getting a dollar a box, and it took two five-gallon cans to fill up a box—about 150 clams to a can. . . .

"I dug as many as eight boxes a day, that's 16 cans, at that age. And my brother, he made quite a bit more than I did. He was one of the top three diggers, even at his age.

"We stayed with Sargus Kvasnikoff. His father was in charge of our camp. We had tents, and we both just loved it.

"The second year we dug there, they paid us off and the checks bounced. The fellow from Seldovia finally made them good, but it took a while."

Fishing was the foundation of village life, originally for subsistence, later for income as well. Ask Walter about recreation when he was a boy and he mentions first of all fishing, although not the storybook version, lazing beside a brook with a safety pin on a line. Cook Inlet salmon were harvested mostly with traps constructed of piling poles and netting, or with gill nets, either towed by boats or "set," that is, secured to the shore. The fishing was seasonal, but preparation and maintenance never ended—repairing nets, cutting and hauling poles for the trap pilings that were replaced each year.

Walter tells of fishing for king salmon with his brother Ed and their cousin George Cooper across the inlet when Walter was 16 or so. "This was over at West Foreland, at one of the sloughs there at Kuskatan. The runs were heavy on that side, and there were a lot of seals in the water. We were catching baby seals in our nets. We'd feed them and try to turn them loose again, but some died. . . .

"We were taking a break on a nice sunny day, sleeping away in the tent with the flaps wide open. I woke up and saw big bear tracks right between us, in that sandy ground we were sleeping on. He might have been attracted by what was left of the seals. We hadn't been too careful about that. We had a gun handy, but we didn't need it. It looked like he just walked through and kept going."

Many of Walter's stories are recounted with an engaging mix of self-assurance and apparent bemusement at his own exploits. For instance:

"I was about 15 years old when I shot my first bear. I was walking up the beach, up to Ninilchik Point where there were some porcupine traps I had set. I climbed up on the hill, and there was a black bear standing there, eating high-bush cranberries. I had a 30-30. I got all excited. I shot, and the bear disappeared. I said, 'Well, he's gone.' But just in case, I ran. And I found him dead, right by a tree."

Yes, he acknowledges, he was lucky the bear was dead and not just wounded. But that's obviously not of primary importance.

"I don't know how it happened, you know. But, 'I shot my first bear! I can't let him go. Gosh, he's laying dead there underneath a tree!'

"I skinned him right there. I had a hunting knife. We always wore a hunting knife on our belts, you know. Skinning a moose or a bear, there's nothing to it. We could even skin a moose with a jackknife, my brother and I, my dad.

"My father and brother went with me the next day to bring the meat back. But I took a paw home to show them, in case nobody believed me."

Fisherman's Prayer

Chorus

> In the name of the Father and the Son
> And the Holy Ghost
> Lord, have mercy on the fisherman
> He don't ask for human favors
> Just let it be . . .
> That the fish run in their season

Early mornin', stormy weather
Fear of surf and sea
Twenty hours we work together
Then try to get some sleep

Wet boots 'n' hot coffee
Another day begins
Body aching, spirit weary
We pause to bow our heads

Chorus

Deep roots make many teachers
Life's lessons learned
May our family grow and prosper
May the fish return

Have mercy on our children
And our way of life
Bless the loved ones gone before us
Living in the light

Chorus

Words and music by Butch Leman, © 2003.
Published by Sturdy Music–BMI

Alice Jackinsky: "I came to all this haltingly"

... *Before meeting the people, I met the land and be-*
came enchanted with it. Think of a salmon-filled stream that
winds through birch- and spruce-covered bluffs and empties into
a body of water once explored and subsequently named after
Captain Cook. Near the mouth of the stream is a tiny village
composed of a handful of homes. Most of them were built from
hand-hewn logs beautifully fitted together.

My first walk over the dirt road that ran through the village
filled me with a sense of peace. Warm summer sunshine, sled
dogs too content to bark as I passed, grass that blew lazily in the
breeze and the melodious lonesome call of the golden-crowned
sparrow. High on the hill was the church, watching serenely over
the lives below.

Fish and game were plentiful then. One had only to set a net
and soon the smell of alder would be in the air as salmon were
being smoked for *balik*. And barrels would be filled to the brim
with salt fish. Moose roamed the area freely. But there was no
display of antlers to tell of prowess with a rifle. Killing was for
food—not sport!

A community garden in a sunny area provided rhubarb for
fresh pies and the winter's supply of potatoes, turnips, cabbage,
rutabagas. Wild berries were everywhere. Low- and high-bush
cranberries, blueberries and *moroshkis*.

And the people used wisely of these resources. Nothing was
wasted, everything shared. Their main source of income was
from commercial fishing supplemented with trapping done in
the wintertime. Fishing was done with set gillnets, a method still
in use, and hand and pile-driven traps, later outlawed.

Food items needed were ordered from the canneries and delivered in the fall. And then the Sears catalog would be brought
out and the whole family would be completely outfitted with
warm winter clothing—enough to get through the seasons until
the next fall and then the cycle would be repeated.

Fuel for heating and cooking was not wood, as one might
suspect, but rather coal. The beach bluffs were lined with coal

veins and an endless supply was on the inlet floor. The fall storms and big tides would deposit much of it on the beach where it was readily available when needed. The men and boys always put up a large supply in the coal sheds.

Most homes had three small buildings in the yard. One for the obvious reason, one for wood and coal, and the third a *banya*, similar to the Finnish steam bath. Once a week it would be fired up and water would be poured over hot rocks. It wasn't at all unusual to see someone in the coldest winter weather emerge from the warmth of the *banya* with face flushed from the heat into the most extreme of contrasts.

Work always came first and there was a time for it. And play came next. Their play consisted of rough drinking. Usually all was happy, but occasionally the air was split with vile accusations or even blows may have been exchanged. And afterwards maybe a few more drinks together with anger in the past. Friends once more. Some new to this particular scene would have possibly felt it was all so ugly—the drinking, careless dress, and the rough accented language. Accented because these people were descendants of the first settlers of the country. Settlers from the "old country" who married with the Aleuts and never left the land that had given them so much. Because they had been raised speaking the language of the Russians, the accent remained a part of them.

In contrast with their favorite recreation was religion. The church holidays meant much to them. It wasn't disloyalty to the American flag when they celebrated according to Russian tradition—it was their heritage. Their Christmas followed ours by a week or so and was a period of prayer, celebration and fun—of the *Masqueradji*—going from house to house in costume and singing before the candlelighted icon. If your identity was undiscovered, treats were in store.

During the Easter vigil there was a candlelighted procession around the outside of the church. And in the morning you would be awakened by the constant pealing of the church bells—a special privilege granted to all to pull the rope on this one day. Later there would be the exchange of *kulich* and Easter eggs, *"Khristos*

Voskrece" and a kiss on each cheek. If you were one of the chosen, you received an invitation to dip your cup into the strong home brew found in most homes as a special treat during this time.

I came to all this haltingly, as a not so young wife and mother of a small child. Haltingly, because the preparation for such a move was limited—my husband and male in-laws spoke with laughter in their voices of the fun times, the drinking of their neighbors. This was the opposite of the way I had been raised. So, with a promise from my husband that this would be only for the last days remaining for his father, who was suffering from a terminal illness, I followed. To fall in love with the country and the people and soon to have the wish never to leave.

We reached our first home in the village in December, and to borrow a phrase popular at the time, it was the usual "three rooms and a path." The necessity to use the path was delayed as long as possible because your objective was white with a quarter inch of frost and most uncomfortable. There was no hot and cold running water, no electricity, no TV, no washing machine. Often an ax would have to be used to cut a hole in the ice for water, which was carried with a shoulder yoke in two five-gallon cans that had formerly contained the substitute for electricity. And the boxes these cans came in provided excellent shelves, stools, or whatever else your imagination chose to fashion from them.

The nights were cold in December and often the wind would whistle through the draw, leaving high, hard-packed snowdrifts. The old potbellied heater would be filled with coal so there would be enough heat to keep things from freezing, but occasionally a hot-water bottle taken to bed as a foot warmer would fall to the floor in the night and be frozen solid in the morning. . . .

By Alice Lorraine McKibben Jackinsky, written in the 1960s for a class at Juneau-Douglas Community College.

Walter's grandfather Gregory Oskolko,
buying just one box of 20 shells a year and parc
his sons. "My uncles Alex and Simeon got two s
they went hunting. One to kill whatever they ....
One in case of emergency."

His grandfather was a strong man, Walter says, and stern.
"Grandpa had an icon in the corner of their log house, the house
they lived in. Mother Mary, I think. I'm trying to picture her. If the
kids got out of hand, or he wanted to punish them, he'd pour rock
salt on the floor, and on their bare knees they'd have to kneel on
this rock salt and look at the icon for 20, maybe 30 minutes.

"He spanked his wife when she did something he didn't like.
Finally Babushka's daughter, my mother, told my dad about it, and
some of the other daughters were pretty unhappy, too. So their husbands got together and said, 'OK, we're going to talk to him.' And
he realized, he knew. . . .

"About four or five sons-in-law were coming after him, so he
walked up the beach, pulled his hip boots up, and waded out in the
ocean. He said, 'I know what you guys are up to.' And they told
him, 'If you do this anymore, you're going to get in trouble.' He
said, 'I promise I won't do it anymore.' But we understood that he
did it once more after that.

"We got spanked when we were small, Ed and I, but not by our
parents. Mama would call our godfather—we both had godfathers.
Mine was Vanik Astrogin. (Sometimes people called him Pegleg,
but not to his face. He had one twisted leg, and he made a sort of
wooden leg for himself.) Vanik would come and spank me. A
spanking, not a beating, and only a couple of times or so. My
brother's godfather was a mean guy. My brother got some terrible
beatings from him. One time he caught too many fish, and my
mother didn't know how to handle it. Not that there was a limit. It
was just more than she could handle. So she called his godfather,
and Edward got a beating for that. He was maybe 12. He loved to
fish, with a hook and line, and he was a good fisherman. He caught
a dozen king salmon, maybe not even that many. Brought them
home, proud as can be, and she said, 'Oh, man,' and called his god-

Gregory Oskolkoff carries a king salmon through Ninilchik village, with the original Russian Orthodox church in the background. Photo courtesy of Ninilchik Native Descendants, with thanks to Irene Brookman Hixson.

father, and he got a beating. Once or twice Pegleg came over and talked to me, but he was a good-hearted fellow, not a spanking kind of guy. . . ."

The Sterling Highway connected Ninilchik to the rest of the world in 1950. In the hundred years before that, travel was most often on foot or by rowboat in summer, by dog team in winter. The book *Once Upon the Kenai* tells of teacher Enid Stryker [McLane—daughter of teacher Bertha Stryker] arriving in the isolated village in 1920 "tied to the mast of the little gas boat that she boarded in Seldovia. Teachers were not easy to come by—no one wanted to lose this one to the storm-tossed Cook Inlet!"

The highway also accelerated the postwar homesteading boom. As Alice Jackinsky wrote in the 1960s:

> Time passed, and the country saw many changes. The road became a much-traveled highway.
>
> The villagers had seen no need for homesteading. The land had always been there. It belonged to everyone.
>
> But suddenly it was too late. Many homesteaders came, from all walks of life. . . . The old community garden became a newcomer's front yard. All had good intentions of staying, but too soon resources would be exhausted and they would go—leaving behind sagging cabins and broken dreams.
>
> But there were hardier ones who stayed on and helped the land develop. They were harmonious with the villagers and were accepted.
>
> Soon the school had to be enlarged and there was a PTA, Homemakers, knitting clubs, square dancing. And then it leveled off to become once again the sleepy wonderful community it remains today.

Ninilchik lies midway between Homer at the southern end of the Kenai Peninsula and Kenai to the north. Before the highway, that meant a hike of about 37 miles along the beach in either direction. That's 37 miles for groceries, 37 miles for medical attention, 37 miles for mail. On foot or even in a dory, a considerable trip. And dories didn't come from a factory.

Coast Pilot 9, 1964, "the earthquake edition"

Ninilchik *(1960 population 169; P.O.)*, **an agricul-**tural settlement at the mouth of a small stream, is connected by the Sterling Highway with Homer and Anchorage. Radiotelephone and radiotelegraph communications are maintained with the Alaska Communication System. The [Russian] church and part of the village are prominent offshore. There are several small hand-pack canneries in the vicinity. Ninilchik Channel Entrance Light (60°03.1′ N., 151°40.0′ W.), 100 feet above the water, shown from a skeleton tower on shore, marks the approach from seaward through scattered off-lying rocks to the entrance to a small-boat basin inside the mouth of the Ninilchik River. The light shows brightest in line with the entrance channel, which should be used only with local knowledge. In October 1963, the controlling depth in the improved channel was 9 feet at mean lower low water to the sill, thence 3 feet within the basin through the low-water stages by the sill.

North of Cape Ninilchik the coast is very foul, being characterized by immense boulders not marked by kelp. The boulders apparently rest on comparatively flat bottom, so that soundings give no indications of them. It is probable that many more exist than were found by the survey.

On the western shore of Cook Inlet, from Cape Douglas to Chisik Island, the mountains generally rise abruptly from the water, and Iliamna and Redoubt Volcanoes tower well above the surrounding peaks, affording excellent marks from all parts of the lower inlet.

From U.S. Coast Pilot 9: Alaska, Cape Spencer to Beaufort Sea, *Seventh Edition, 1964*

"Now we have fiberglass dories," Walter says, "but they used to be homemade, with native spruce.

"For boards, two of my uncles would work on a stand my grandpa built. One would be on top—they had this big old rip-saw—and one's down below doing the same thing [motion of strenuous vertical sawing]. They'd just keep on working 'em, watching that straight line, and keep on working 'em, until they got one board done and then they'd start another. That's boards for dories or for whatever other use they had. I saw the last phases of that. When I got older there was a sawmill, towards Happy Valley. That's where some of our spruce lumber came from. There were homesteaders there operating a sawmill.

"We'd still cut the knees ourselves—the ribs for the dory—from spruce roots, but we sent them to the sawmill to be sliced. Knees aren't too bad. You put that root there and fasten it with what they call dogs, heavy metal spikes, and with a big old hand-saw and a straight line you just cut them up, then use a broad-ax to trim them with. You need a root shaped just right—kind of like an L, you know. Not exactly an L, but pretty close to it. That's where the strength is, right here [gesturing to demonstrate the turn of the root, or the rib]. And that thing's so doggone strong, with the grain going this way, you just can't break it. It would take a lot of force to break it. . . .

"A 19-foot dory is heavy, but not too bad. Four men could handle it pretty good. Two men could, though not too easy. You'd have to have rollers—whatever poles you find on the beach for rollers—to get it over the gravel and down to the beach."

By the 1940s, Woodley Airways was making regular mail deliveries to a rough airstrip near the beach at Ninilchik. (Woodley soon became Pacific Northern Airways and then Pacific Northern Airlines before merging in the 1960s with Western Airlines.) But even after the advent of airplanes, sled dogs earned their keep. The Jackinsky family had a team as far back as Walter can remember. "That was the means of transportation—all our coal from the beach, our wood, moose meat . . ." Coal found along the inlet north and south of Ninilchik comes from big veins in the bluff, some running all the way across the beach into the water. "There was

Walter Jackinsky Jr. drives the family dog team with sister Margaret in the sled. "This is the team that won the race in Homer," Walter says of the family photo. "The lead dog is Smiley, a female."

enough there for everybody to pick up, especially when the tide was out," Walter says. "It was scattered in different sizes, sometimes in big chunks you'd have to break up." As L.H. Allen wrote in her 1946 book, *Alaska's Kenai Peninsula*, "Coal abounds at Ninilchik, an excellent lignite. It is without cost to those who pick it up for themselves." The picking up could be arduous, however, especially if the coal collected in the fall ran out before winter weather did. *Chainik Keepeet* quotes elder Dean Kvasnikoff's tongue-in-cheek recollection: "Until I was 15, I thought my name was 'Get Coal.'"

The dog sled was also the Jackinsky family school bus. "We usually moved to the fox ranch about the fifth of March and that was our home until maybe September. March was the start of mating time for the foxes. We had to watch them, write down every time you saw that they were mating, to know exactly when they'd have their pups—be ready to take care of them.

"In March the days were getting longer, and warmer, so it was easy for us to go back and forth to school from the homestead. Going back and forth was by dog team. We'd hitch our four dogs and load the girls [Margaret and Cora] in the sled. Ed and I would either run or push or ride the runners. It's only a three-mile run, so it was kind of fun for us. Then we walked up the hill to the school and left the sled and the dogs tied in a pen at our house in the village."

Apparently the dogs sometimes made it up the hill, because Walter also recalls, with a look of boyish glee: "Going down that steep hill with the sled, down into Ninilchik, could be exciting! It wasn't safe to leave anybody in the sled going downhill. You were going so fast. And even if you used the brake you still couldn't control the sled good. Well, sometimes we got the girls to ride. If the conditions were so that it wasn't that fast, then they could do it. Most of the time we were hanging on to the back handlebars and either drug our feet to kind of control the sled, or used the brake. Sometimes the sled went faster than the dogs. But the dogs got out of the way! If the path going downhill got icy, then we had to put chains around the runners."

"Everyone had to climb that hill in the morning, then at noon," he says. "Going down on foot was easy. You could slide down or whatever you wanted to do.

"At lunchtime the fellow that my dad had hired would have lunch ready for us. Mostly just lunchtime. If the weather got stormy and we had to stay overnight [at the Jackinsky house in the village] then it would be dinner, too. This is when I was sixth, seventh, eighth grade.

"One of the men was Long Trip Carlson—C.J. Carlson. 'C.J.' was for Charlie John. In his early days he used to work in the square-riggers, the sailing ships, but he somehow ended up in Bristol Bay—a cannery worker who came up from San Francisco or somewhere. Then he decided to leave Bristol Bay. He was married, and some kind of trouble came up. He heard about Ninilchik from some of the fishermen, so he got himself a boat fixed with an engine and he ran it all the way from Bristol Bay down through Unimak Pass, up the Aleutian Chain, into Kodiak and on to Ninilchik. That's how he got his name, Long Trip Carlson. His boat was *Fog Auger*. My dad liked him. He had a Swedish name, but he was part Lithuanian.

"Long Trip Carlson's favorite dish was rice and curry. At least once a week, maybe more, we'd have rice and curry, either fish or meat. Fish was good. I'm surprised how good it was. He'd process salt fish and cube it and cook it in his curry gravy. I think he had his own spices. He loved that curry. Other times we had boiled fish. Lots of moose meat. Potatoes.

"He got to where he wasn't well when he was with us, and the only place they could think of that might do him some good was Tenakee Hot Springs. That's not too far from Juneau—a lot of miners used to go there for their rheumatism. So Dad talked him into going there, but it didn't do much good. He had circulation problems—his legs were swelling up. He came back, and he died right there in our house in Ninilchik. I came home from school and saw blankets hanging out, and my dad told me he had died. They couldn't bury him in the Russian cemetery. He's buried about half a mile north of the church. A man they called Black Alex is buried there, too. That was before my time." In addition to the plot farther away where C.J. Carlson is buried, there is now an American

Legion cemetery adjoining the Russian Orthodox cemetery at Ninilchik, as well as a section in the Orthodox cemetery for non-members of the church.

"While Long Trip Carlson was gone to Tenakee Springs we had, first, Tom Dootka. He was kind of a bachelor. My dad picked him out—he knew he was safe to cook for us. We had him one season. Tom Dootka's side business was making home brew. He'd make that and sell it to the local people, if they had any money. He always had a barrel going. His most popular dish for us was soaked-out salmon—salt salmon, you know—and then he fried it. Then he'd boil some potatoes and maybe he'd make gravy. Beans was a popular dish, with some moose meat in. Or he'd fry some steaks.

"Just about everybody, every family, had a root cellar—that's where we kept the potatoes. Dig a hole in the ground, up on the hillside somewhere, not too far away, and make little shelves or bins in there. You don't even board it. Just kind of a hole in the ground where you know nothing will freeze. It doesn't have to be too deep. Or ours wasn't. When you cover it up, you put a lot of hay, and then you have a little door that's covered, too, for the entryway.

"Anyway, there was another fellow, John Malachy. He was a good worker, and Dad hired him first to help build our fox fence. Then Dad said, 'Well, you're handy around here. Why don't you cook for the kids one spring?' And he did. He wasn't as good as the others, but he did OK. He liked moose steaks. Just about every time, he'd get moose steaks from somewhere. His specialty was frying moose meat. And maybe boiling potatoes. That was easy.

"If it happened that our lunch wasn't ready, if Tom Dootka maybe was partying somewhere, our neighbor Julia Steik would grab a big pan, one of those skillets. She'd throw some moose meat in there, fry it up fast, add flour and make gravy, and that would be our lunch. Good! Something hot for us to eat. And then back up the hill."

To Walter's best recollection, the Jackinskys were the only ones who came to school by dog team. "But just about everyone had some kind of a dog team, and there were a lot of dogs working around there, hauling food, fish-trap poles, stuff like that." Sled dogs are not necessarily cuddly pets. In the first issue of *Chainik Keepeet* Walter tells of a team that leaped on him on his way home from school one day and left his back permanently scarred. The dogs were still in the harnesses they'd worn to haul trap poles. "My dad sent Edward over to tell [the owner] that we'd kill his dogs for doing that, but [the owner] begged him not to because then he wouldn't have anything to work with."

Chainik Keepeet also recalls an emergency run with a dog team in 1928, when a teacher named Bess Howe accidentally wounded herself in the stomach while cleaning a pistol. "They took her to Ninilchik Lake by dog team and put her on a plane," Walter is quoted as saying. "We gave some of our dogs to make a big team." *Chainik Keepeet* notes that the teacher recovered but did not return to the village.

When Walter and Edward were 16 and 17, they set out for what they thought would be a day trip with their father's sled.

"My brother and I were out hunting—this was around early March—and we found a bear's den. We knew there was a bear in there. So, 'Let's get this bear, if we can.' We got ourselves situated. I had a gun, the 30-30, and I think Ed had a 30-06. And we turned our dogs loose. The dogs were anxious to get the bear out of there. They were excited, barking like anything around the mouth of the den. Pretty soon we heard that rumbling, you know, and a big old monstrous brown bear came out of there. He was mad. He wanted to sleep some more. The one advantage we had was, you know, they can't see at first. They're kind of blind. But they're raging mad because they're not ready to come out.

"Half his body came out. And we should have waited. The old-timers said to wait until he comes completely out of the hole. We were a little excited, so we killed him when he was about halfway out.

"Afterward we got him out, but it was a lot of trouble. We had to get the dogs hitched in their harnesses, and we finally dragged him out of there. We spent the next five or six hours skinning that bear. He had to be taken care of. He was a big brownie, heavy. He must have weighed maybe 800 pounds.

"We were in the Caribou Hills, about 18 miles from home, and it got dark on us. We thought, 'Where are we going to sleep?' We went right inside that den. That den was beautiful to sleep in. A lot of nice clean straw."

The brothers worried briefly about another bear showing up, but "we had our dogs. We knew the dogs would warn us."

The bear hide and the meat arrived home the next day on the sled. The dogs and the foxes got most of the meat. "We tried cooking some, but brown bear meat has a strong taste. Black bear is delicious. Like pork."

Two years later, in 1934, a local reporter obviously enjoyed writing about another Jackinsky brothers expedition. As quoted in *Alaska's No. 1 Guide: The History and Journals of Andrew Berg, 1869-1939*:

Three Ninilchik boys, Walter Jackinsky, Edward Jackinsky, his brother, and Lee Hancock made the first continuous trip on record from Ninilchik to Seward which took nine days . . . With six dogs carrying their provisions and mushing through a virgin country for 150 miles via the Skilak Lake region, these northern courier de bois traversed a section but little traveled by other than trappers, explorers, or prospectors. The country they crossed is perhaps the greatest moose and bear country on the American continent.

Leaving the well traveled trail terminus at Kenai, they turned their dogs in the direction of their destination. They were soon lost in the almost interminable solitudes of the Alaskan wilds. To these lads the vast stretches of the Northland hold no fears. They are at home anywhere in that vastness in which, to many another, would be many uncertain omens.

All along the trail, wherever perchance the abode of human beings was found, they were greeted with welcome and the hospitality that only this great Northland knows. In the evenings came stories of adventures and new thrills, then off again in the early light of the morning ready for the thrills incident to the day.

Past Lakes Skilak, Tustumena, and Caribou Island, bidding good day to the fading sun, and bon jour to the morning light, they pursued their onward way. After a halt at Kenai Lake, they passed the night at Lawing. In sub-zero temperatures, thru nine long, but to

them not weary days, these sons of the North held the battle of the
day, and the rigors of the night as nothing, snug asleep in their bags
as their faithful dogs kept watch through the frosty silence of the
night . . .

"The old-timers were good to us," Walter says in *Chainik
Keepeet*. "They fed us sheep meat, moose meat and fish they caught
in [Tustumena] Lake. It was just really choice. The best they had."

The three intrepid "sons of the North"—and their intrepid
dogs—returned from Seward via the Alaska Steamship Co. vessel
the SS *Northwestern* to Seldovia. From Seldovia they hitched a ride
on a mailboat to Homer and then mushed home to Ninilchik.

Ed and Walter were often close companions. But they were also
highly competitive. "I thought he was so darn bossy, and I hated to
be bossed around *too* much. But he figured because he was older—
and our parents felt that way, too. Whenever they left us, he was in
charge. 'Listen to him, whatever he says . . .'

"We got along at times. We could go and hunt together and do
pretty good. But there were times when we'd get mad—we fought
a lot, we fought a lot. Brothers fight a lot, I guess. Even in our
teens. It was hard for us, I don't know why. We were both pretty
strong. We had our dad worried sometimes."

Walter Sr. introduced the boys to boxing, and they practiced on
each other—those were the *regulated* fights. "We had boxing gloves
at home all the time," Walter Jr. says. "We'd put 'em on and say,
'C'mon, Dad!' He would box sometimes, and then he wouldn't.
But my brother and I would, and there were a lot of other kids that
loved it. I especially—I thought it was great, and I always did
good." Their father also taught the boys to swim. "There's a little
lake back here, not too far away. That's where we started. It doesn't
have a name. It's just a little place. And then we swam a lot in the
river, when the tide came in, or even when the tide was out. That
was a good spot. It was cold in the ocean, once you got in it. Temperature of about 50. But we liked it."

A young man named Fred Lange who stayed with the Jackinskys one winter was an especially good boxer, Walter says: "I
learned a lot from him." Fred had taken up boxing in a PE class at

From left, Nels Nordeen, Lee Hancock, Otto Nilson, Walter Jackinsky Sr., and Larry Slevin. Jackinsky family photo, which Walter believes was taken at Seldovia.

Walter Jackinsky and fellow boxer Karl Nielsen of Homer, c. 1936. Jackinsky family photo.

Seward High School, where an ex-pro named Roland Nipps, who also taught math, was the instructor. Fred went on to box as a "paid amateur" in Kodiak.

In his late teens Walter boxed at a gym in Anchorage and also around Palmer, where he got some notice as a welterweight (140-147 pounds). He and a friend, Karl Nielsen of Homer, were asked to participate in Palmer's winter carnival. "They said, 'You two are good boxers. You [Walter] represent Ninilchik, and you represent Homer.' So we went up there.

"Karl Nielsen was a Finnish person, a little short guy, about 5-foot-2, I guess, and nothing but muscle. Man oh man, he was strong. He was a good one to train with."

Walter, at about 5-foot-7, was paired with a 6-footer from Wasilla. "I did OK. The fights only went three rounds. . . . I just dropped him on the floor, and that was it. That was my match for that bout. And Karl did good, too. We felt pretty proud.

"Then we came back here, and Homer had a winter carnival. They said, 'You guys gotta get into the dog races.' So I took our team from here to Homer. There must have been at least 10, 12 teams entered. Karl was there. Jesse Lee Home [a children's home] from Seward had a team. Fred Lange's brother had a team. . . .

"Darned if I didn't win that race. Twenty miles. One hour, 54 minutes, 33 seconds. They gave me a trophy, but they said, 'We have to keep the trophy here. We can't let the trophy go out of Homer. You won it, but you can't keep it.'"

Fred Lange, now living in Cordova, remembers that his older brother, Charles, finished the race sprayed with blood from his dogs' feet. "The race was run over thin ice up Homer Slough," Fred says. "His dogs were German police and Siberian husky mix—they had pretty soft feet." (Brother Charles Anthony Lange was nick-named Tubal, Fred says, "from a poem he had to recite in the third grade: 'Old Tubal Cain was a man of might, in the days when earth was young, . . .'" from Charles Mackay's 19th century story in rhyme of the sword-maker who repented and turned his skill to ploughshares.) Fred later had a team of his own, "three malamutes from Jackinskys' litter—Jynx, Don and Babe."

Walter Jackinsky Sr. established his fox ranch around 1925, on land he had homesteaded a few miles north of the village. "I was 9 or 10 years old," Walter Jr. says. "Ed and I worked like anything. We built pens, we dug trenches, we did everything. Dad had as many as 30-some breeders, I believe. And the foxes had to be taken care of, you know.

"But there was a lot of game here. There were porcupine, and there were groundhogs, and there were moose, and everything you wanted, right handy, right at home. They'd come right up to our house [on the homestead]. It was easy. Fish—you could put a net across the mouth of the river and catch all the fish you wanted real fast." Ninilchik families didn't have to compete for salmon, he says. "It didn't take long. You put a net across the mouth of the river, in half an hour your net was getting filled up, you know. So you'd have to get it out of there. And someone else would do the same. . . ."

Fred Lange well remembers his winter with the Jackinskys on the fox ranch, and the long day's journey from Homer with the Jackinsky dog sled. "Walter and I made the trip to Ninilchik with his team on the beach ice," he says. "The weather was very cold—20 below and windy. We had to stop at Diamond Creek, seven miles from Homer, and kill a couple of rabbits to use the fur to warm our plumbing in order to pee."

Fred was kept as busy as the Jackinsky boys on the fox ranch, and he loved it. "I was healthy as a horse when I came out of there," he says. "We worked hard, hauling coal, hunting, trapping, cutting wood, taking care of the silver foxes and the dog team, and a hundred other jobs. What a good, healthy life! We were in bed early by choice. Every evening about eight o'clock we had to be very quiet as the dad had to listen to the Russian radio from Khabarovsk, Siberia. . . . And we ate fox food!" Fox food meant moose meat and porcupine and fish, but it also meant good Russian black bread, and that was especially impressive to the young visitor. Walter Sr. would make a big batch, Walter says, and apportion the loaves—so many slices for the family, so many for the foxes.

Fred Lange had intended to spend a week or two on the homestead. "But I couldn't get away," he says with recollected delight.

Adolph Jackinsky in Ninilchik village, c. 1930. Jackinsky family photo.

Langes celebrate 50th Anniversary

Fred and Mae Lange celebrated their 50th wedding anniversary on Aug. 17 at the Cookhouse Cafe in Cordova. The Langes were married in Anchorage on Aug. 15, 1947. They honeymooned while silver fishing on the Copper River Flats, beginning a lifelong partnership of commercial fishing and raising a family in Cordova.

Mae was born in Katalla (80 miles east of Cordova) and Fred was born on Peak Island in Prince William Sound. The couple retired from commercial fishing in 1996 and now they enjoy spending time with their grandchildren, putting up home packs and traveling in order to "get a little sun in the wintertime." Fred keeps busy with his consulting work for such clients as Cannery Row Fish Company and Odiak Maritime.

Attending the celebration were the couple's daughters, Karla Herron and Sylvia Lange; Mae's sons Bob, Pete, Tom and Teeny Andersen; Mae's sister Stella Jansen; Bud Jansen; and many grandchildren, great-grandchildren, and family well-wishers.

"Old Walter, the dad—oh, I loved him. He just kept me! He said, 'Go next week, next week, next week.' . . . They were a wonderful family—the father, Walter and Ed, the two girls. There was another brother [Adolph], but he died in a plane crash." Fred's own father had died when he was a boy; his mother, born at Unga in the Shumagin Islands, wasn't able to care for all 12 of her children, and Fred and three siblings grew up at the Methodist-run Jesse Lee Home for Native children, which had recently been moved from Unalaska to Seward. After graduating from Seward High School he was trapping with his brother around Homer when he and Walter first met.

Even midway through the Depression years, Walter says, the fox ranch was successful. "We were selling pelts for as much as $300 apiece. The style for foxes was pretty strong then, in Europe especially. We sold them to the New York fur exchange, to London, to the Seattle fur exchange. These were silver-black fox—the more silver, the more valuable. The highest was maybe $300 and some for one skin, and gosh, for $300 we could buy our winter's groceries."

But eventually the Depression won out. When the Alaska Road Commission commenced work on the Sterling Highway in the late 1940s, the foxes were long gone. "Ralph Soberg [Road Commission general foreman] came over and talked to my dad: 'We have to go through where your pens are. Can we get your permission to go right on through?' Dad said, 'You bet. Do whatever you want.' The road went right across our land—right through those pens!"

Walter was 8 or 9 years old when his parents separated. Walter Sr. kept Edward, Walter, Margaret, Cora and Adolph with him. Walter Jr.'s respect for his father is at all times evident, and he speaks reluctantly of this period, saying only that the children longed for their mother. "We missed her. All of us. It was hard." Fred Lange recalls that "there was no mother or woman around or even mentioned when I was there."

Mary Oskolkoff Jackinsky Linstrang was 35 years old when she died in Ninilchik in 1932 after giving birth to daughter Clara.

Some years after he and Mary divorced, Walter Sr. opened a general store in the Jackinsky house in the village. After a period of ill health, he died in Ninilchik in 1950, age 58.

"He had cancer of the pancreas," Walter says. "He went to the Mayo Clinic, but it had gone too far. They couldn't do too much about it then anyway. Now maybe they can. He died upstairs in his house in Ninilchik. I was with him.

"He just kept getting weaker, getting frail. He lost all his strength. But his mind was good. He was such a strong man when he was young. Powerful, and strong.

"I was crying and everything else. But that doesn't do any good. . . .

"You get so attached. He's the only parent you have."

Brother Ed was in Ninilchik at that time, too, although not at the house when their father died. "Ed and I took care of things. The girls weren't able to be there. Margaret and Al were married by then, and Cora and Don, too. . . ."

Walter Sr.'s marker in the Russian Orthodox cemetery on the hill above Ninilchik is inscribed "Loving Dad / Walter Jackinsky / 1891-1950."

Walter vividly recalls his last glimpse of his grandfather Gregory Oskolkoff, Mary's father. "He got Alzheimer's, something like Alzheimer's, and they couldn't take care of him. He went out hunting, got lost, and never was the same afterward. I think it was Allan Petersen and Ralph Andersen from Seldovia who came by boat to take him, and then he was sent to Morningside Hospital in Portland. I was on the beach when they were taking him, and he was saying in Russian, 'The devils are taking me!—*Cherti menya zabirout!*' He was wearing big shoepacs, and they had handcuffs on him. That was the last time I saw him." Gregory Oskoloff is believed to have died around 1940. He would have been 80 years old.

"Babushka," Gregory's wife, Matrona, who had been orphaned early in her own life, outlived them all. During the last years of her widowhood, which she spent with her daughter Milanya in the village, she kept busy braiding rugs for the family from outgrown clothing and remnants of cloth that they brought her. She died in 1963 at age 86.

"And Life Goes On"

Although faced with the soon to be loss of a loved one, we moved toward that day, hoping for as little pain and suffering as the Lord would allow. And He was good, because if the pain was too great to bear, a peace and acceptance of his lot had been given to my father-in-law that made it so much easier for him and those of us standing by trying to help. And the end came quietly very early on a day in January.

He was not a village man in the true sense of the word, but had been a leader there and held much respect. He had passed on a love and longing for knowledge to his children, encouraging them to go forth and find what they wanted of life, rather than waiting for it to come to them.

Death in the village was harder than elsewhere because of the stark reality. Church leaders and men of the family prepared the body for burial. The local carpenter built the casket and Russian cross and the women gathered straw for a pillow and lined the casket with unbleached muslin. Everyone gathered in the home and as the church bells tolled, the procession made its way up the hill to the little church and cemetery. A young man carrying the cross led the way, followed by the pallbearers with their burden and then the family and friends.

After the service everyone returned to the family home, bringing pickled fish, cheese, cakes, cookies—and all drank *chai*, strong tea brewed on the back of the stove. There was laughter, the women cleaning—all helped to erase the thoughts of what had transpired shortly before. . . .

And life goes on. Shortly after this our little girl, who had just passed her first birthday, was baptized in the Russian Orthodox church in a baptismal tub built by her great-grandfather 50 years earlier. This ceremony was followed by christening as Tatiana in the Kenai church by Father Shadura. A cause for celebration and *chai* again. If one has never attended services in this church, it is an experience long to be remembered. . . .

By Alice Lorraine McKibben Jackinsky.

Transfiguration of Our Lord Russian Orthodox Church and cemetery, September 2003, with gravestone for Matrona Balashoff Oskolkoff. Photos by J.R.B. Pels.

SAILBOATS AND LIBERTY SHIPS

3

If I had a talking picture of you,
I would run it every time I felt blue.
I would sit there in the gloom of my lonely little room
And applaud each time you whispered, "I love you (love you)."

On the screen the moment you came in view,
We would talk the whole thing over, we two.
I would give ten shows a day, and a midnight matinee,
If I had a talking picture of you.

("If I Had a Talking Picture of You," words and music by Ray Hen-
derson, Lew Brown and B.G. DeSylva, 1929.)

"I was pretty much gone after ninth grade. I'd leave home and
then come back. Summers I fished with my dad at Kalifonsky
Beach and Salamatof. In 1935, '36, I worked for the colonists,
when the colonists were coming to Palmer [in the Matanuska Val-
ley]. I drove truck there for the CCC—Civilian Conservation
Corps—two different seasons. We worked hard trying to get them
settled. . . ."

Walter was 19 in 1935. At 87 he's still enthusiastic about those
early jobs. In the telling, it was hard work, but never drudgery.
And then as now, he loved music, loved to dance. People congre-
gated at a hall by the river in Ninilchik for community dances,
with homegrown musicians. Walter learned to play guitar a bit as
a boy. "I must have been 12 years old, maybe 13. We had our own
group, mostly guitars and an accordion. An elderly fellow had a vi-
olin, and he joined us. He played fast!

"Alex Kvasnikof was my age. He played the guitar well. Bob Resoff. He and I were in the same grade and were the same age. After the service he went into the king crab business and made millions. He came out good after years of doing that. He sold all his interest to one of the big companies, I don't remember which one.

"And there was Nick Leman, Charlie Resoff, Bill Kvasnikoff. They were all pretty good guitar players.

"John Kelly played the mandolin. He was always kind of a lead person. He was older than me, and he was real smart. Peter Cooper played accordion. My Uncle Jack [Oskolkoff] was a good guitar player, too. We all took turns."

In Kenai, a pickup band played regularly at Joe Consiel's dance hall and bar, known to some as Smokey Joe's, or as the sign above the door announced, "Keen [eye] Joe's." From one weekend to another the group might include some of the Ninilchik musicians. One popular guitar player, Johnny Lund, was from Seldovia by way of Ninilchik.

"Johnny Lund had relatives there in Kenai, and he wasn't getting along too good with his family in Seldovia. He came along the beach one winter. Walked all the way from Homer to Kenai. He stayed with us for a while, hunted a little while—he and I went and killed a moose. Then he went on to Kenai and made his home there, pretty much."

The young men had an unofficial uniform for those nights out: bell-bottom jeans—Walter doesn't recall what brand—"with a little red V, an upside-down V, right here down this side [gesturing toward a trouser hem]. We thought they were just beautiful. Some had red all the way down on the outside there along the seams. And dark shiny shoes. Usually we wore a jean shirt—not a jean shirt, but a blue [probably chambray] shirt. A white shirt looked good with it, too. We wore a lot of white shirts. No ties."

He has to think a little harder to envision the female uniform: "Nice dresses, probably. They didn't wear slacks very much then."

Walter didn't have a steady date, but one of the dance partners he particularly remembers was Louise Darien, from a Kenai family. She later married Erling Frostad. "And there was another gal there

Walter Jackinsky Jr. and Sr., in Portland, Ore. Jackinsky family photo.

that my uncle liked, my Uncle Jack. Her name was Farting Fanny. She was quite a gal. Everybody liked her. She was kind of a little thing, but lively. Loved to dance. She'd come over and have some beer with us, you know, then she'd start rubbing her stomach and say, 'I have gas.'

"Her family moved to Seldovia, I believe. They spent a winter in Ninilchik and then moved to Seldovia, or maybe Kodiak. That's the end of what I heard about her."

Today, with his new guitar from the Music Box in Homer and a little coaxing, Walter can still sing and strum his favorite dance tunes from that period:

"'If I had a talking picture of you-ooo, I would run it every time I felt blue-ooo [through both choruses] . . .'—that's a good one. You could hear Johnny Lund and some of the other guys singing that around town all summer long, kind of yodeling, you know: 'We would talk the whole thing over, we two-woo-ooo-ooo . . .'

"'Don't send my boy to prison . . . never again will he roam. . . .' *Skal vi gå på lofte.*' That's Norwegian: 'Let's go up in the loft.' A schottische. 'Love Letters in the Sand.' 'Barbara'—that's another good one. . . .

"My dad had a fisherman from Seldovia named Sammy Hunter working for him for a while, helping him build two hand traps [small-scale fish traps]. Dad would say, 'OK, Sammy, when are you going to fix breakfast for us?' And Sammy would fix breakfast and then get his guitar and start playing. He was so good. He'd come to the village sometimes and play his guitar and sing. 'Barbara' was his favorite song. And the kids would just swarm around him, and sing. [crooning] 'Barbara, the moon is shining, Barbara. . . .'

"Some of the Hunters still live in Kenai. Ed Hunter—he married someone in Kenai."

Ninilchik was a way-station for many travelers. Victor Segura, originally from the Philippines, worked at Libby, McNeil & Libby cannery at Kenai one season around 1930 and fell in love with a Kenai girl, Matrona Evinor. "When the summer contract was up the crews all had to leave—the cannery shipped them back to Seattle or wherever they were hired. Toward winter Victor decided he'd better come on back. He told us he traveled steerage on Alaska

Steam to get to Seldovia, then got a ride on Charlie Munson's mailboat to Homer. From Homer he just started walking. Spent a night at Anchor Point with Fred Winslow, who took care of the lighthouse there, then on to Ninilchik.

"He stayed a couple of days in Ninilchik to rest up. They had a dance while he was here, and my kid sisters got him to dance with them. They liked him—he had a fancy way of dancing, a kind of different style. Good dancer. When he was rested he went on to Kasilof and stayed overnight with Odman Kooly at the Alaska Packers Cannery. Odman Kooly was a watchman there for many years, and that's where people usually stayed.

"From there to Kenai was easy—about 12 miles, and he had a winter trail, a dog-team trail, to go on. I guess when he got to Kenai and found his sweetheart, he got married!"

Mentioning Fred Winslow in the course of Victor Segura's odyssey reminds Walter of a time when he and his brother Edward and Sargus Kvasnikoff went from Ninilchik down to fish at Anchor River for steelhead, about 1933. "We rowed our way down there—that's around 16, 17 miles from Ninilchik. We watched the tide and rowed down there. It took the biggest part of the day to get there. We fished quite a bit, stayed one or two nights with Fred Winslow, and then one morning the wind was nice, blowing from the south, so we took off for Ninilchik. We had an old moose hide that we slept on, and we used that as a sail. We sailed right on home without even rowing. That sail was enough to bring us home.

"We came home with a load of at least 250 steelhead, maybe more. There were steelhead everywhere, but hardly anyone fished Anchor River then and it was just chuck full with steelhead.

"A few years later, Charlie Cooper and two or three of his boys—Alfred, Peter, probably Martin—went down to Anchor River for steelhead. Fred Winslow had some homemade beer—*makoola*—that was just about done, so they started sampling it that night. They drank, and ate, and next morning, gosh, Fred Winslow was dead. They had to bury him there."

Many families made their own home brew, Walter says, from whatever was available that might ferment: potatoes (and potato peels), berries, raisins—there are even tales of finding old socks in the *makoola* barrel. In addition, two brothers in a family near Anchor Point had a large still and ran a successful bootleg whiskey operation during the Prohibition days of the 1920s and early '30s. Their boats *Snowbird* and *Foxtrot* were a familiar sight up and down the Inlet. Young as he was, Walter remembers *Snowbird* in particular, anchored for business at the mouth of the Ninilchik River.

The roadhouse in Ninilchik where Victor Segura stayed on his way north has a history of its own. "The Cooper family added on to their house, made a pool hall, and I think they had four rooms upstairs that they rented. After Joseph Cooper Jr. died, Lizzie Cooper lived there alone until she married Stepan Churkin. He was from Russia but he lived in Kenai for a while.

"They had that big pool table, and they did some gambling there occasionally, blackjack and poker. They got my brother in there, and I felt so unhappy. Gosh, I didn't know that much about gambling, and I saw my brother playing with a bunch of gamblers there! [Laughter—apparently Edward's brush with "a bunch of gamblers" didn't lead him astray.] I told my dad about it. I was maybe 15 or 16.

"Then one time, let's see, the mail plane came—I must have been 19 by then, 1935 or so—and some of us said, 'Well, let's go and get some wine. We'll charter this plane and go and get some wine and have a little fun here.' So about six of us chartered the mail plane, a Woodley Airways Travel Air plane, flew to Kenai and got a bunch of wine, and brought it back to Ninilchik. It cost around $75 for the charter, maybe more. But nobody had had anything to drink for a long time, and they felt like they wanted to do something different. We came back with a bunch of wine, and Churkins' was the only place where we could have a good dance, you know, a big dance. We got the tables moved, and got it ready.

"My dad was just as mad as can be at me for doing that. He wouldn't even talk to me. But later he had a little bit of wine, and he came to the dance. I could see him dancing with Polly Crawford. She was a widow, a beautiful woman. She had two children, and she and Dad were kind of friendly. I'm dancing with Fedora Kvasnikoff, my sister's best friend, and we're having a good time, but I was kind of scared to see what Dad would do, you know. But then every time he danced by he'd wink at me, and smile, and I thought, 'Well, I guess things are OK now.'

"The whole village came to that dance!"

Eventually Churkins' roadhouse became Sam Kraskoff's place.

"Sam Kraskoff came from South America. He ran away from Russia and went to South America with a group, and from South America he came to the United States in the 1920s—somewhere around there. Somehow he ended up in Bristol Bay—must've got hired by one of the cannery offices in San Francisco. He didn't fish that first year. He did fish for a while after he'd been there a couple of years. He even fished with me for three, four days one season as a relief partner. My partner got seasick—Ray Coleman. He had never fished much before. So Sam and I got to know each other quite a bit, and Ninilchik kind of interested him because of the Russian people there. Some Coopers were at Bristol Bay, and they talked Sam into coming to Ninilchik. He visited a few times.

"We met each other again when we were working at the Air Force base in Anchorage—they were just building that Elmendorf Air Force Base then, 1940, '41. I worked there for about a year, spreading concrete for those big runways. Sam was doing carpentry work. In the meantime he had met a gal from Palmer—heck, she was about half his age, maybe late 20s and he was 40s, 50s—and they got married. He said, 'Now I'm going to take you down to a good place where you can really enjoy yourself.' They got down to Ninilchik and things weren't going too good. The big thing was she didn't know how to make Russian bread. He wanted bread like they did it in Russia, but she only knew one way to make bread. He gave her a hard time about that. Finally she took her bags and went back to Palmer. That marriage didn't last too long.

"Sam stayed in Ninilchik. He rented for a while, a cabin in the village, and then he bought the Churkin house. Lizzie and Steve [Stepan] Churkin had both died, I believe, so Sam Kraskoff bought the place and rebuilt it. Made a nice boarding house out of it and did real good.

"Every spring people come to Ninilchik to go clam digging. They did then and they still do. They come in from Anchorage and

Fedora Kvasnikoff and Margaret (Jackie) Jackinsky with clam shovels and the tide coming in. Photo courtesy of Ninilchik Native Descendants.

Seward and everywhere. There's about an 18-mile stretch of beach just full of razor clams, from Ninilchik in either direction, but mostly north—all the way to Kasilof. Clam Gulch is just loaded with clams. One spring after the highway was in, some nurses came from Seward to stay a couple of nights and get some clams. They stayed with Sam. Some of the nurses had colds, and Sam thought they weren't really well enough to go clam digging on the beach. But they did, and when they came back to his place, sneezing and coughing, you know, he was disgusted. He told 'em, 'I'll tell you how you can take care of those colds you have.' He said, 'Look at me, look how healthy I am.' And he grabbed a raw egg, broke it, and drank it down. Then he took another raw egg, broke it, and drank it. They were looking at him, turning green, but he said, 'Look at you—pale, and coughing. If you just do what I do you'll be healthy in a short while.' That was his medicine for just about everything. 'That's how they do it in Russia,' he said.

"Sam had quite a Russian accent, but he also spoke Spanish because of his time in South America. He had a favorite saying, no matter what you asked him: 'Maybe yes, maybe no, altogedda make it go.'" Not to be confused with "Absolutely Frank" Cooper, brother of Charlie Cooper, whose usual rejoinder was, according to Walter, "Absolutely!"

"Later Sam got married again. He ordered a wife. He joined some kind of a club where they had wives you could order, and he found one who came from Russia. So he ordered, and she came, Irene came, and she was a good woman. He met her in Anchorage, and she stayed with him till he died, 1964. They got a general store going, and he left her $200,000 that he had saved, and the whole store and everything. They were a good pair. They would invite us a lot of times for dinner [in the 1950s]. She was a good cook. Pork and sauerkraut was her big dish."

Did she make Russian bread? "She sure did!"

The village also attracted longer-term lodgers. "In Ninilchik when I was small there were quite a few Scandinavians who used to come and spend the winter. There'd be Swansons and Johnsons and Petersens and Nelsons, six or eight or 10 men from various fishing areas who'd come to Ninilchik to winter there. Two or three of

"The old dance hall by the river" in Ninilchik village, 2003. Photo by J.R.B. Pels.

them would rent a house together until spring. They were all nice guys. Some were from Bristol Bay, some from the Aleutians, I guess. They just wanted to find a place where they could settle down for the winter. Somehow they found out about Ninilchik and they kind of liked it. This lasted for 10, 12 years and then they found other places.

"John Johnson was one of them, a Norwegian. He built a salmon cannery in Ninilchik, and Long Trip Carlson ran a tender for him. In the summer John Johnson hired five or six Alutiiq men from English Bay, and they stayed in a little cabin where our house is.

"John Johnson married a nurse, Edna, from Seattle or somewhere. Her sister was Alyce Andersen, one of our first teachers.

"He played accordion for some of the dances. His favorite song was '*Skal vi gå på lofte.*' If he had a couple of beers he'd play faster and faster and we'd be spinning around that room—'C'mon, Inga, let's dance!'"

Inga? Teacher Inga Tornsvold?

"We didn't call her Inga in school! But we were finished with school and she was still teaching, only in her 20s, I think. We all liked her. She was great. She stayed and met Captain Bert Hansen—he had a fishing boat. When he got into town he'd go up on the hill to surprise her. (He had a big nose. We called him 'Captain Cleeyune'—*cleeyune* is the word for when an eagle bites with its beak.) They got married and settled in Homer and had two children. The boy, called Buoy, grew up and worked on tugboats. I've known him quite a bit. The girl worked in a bank in Homer.

"Those dances were at the old hall by the river. Mike Oskolkoff, the postmaster, owned it. He and Zoya would come down from their home before the dance was over, to say hello. They had a nice house but after they left somebody turned it into a horse barn."

Walter's own first season on Bristol Bay was the summer of 1935. "When I started in Bristol Bay I was just kind of an extra there. If any of the fishermen were sick I would be the relief. Then I got acquainted with George Osterback, and he and I fished together the next year, 1936. We were second-high boat that year for the cannery we fished for, the Red Salmon Canning Co. We were just good workers."

This was on a 30-foot gillnetter, a two-man lateen-rigged sailboat towing a drift gillnet and equipped with 16-foot oars for times when the infamous Bristol Bay winds weren't in the fishermen's favor. The boats were owned by the cannery.

"I fished Bristol Bay seven seasons, I think, and I enjoyed it. I went there again in the '60s. They had power then [after 1951]. But this was sails. That's a rugged life. And we went out for three days at a time, you know. Get a day's break and then back again for three days.

"In '37 I got my brother there. They said, 'You're pretty good. You can have a boat of your own.' So in '37 I got a boat of my own and took my brother up there with me to fish. He wanted to go. And we did good."

At the end of one fishing period, the brothers headed in as usual to unload their catch on a power scow anchored outside of Libbyville. "Ed did a good landing. We unloaded and tied behind the power scow—there were several other boats tied behind. We'd peugh the fish aboard the scow, and they'd have a big pot of fish chowder, you know—we'd eat that and then get back in the boat.

"In the meantime there's another boat coming right behind us—Charlie Wamser. He was pretty well known around the bay. He was a German but he was a real top fisherman. He was coming in, and somehow he missed the scow.

"Now, you don't have any power. You have to wait until the tide changes or you get more wind there. He missed it, and they started drifting up towards Graveyard, up Kvichak River. He had Tommy von Scheele with him—he was an Alutiiq fellow, Charlie's brother-in-law—and Charlie hollered at him, 'Drop the anchor! We're going to have to wait here till the tide changes.' Tommy said, 'Well, look here,' he said, 'the anchor line isn't tied to the anchor.' Charlie said, 'I'm the captain, goddam it. Drop that anchor when I give you an order!' So Tommy just threw that anchor—no anchor line or nothing.

"Well, then the captain got mad. He said, 'You dumb son of a so-and-so,' and he stood up and they started fighting. Charlie was so doggone strong, but Tommy tried to fight him.

"Charlie grabbed the belaying pin—that's a piece of wood about a foot and a half long—and he hit Tommy across the shoulder and broke his arm. That ended the fight. They found another anchor, a spare, got it together and threw it. Charlie told Tommy, 'You're gonna work the season even if your arm is broken.' And Tommy did. The public health nurse wrapped it up good, whatever it needed, when they got to the cannery, and he worked the whole season with that broken arm."

Walter laughs sympathetically, telling that story. A listener isn't sure whether he's identifying with the captain or the hapless crew. But he grows solemn at another Bristol Bay recollection.

"About seven or eight miles from shore are big sandbars. They call them 'Dead Man's Sand,' and you're supposed to stay away from them. Big waves come over there, and if you ever get stuck on them you've just about had it. But the fishing is good there. The fishermen try to come as close as they can and do their fishing there before the fish start coming into the bay itself.

"One boat finally got stuck—the tide was going out like anything. It got stuck and went dry right on Dead Man's Sand. They said, 'What are we going to do? We're just going to have to wait and see what happens.' The tide changed and here come these big rolls, coming right towards where they were, you know. One guy jumped up and said, 'I'll help from the sandbar. Maybe we can get the sail up and get out of here somehow.' The guy on the boat was maneuvering, and the guy on the sandbar was pushing, and pretty soon the boat took off. The guy was left standing on the sandbar and that was the end. That was it.

"He should have had a line around him or something when he was doing it. He knew that. He should have known. The guy couldn't come back to get him. He would have swamped and lost the whole thing. So he kept going and the guy on Dead Man's Sand took the consequences.

"You can ask my brother. We were around there, and he knew all about it."

Tim Troll: "Work Boats First and Foremost"

During the first half of the century, the commercial salmon fishery of Bristol Bay was exploited primarily by sailboats. Most beautiful among them were the "double-enders," single-masted gillnetters distinguished by a bow-shaped stern and the winged profile of a sprit-rigged sail.

Patterned after a Columbia River design, the 30-foot fishing boats were constructed of rot-resistant Port Orford yellow cedar planking graciously shaped by oak ribs and a hardwood keel. Old pictures of them contrast sharply with the powerful aluminum-sided gadget- and gizmo-driven gillnetters that dominate Bristol Bay as the century comes to a close.

The beauty of the double-enders, however, is not always the first memory of the old fishermen who sailed them. They were work boats first and foremost, and in those days fishing was extremely hard, miserable work. The sailboats were open and exposed to the often cold and wet weather of Bristol Bay. Catching fish in them was arduous. Nets were made of water-absorbent linen with wax-coated wooden floats and were heavy even without fish in them. They were set and pulled by hand.

All of this seems more incredible when you consider that fishing generally was a 24-hour-a-day, six-day-a-week proposition. Six days rolling on the waves in the rain and wind. Six days sleeping among the fish scales and slime. Six days with only an unshaven, unbathed partner for company. Fishermen got a break on Sunday, but it was back out on Monday for another six days.

Providence made Bristol Bay the motherlode of the world's salmon fisheries, but it did so with a fiendish touch. Fishing is dangerous work, and Bristol Bay is one of the most dangerous fishing grounds in the world. A bay fisherman must negotiate a maze of shallow waters, rip tides, shifting sand bars and windswept waves. Many fisherman have failed, a good number giving their lives in the attempt.

The task was especially difficult in a double-ender. Without power or access to a radio to call for help, a fisherman had to rely on his skill at the sail and tiller or on a strong back at the oars to avert tragedy. Death was always present, the invisible third deckhand. No wonder, in the lore of fishing in Bristol Bay, the sailing days represent a romantic era—the time of "iron men in wooden boats" in contrast to the post-sailing "wooden men in iron boats."

As romantic as the sailboat may have been, it nevertheless was a craft of servitude. The double-ender was a boat preserved long after its obsolescence by a federal law that prohibited the use of motorized fishing craft in Bristol Bay—a law pushed and safeguarded by the salmon canneries.

The statute was sugarcoated as a resource protection measure but, in fact, was an industry protection measure. Each cannery owned a fleet of double-enders, and each decided who would get to use them. They towed the boats they owned with the fishermen they chose to the fishing grounds.

Motorized fishing boats finally were legalized in 1951. Power bestowed independence on the fisherman—the ability to move quickly around the fishing grounds and sell to the cannery offering the best price. Motorized power reduced the leverage of the canneries over the fisherman, though perhaps only from a stranglehold to a wristlock.

Independence from the canneries, however, didn't come without a price. Motorized power also made Bristol Bay accessible to a lot more fishermen, and they came—many, if not most, from Outside. Twenty years after the legalization of motorized power, the limited-entry system was enacted to protect the bay from overfishing. Almost 30 years after limited entry, the bay still seems crowded. For at least 10 years there has been talk of buying back permits, but nobody has figured out how to do it.

For these reasons, some old fishermen lament the loss of the double-ender.

John Nicholson of Dillingham is one. He's 93 and has more than a half-century of experience fishing in Bristol Bay. He wrote a book called "No Half Truths," expressing his opinion on the matter. He writes:

"The reason I was against power boats was because every Tom, Dick and Harry might fish. After legalization of power and the establishment of limited entry, it seems there are now twice as many fishermen. These include doctors, lawyers and other professionals; it seemed all the pencil pushers started fishing.

"During sailboat days, they wouldn't have been able to fish because they might have been afraid to sail. The rigors of sailing and living in an open boat would have been overwhelming. I may be old-fashioned, but I still feel that it's only those guys who know how to harness the wind who really know how to fish."

In the sailing days, everybody fished the same gear; the playing field was relatively even. The bounty of the fishery went to those with skill, courage and knowledge. Today, better gear can make up for a lack of those attributes. Perhaps in time, market forces or the tenacity of the salmon to defy all predictions will weed out some of the Toms, Dicks and Harrys.

In the meantime I can't help but wonder what it was like to fish in a double-ender. I imagine the sounds that have become extinct—the ripple and then the snap of the sail as the wind brings it taut, the clack of wooden corks spilling over the gunwale, the slap of waves against the cedar hull or the creak of a bent mast sailing before a brisk wind.

Or imagine the sounds that weren't heard—the chug of a diesel engine, the clatter and chat of the VHF radio and the echo of waves rapping an aluminum hull. Fishing in a sailboat must have been a quiet undertaking. And what about smells like damp wood and wet canvas or even the smell of sea itself. All gone, replaced by the odor of diesel fuel and gasoline. And finally there is the vision of sails on the water in Bristol Bay, dozens of sails. A sight never to be seen again.

Of course, my imagination is colored by warm, sunny days and blue skies. One old sailor, Judge Roy Madsen of Kodiak, told me his memories of fishing in Bristol Bay were gray, wet and bone-chilling. The experience was so miserable, he said with a smile, that he went to law school so that he wouldn't have to spend his life fishing.

Yes, there was something about those sailboats. They made some good fishermen, and they made some good lawyers.

Artist and writer Tim Troll is chief executive officer of Chogglung Ltd., a Native village corporation in Dillingham. This essay was published under another title in "We Alaskans," Anchorage Daily News, *Oct. 3, 1999.*

The Bristol Bay salmon runs of that era are the stuff of legend. "I fished there several times when they would take all the limits off. You could fish anywhere, any amount you wanted, and the canneries couldn't even handle all the fish we were catching.

"Those were good years. The price of fish was nothing, but I made maybe 12 hundred dollars, and that was a lot of money for that time, for a fellow who was only 21, 22 years old. And I got in on some more fishing then and made another five or six hundred dollars, fishing at Unga.

"My dad was starting a store in Ninilchik. I come by here, and he was trying to get a store going, and I said, 'Here—here's all my pay. You have that. I'm going to go to work in Palmer.' I gave him whatever I earned that summer."

With George Osterback, Walter fished around Unga Island in the Shumagin chain in 1935 and 1936, after the monthlong season in Bristol Bay. "We got away from Red Salmon as quick as we could. We wanted more fishing. They want you to stay there and load all their canned salmon and everything else until they're ready to leave. It's kind of an unwritten contract: If you want to come back the next year. . . .

"But we got permission. They said, 'If you guys want to go, go.' The season's over the 25th of July, and by the first of August we were in Squaw Harbor, seining for reds and humpies, I believe, for the Squaw Harbor cannery. We were fortunate, getting there so fast—once there was a fishing boat going out there, and another trip we caught the mailboat just in time. The *Starr*.

"We already knew a lot of Unga men from fishing in Bristol Bay—Fred the Whaler and John the Sneller and plenty others. And Adolph Rodgers, from Sand Point. We fished with Walter Osterback, George's older brother. When we got there he only had a crew of one. So we fished with him for the Squaw Harbor cannery.

"Adolph Rodgers had a beautiful sister, Elizabeth, the most beautiful person I'd ever seen, I guess. But I never was around very long, and there was another guy, Andrew Gronholdt. I knew his brother Peter in Bristol Bay.

"Andrew was in love with her also. He and I were competing. She asked me to go berry-picking with her once at Sand Point, and

Walter Jackinsky Jr., c. 1942. Jackinsky family photo.

Andrew Gronholdt wasn't happy al
they got along good, and I was ther'
I was gone. . . . I don't know what
they got married. He died not too
know.

"He was kind of frail, at leas.
He couldn't fish too much. He playc.
played real well. He and I used to play a little b.

(Andrew Gronholdt and Elizabeth Rodgers did ma..,
has learned. And Andrew apparently recovered his health. A bi.c
raphical note on the Unalaska City School District's website says
that after beginning work as a deckhand on a fishing boat at age
16, Andrew Gronholdt went on to deliver mail to trappers and fox
farmers throughout the Alaska Peninsula and in the Shumagin Islands. "He was always fond of hiking, and one time while walking
on a beach on Unga Island he found a 30 million-year-old petrified
redwood stump," the writer continues. "Later he even found his
wife through his affinity for thinking and walking: By reversing
the batteries in her flashlight and making it useless, he walked her
home.")

"We all went to dances in that big beautiful dance hall, that
round dance hall in Unga," Walter says. "I knew quite a few of the
local people. There was a big family of Berntsens. Walter Berntsen
loved to sing. His favorite song was 'Amapola.' He loved to sing
'Amapola'! He had a sister, Margaret Berntsen, about our age. We
used to dance and have fun. They had some good musicians, too."

In 1960 Walter had another musical adventure of sorts on his
way to Bristol Bay from Ninilchik, crossing the Alaska Peninsula.

"Two of us took our boats to Iliamna Bay and then had to
portage from Iliamna Bay across the Alaska Range into Pedro Bay
on Iliamna Lake. Iliamna Lake is 80 miles long, 50 miles wide. It's
big, like a little ocean, and this time it was wild. We got to Pile
Bay and had to wait for weather. At the village where we stopped
and stayed a couple of nights, all the men were already in Bristol
Bay, fishing. There was nothing but women and kids around there.
Well, the commissioner, Halle Foss, was there. In fact, I hired him
as a guide to take us down the Kvichak River.

.the daughters who were in some school in Sitka or
e, they were all there for the summer. And we danced!
his boy played the guitar, and we had quite a time there.
d the cannery's calling us: 'Where are those guys? We're
ng for their expenses here and they're running us around. They
tter come over here.' We got there just before the Fourth and
there was a lot of fish. I went to the cannery and got our gear, and
we started fishing that night and were loaded with fish from then
on."

Walter talks of his friend Adolph Rodgers with regard, even
aside from Adolph's being brother to the beauteous Elizabeth. In
1938 the two young men both went to flying school, although in
different states. While Walter was earning a private pilot's license
at Swann Island Airport near Portland, Adolph was doing the same
at Boeing Field in Seattle, and they visited back and forth. Walter
soloed after eight hours of flying time. "That's a thrill when they
send you on a plane by yourself: 'Oh, you didn't even tell me I was
ready for it!' But you get in that plane, the instructor gets out, and
he says, 'I'm getting off. You go and make three landings—circle
around the airport and make three landings.'

"Up in the air, my thumb and my foot were shaking a little bit,
nervous, but I did it. From then on it got better."

Later that year, 1938, 22-year-old Walter Jackinsky married
Marie von Scheele, a schoolteacher two years his senior from a
Swedish-Alutiiq family on Afognak Island, in the Kodiak Archi-
pelago. It was a short-lived marriage, and again Walter is reticent
about this period. The couple had two children, Vonnie, who was
born Jan. 23, 1939, and died Oct. 24, 1995, and Adolph Wallace
(Duffy), born Jan. 6, 1941. Marie von Scheele remarried in 1947,
to Archibald (Scotty) Brunton, and lived the last 27 years of her life
in Santa Cruz, Calif., where she died on Sept. 23, 1996. Walter has
had little contact with the children and their families over the
years, but his oldest grandson, Vonnie's son Tom Peterson, says his
mother's first memory was of being "wrapped in furs as a baby on a
dogsled in Alaska, with Grandpa Walter's father driving the dog
team." An Afognak history titled *Derevnia's Daughters*, published in
2000, tells the story of the von Scheele clan.

Walter Jackinsky Jr. at Swann Island Airport, Portland, Ore., 1938. The plane is a Fleet Model 10 trainer, with a 125-hp Kinner engine. "Most Fleets did not have the head rest aft of the back cockpit [the 'bump' over Walter's right shoulder]," says aeronautical consultant Brad Poling, "but that could have been added after the fact." Jackinsky family photo.

"They have delivered the goods"

. . . They are largely forgotten heroes, men who made victory in World War II technically possible, who suffered a higher percentage of their number killed than any branch of the armed services—and got little credit for it.

They are the surviving wartime members of the Merchant Marine.

"We built the largest fleet of merchant ships ever and operated them to take cargoes and passengers to every part of the wartime globe," said James V. Shannon, who enlisted at age 17 from his home town of Galveston, Texas, exactly 55 years ago. . . .

Merchant mariners have never gotten much respect. During the war they had to endure the taunts of those who called them "draft dodgers" and, afterward, had to fight for decades before a federal court in 1988 and an act of Congress in 1998 finally led to "limited" recognition as veterans for mariners who served in wartime. . . .

According to unofficial statistics, 8,851 mariners were killed at sea—more than one out of every 25 of the 215,000 who served. That's a higher rate than the Marines, who lost one in 34. Other branches of the service had a much lower casualty rate.

President Franklin Roosevelt, a sailor himself, understood the mariners' contribution. "They have delivered the goods when and where needed in every theater of operations, and across every ocean in the biggest, the most difficult, and most dangerous job ever undertaken."

. . . "Just remember two things," [one seaman said]. "We were there, and every man was a volunteer."

From "Credit due mariners who delivered the goods,"
by Jack Lessenberry, Toledo *[Ohio]* Blade, *June 25, 2000.*

After Pearl Harbor was attacked in December 1941, Walter's friend Adolph Rodgers enlisted in the Army Air Corps. Walter worked for several months with a Morrison Knudsen construction crew at Dutch Harbor on Unalaska Island, building gun emplacements and ammunition storage bins, and then joined the U.S. Merchant Marine. Dutch Harbor was bombed in June 1942, a month after he left.

"My dad and I made the trip to Seattle on Alaska Steam, and I signed up there. I was interested in flying, but the Merchant Marine seemed like the best place for me. I had good letters from different companies I fished with in Bristol Bay, and from a company I was seining with at Bellingham one season. That helped a lot.

"They sent me to maritime school at Lake Washington for about a month. From there I spent a year on a tanker, the SS *Plattsburg*. I got on that at Bremerton before it was even completely finished. We made a trip to Pearl Harbor and one to the Marshall Islands, and then we took her down to Wilmington, Calif.—near Long Beach—loaded with fuel, and that's where I got off. They said, 'We want you on this Liberty ship.'"

"This Liberty ship," the SS *Henry L. Abbott*, was one of almost 3,000 such vessels built in the war years under the direction of industrialist Henry J. Kaiser. "They were built fast," Walter says, "but they weren't built for speed. They were built to carry a big load." In the case of the *Henry L. Abbott* in the spring of 1945, that meant 9,000 tons of medical supplies bound for the beleaguered Philippines.

AB Walter Jackinsky wrote a first-person account of what happened as the *Henry L. Abbott* steamed across the Pacific. The voyage and his account ended abruptly in Manila harbor.

It was a cold, rainy and foggy day as the SS *Henry L. Abbott*, a Liberty ship heavily loaded with war supplies for the South Pacific, let its lines go and slowly pulled away from one of the Army piers in Oakland. As it slowly got out into the bay the compass inspectors came out and met us from San Francisco. It took just a short while for them to swing the compass by the different bearings on the surrounding country and enter the variations and deviations for the correction into the compass log. Their job done, they wished us good voyage and were gone.

The ship steadily gaining speed passed underneath the San Francisco-Oakland Bay Bridge, then the Golden Gate Bridge, and out into the Pacific. By this time the ship had reached its top speed of approximately 10 knots.

SS *Henry L. Abbott* was built at Portland, Ore., August 1943, . . . for the War Shipping Administration and was named after U.S. Army Lieutenant Henry L. Abbott. This was the fourth voyage of the SS *Henry L. Abbott*. The Merchant Marine crew on the ship consisted of master or captain of the ship, first, second and third mates, purser, three radio operators, 10 men in the deck department, bosun, six able seamen and three ordinary seamen. [Also] Chief, first, second and third engineers, and nine other men in the engine department—three oilers, three firemen, deck engineer and two wipers. [And] Steward, first, second and third cook, three mess men and one utility and galley man. There were also 27 Navy armed guard personnel, including a Navy lieutenant and gunner's mates to man the ship's guns. Also an Army lieutenant cargo officer, as the ship was carrying Army supplies.

The weather continued to be very favorable and it got warmer day by day as we proceeded on our voyage. Flying fish could be seen most of the time and everyone started taking their shirts off. On the 10th day the Hawaiian Islands were sighted, and as we got closer Diamond Head could be distinguished, and then as we proceeded through the Kauai Channel, Molokai Island on the port side and Oahu on starboard, the city of Honolulu could be plainly seen, and then Pearl Harbor.

We slowed down, expecting possibly a change in orders, but as nothing happened the ship continued again at the regular full speed to our destination, which is usually given to the captain at the port of departure in a sealed envelope. This isn't opened until the ship is out at sea.

One day someone announced that we were crossing the international dateline and also the weather had gotten considerably warmer. By then everyone was out on deck as much as possible . . . getting suntanned. Also the fo'c's'les or the quarters were usually too hot, regardless of the continuous use of the fan, to even sleep in at night. And so eventually we were all sleeping outside. The only disappointment . . . was a heavy downpour of rain at night. The whole thing usually ended up by everyone making a mad rush with all their covers cussing and mumbling to themselves and going back to their quarters. These rainbursts usually lasted only a short while but it made things quite disappointing anyhow. The flying fish could be seen at all times and even could be found on the deck of the ship, as some unfortunate ones especially at night took the wrong direction. One early morning I was awakened unexpectedly to find a live one laying on top of my covers.

We now knew we were in the Marshall Islands, and we had been seeing different ones during the day. Next day at noon we anchored at Eniwetok. This was one of the American bases and we would get our further sailing orders from here. At noon the following day we hauled anchor as we were informed to proceed further to another given destination.

I had just sat down to a noon meal of boiled codfish, potatoes and other vegetables as it was Friday (the 13th) when all at once the ship gave a sudden heave, listed to one side and stopped. Everyone made a mad rush to get out on deck and to see what had happened. We had taken the wrong channel and were aground on a coral reef. The base control signal tower was immediately contacted and informed of our desperate situation and misfortune. In the meantime we took lead line soundings of the depth of water all around the ship and that way knew exactly how much and what part of the ship was on the reef. Three tugboats were sent to help us at once. We took their tow lines, secured them to our stern bits, and gave them the signal to pull away. We also could and did use our own power as the ship's stern was in deep water.

This pulling and using our own engine continued for about two hours with very little results. So far the ship would only move just a little bit from side to side. In the meantime during all this excitement we got a very sad message that our president of the United States, Franklin D. Roosevelt, had died [the day before, April 12, 1945]. This was certainly one Friday the 13th that made us wonder and believe about it being such an unlucky day.

U.S. Naval Historical Center photo NH 98700.

According to maritime historian William Hultgren, there are no known photographs of the SS Henry L. Abbott. *Official Liberty ship files were unaccountably earmarked for destruction shortly after World War II, Mr. Hultgren says, although by a stroke of good fortune many were intercepted and saved. The representative photo above, taken in San Francisco Bay in late 1945 or early 1946, is of the Liberty ship SS* Carlos Carrillo *and was donated to the U.S. Naval Historical Center by Bosun's Mate First Class Robert G. Tippins, USN (Ret.). The* Carlos Carrillo *was launched at Terminal Island, Los Angeles, in January 1943 and scrapped at Portland, Ore., in 1963. Mr. Hultgren offered further data on Walter Jackinsky's ship:*

The SS Henry L. Abbott *was launched Aug. 12, 1943, at the Oregon Shipbuilding Corp. in Portland and delivered seven days later to the Alaska Steamship Co. as operating agent for the U.S. War Shipping Administration. Its first voyage was to Brisbane, Australia, from San Francisco. On May 1, 1945, said Mr. Hultgren in corroboration of Walter's account, the* Henry L. Abbott *was 1,000 yards off Pier 7 at Manila when a mine blew an 8x10-foot hole into the engine room and killed two crewmen.*

On Sept. 7, 1949, the ship is known to have been thrown aground and severely damaged by a typhoon while in Hong Kong harbor. "Since the [1945] explosion was under the engine room," Mr. Hultgren says, "I seriously doubt that the ship was ever repaired and would assume she was originally at Hong Kong for scrapping." In 1950 the Henry L. Abbott *was sold to shipbreakers in Shanghai for scrap, but its story did not end there. On Sept. 26, 1950, it was intercepted by Nationalist Chinese warships while en route to Shanghai in the tow of tug* Christine Moller, *180 miles off Keelung, Taiwan, in international waters. The tug was ordered to cut the towline, and the ship was cast adrift. On April 10, 1951, it was captured by a Nationalist Chinese tug and taken to Keelung, then released and towed to the British crown colony of Hong Kong where it finally was scrapped, September 1951.*

The tugboats continued to pull us, and our own power was used to the extreme. The ship finally slowly started swaying more and more, started to move slowly, righted itself and was at last pulled off the reef. The tugboats were then turned loose as we were able to manage under our own power, being in deep water again. We went a short ways and anchored. The next day the Navy divers came out to check the bottom of the ship for serious damage to the hull. Their report showed that everything was all right, with the exception of a few bottom plates bent a little, so we were ordered to continue again on our voyage the next day.

Our next stop was at Palau Islands, and we anchored in the Palau Passage from where we traveled in convoy of about 40 ships [led by the flagship *Monterey*, so called because it signaled course changes to the other ships via coded flags; radio communications were forbidden]. At Leyte (one of the many islands in the Philippines group and the first one we came to), it being our (U.S.) first base in the Philippines during the invasion, the convoy split up to about half. Later on the convoy again split up and only about 10 of us continued to Manila.

One evening as we were coming around the point of Negros Island quite close to land, we were met by hundreds of Filipinos in their little outriggers. They seemed so happy to see us. We threw cigarettes, apples and a few different things to them. One of the fellows on the ship got so excited that he even threw away his expensive guitar.

During one stormy night the engine slowed down considerably due to trouble in the fuel lines, and before we knew or had a chance to do anything, the ship back of us in the convoy nearly ran into us. When we finally tried getting back into our position again, our ship nearly ran into one of the ships ahead of us. We finally managed to get into our place again. (We were in a zigzag course to confuse the submarines.)

It was sure good and exciting to be entering Manila Bay. As I looked at Corregidor through the telescope I could plainly see and distinguish the bare structures and ruins of different buildings. Everything had been completely destroyed by the Japanese bombs. Bataan Peninsula could also be seen very plainly. Inside Manila harbor there were approximately 400 Japanese sunken ships, bombed by our planes during the invasion. Some were lying on their side, some with only the mast sticking out of the water, some with the bow sticking out, others with just the stern showing and still others right alongside of the docks where they were unloading and now sunken. Guns could be heard in the distance. Our Army was fighting there about four miles from Manila for the city's water rights.

We anchored amongst the other merchant ships and that evening were informed that our ship would be taken inside the breakwater early the next morning, where they would immediately start unloading the cargo. When the pilot came aboard the next morning we hauled anchor and slowly proceeded to get inside the breakwater and toward the docks. We were about seven or eight hundred feet off of Pier 7 when all at once there was an explosion. The ship trembled and shook all over, raised out of the water, and finally settled down again, helpless. I and a few others were forward at the bow of the ship at that time and were quite badly shaken up but not hurt.

I immediately went back to midships to find out what had happened. Everyone there seemed puzzled, excited and uncertain as to what to do next. The engine room had flooded full with water and fuel oil and for a while we expected the boilers to blow up. There were pieces of iron and fuel oil all over the boat deck, and just then I heard the chief engineer ask some of his men if they had seen the first or the third engineer. I walked forward through the oil on the starboard side of the boat deck and there I found the fireman and oiler who had just come up from the engine room and were completely covered from head to foot with the black fuel oil. I did all I could to help wipe the oil off their faces and eyes and they told me then that the two engineers were still down in the engine room. In the meantime one of the Navy rescue boats had come alongside and also we had launched one of our lifeboats as the order to abandon ship was given although it wasn't carried out. The engine room filled up full with water but the ship still kept afloat.

By Walter's description the captain of the *Henry L. Abbott* was not himself after the ship went aground in the Marshall Islands. After the explosion in Manila harbor he had a complete nervous breakdown and was hospitalized and then sent home. The first mate, Patton, took over.

"And then, on top of the captain, the head steward went to pieces. Several days afterward [after the explosion] he got into the doggone vanilla extract—that's about 30 percent alcohol, you know—and we had to get rid of him, too. The first cook took over as steward.

"There were 12 of us picked to stay with the ship. The rest were reassigned after the explosion. I became bosun and had a sailor, AB Ed Fanticoni, and ship's carpenter, Campion, as deck crew. Then there was chief engineer, first assistant engineer and two oilers, and also a deck engineer. Steward's department consisted of chief steward and cook and combination waiter, galley maintenance, dishwasher and helper in galley."

The first order of business was to get the medical cargo unloaded.

"Manila hadn't had any medical supplies for three and a half years. Can you imagine that? Sewage, water, everything was bad. People were just in terrible shape. Broken out in sores. . . .

"We organized a Filipino crew of about 45 men and prepared to start unloading. It took approximately 40 days, around the clock, to move all the cargo. The Filipino workers were fed where they worked, mostly tubs of rice with canned salmon. Some of us made trips to uptown Manila to observe what was happening—took what clothes and other items we could spare, to help. There were a couple of hundred bed sheets aboard, and when we left [Manila] there were maybe two left. The Philippine women were making beautiful things with them. . . ."

Meanwhile, and through the months that followed, the bodies of the two crewmen remained in the engine room, inaccessible until the ship went into dry dock. Although the blast had flooded the engine room, sealed compartments around the damaged area kept the *Henry L. Abbott* from sinking.

The ship was taken under tow by a Moran Co. tug out of New York, headed to dry dock in the Admiralty Islands, below the equator. After four days of slow progress, orders came to turn around and travel back to Tacloban in the Philippines, where the United States had a floating dry dock—with a dozen ships in line ahead of the *Henry L. Abbott*.

Edward Jackinsky served on an 11th Air Corps rescue boat in the Aleutians—at Adak, Attu and Shemya—during World War II. On the back of this photo from his collection is written: "85' #511 PT boat / 15-16 on boat / captain, medic, cook, bosun's mate—Ed / 2-50 cal machine guns / twin Packard engines / built in Miss."

While Walter and the rest of the crew waited their turn, living aboard ship, "the Philippine natives would occasionally visit us in their outriggers, and we would barter for whatever each had. I got several bolo knives and a Japanese flag. They needed food and clothing. We got weekly service by U.S. Army T-boat to deliver and pick up mail and whatever stores we needed. Even got a case of beer each a month.

"In our spare time the ship's carpenter, Campion, and I built a small boat with a sail and oars and eventually found a small outboard motor, so at times we took turns and visited some of the small islands and villages.

"It was more than six months before we were able to go on dry dock and get to the remains of the bodies. . . ." At that time Walter attended the burial service in Manila for the crewmen, Albert Rutledge of Washington and John Larkin of Wisconsin.

In August, halfway through the wait for a dry dock berth, the United States bombed Hiroshima and Nagasaki. Two weeks later the war was officially over. The *Henry L. Abbott* did not make the return trip to the States. To Walter's knowledge, after Navy Seabees spent a month working on repairs in dry dock, the ship was either leased or sold to the Philippine government.

When word came for the remaining dozen crewmembers to leave the Philippines in December 1945, they traveled back to San Francisco on another Liberty ship. The crossing in winter seas was a rough one. In San Francisco they were officially discharged and received their first pay in 14 months. "We were in a 100 percent war zone, entitled to double pay," Walter says, "so payday was surprisingly good." An allotment had gone each month to Ninilchik, where Walter Sr. forwarded it to Marie von Scheele. "I didn't know where she was," Walter says.

"After a short time in San Francisco I headed for Seattle, where my dad and brother Ed were. Ed had just gotten out of the Army. In Seattle a planeload of us got together and chartered a DC-3 to fly us home. It took us maybe six, seven, eight hours to Anchorage—we stopped several places to fuel up. The three of us came home to Ninilchik. Before long we were making plans for the fishing season—building dories, hanging nets, and enjoying the good life."

Alice Lorraine McKibben (left) at a shipyard in the Oakland, Calif., area, c. 1944. On the back of the photo is written: "[corner torn and word or words missing] ... as Kip Kipley, 6524 Knott Ave., El Cerrito, Calif. Phone No. 5734," presumably the name and address of the young woman at right, and an inscription in another hand: "To a mighty nice little girl and a swell worker; may the man who marries you be worthy of you. Phil Kane[?]." Jackinsky family photo.

TALES OF THE 'BLUE CANOES'

4

. . . It was, and continues to be, the mission of the Alaska Marine Highway System to provide safe, reliable and efficient transportation to those transiting coastal Alaska. For over 30 years, this mission has been met in an exemplary manner by the consistent, dedicated and professional efforts of the men and women who operate the Alaska Marine Highway System.

A lifeline to Alaskan communities with no other viable transportation options available to supply basic service, the marine highways represent a critical component of Alaska's infrastructure by linking, in a strategic manner, its populace, industrial base, and trade. The Alaska Marine Highway System now employs more than 900 individuals, operates eight vessels, and serves 30 Alaskan ports covering 3,500 nautical miles. The system's impact on the state's economy can be felt from the southernmost port of Ketchikan, to deep within the interior and out the Aleutian chain to Dutch Harbor. In addition, the system operates upon intense and awe-inspiring waters winding through some of the most beautiful territory in the world. . . .

From System Director Gregory A. Dronkert's Preface to Highway on the Sea: A Pictorial History of the Alaska Marine Highway System, *by Stan Cohen (1994).*

Few enterprises top fishing, in Walter's view. But he had other postwar plans as well. While at flying school in 1938 he had become acquainted with a shy young country-western singer in Roseburg, Ore., and they had kept in touch through the war. "She was just really beautiful," Walter says. "And smart! She finished high school in three years. She was 17 when she graduated."

On Jan. 21, 1947, almost nine years after their first meeting, he and Alice Lorraine McKibben were married at the home of her brother, Harry McKibben Jr. (first name Francis, but known as Sonny), in Albany, Ore. Alice was 28, Walter was 30. "Even then, I wasn't quite ready to marry, I don't think. But then I figured maybe I'd better, and I did. And I was glad I did."

The newlyweds lived in Anchorage for a couple of years, 1947-49. Walter fished at Kalifonsky Beach during the summer and worked for the Morrison Knudsen construction company in the winter, repairing bridges on a road out of Yakutaga, on the Gulf of Alaska, to an oil drilling site near Malaspina Glacier, 26 miles from shore. "They flew us back and forth in helicopters—they were in a big hurry. When we got there, the boss said, 'Work those guys until they get loggy.'"

Their first daughter, Autumn Diane, was born Feb. 1, 1949, in Myrtle Point, Ore. While a student at the University of Arizona, Phoenix, in 1986, she legally added McKibben as her first name, "to honor my mother's side of the family." Son Shawn W. was born five years later, July 27, 1954, and daughter Risa Ann on Sept. 14, 1956, both in Seward. Shawn's middle initial is exactly that, an initial. He says he's always wished his parents had made it Walter. Walter says the W was Alice's idea.

By this time all the Jackinsky siblings of Walter's generation had married and begun families. Margaret—known since college by her nickname of Jackie—and her husband, Albert Pearl, had two daughters, Carroll and Patricia, born in 1943 and 1958 respectively. Cora and husband Donald Cook lost two young sons to polio in the epidemic years of the 1940s. Their sons Galen and Donald Jr. were born in 1954 and 1957. George Jackinsky brought his college sweetheart, Jeanne MacPhee, home to the Kenai after their marriage in 1950, and their daughters Traci (1951) and Lisa (1959) and sons Craig (1956) and Jon (1961) all were born in Alaska. And Edward, the eldest, was also married in 1950, to Wade (Anna Wade) Cline. Their six children are listed in Chapter 7, "Ninilchik, 2003."

The year before McKibben was born, Walter and Alice visited San Bernardino, Calif., where Alice's father was helping care for his

Alice Lorraine McKibben with the band in Oregon, c. 1938. Jackinsky family photo.

*Alice and Walter Jackinsky Jr. on their wedding day, Jan. 21, 1947, Albany, Ore.
Jackinsky family photo.*

mother, Alice's grandmother. "I got bored there," Walter says. "I needed something to do. So I got a job spraying fruit trees."

After another visit Outside, in late winter 1951, 2-year-old McKibben and her parents traveled home to Alaska in caravan with Ed and Wade and their infant son, Tim.

"I asked the cannery I was fishing for to advance me the money, and we bought a Plymouth sedan for $2,400. I paid it off when I finished fishing the next season. Ed and Wade had a new car, too. We met in Coeur d'Alene, Idaho, and went into Canada from there. The Alcan was a mess in the summer, but it wasn't bad when we drove it. Everything was frozen."

The cannery was Squeakey Anderson's in Seldovia. Walter recalls that writer Elsa Pedersen, known later for her popular series of Alaskan novels for young readers, was working then as bookkeeper for Squeakey Anderson, as retired Admiral Carl Anderson was known throughout Southcentral Alaska and beyond. And he likes to tell the story of Squeakey Anderson's crew of drift-netters in Cook Inlet who didn't want to knock off fishing because the run was so good but had the tender send an SOS to the cannery: "We're out of snoose!" According to Walter, Squeakey didn't dip tobacco himself but knew an emergency when he heard one. "He radioed back, 'Hold on! I'll send some right away.'"

After Alice and Walter's return to Alaska courtesy of Squeakey Anderson, the little family moved to Ninilchik to be near Walter Sr., whose health was beginning to fail. That first fishing season, the three of them—Alice, Walter Jr. and McKibben—lived in a tent on the beach at Point Harriet, across the Inlet from the Jackinsky homestead. Alice made the adjustment to life in Alaska remarkably well, Walter says. And why not? She loved to fish. "That was one of their favorite things to do together," says their son, Shawn. "They didn't see eye to eye on every subject, but when it came to fishing—well, they both loved it. Commercial or sport, they just loved to fish." In later years, when Walter was away on his ferry job or fishing in Bristol Bay, Alice would take the children out with their poles to one or another of the streams around

From left, Walter Jackinsky Jr., Alice Jackinsky, a 290-pound halibut, and Walter Jackinsky Sr., at Kalifonsky Beach on Cook Inlet, late 1940s. Jackinsky family photo.

Juneau, "just the way Grandpa McKibben used to take her and her sister and brother in his Model T out to the rivers in central Oregon," Shawn says.

Walter has a heart-stopping story from Shawn's childhood:

Alice and the children were at Ninilchik School—the present school, along the highway above the village—for a midwinter evening basketball game, and Walter was in Anchorage on business. In the hubbub of preparations for halftime refreshments in a room adjoining the makeshift gym, no one noticed when 2-year-old Shawn wandered over to an old upright piano in the corner and managed to loosen a stack of shims that was supporting one of its legs. The piano fell backward and pinned Shawn in position, bent double with the piano resting on his back, like a miniature Atlas supporting the world.

Shawn's world burst into action. His sister McKibben, 7 at the time, remembers parts of the scene with clarity, other parts from family retellings. Someone took baby Risa from Alice's arms and shepherded the two girls, while half a dozen men raised the piano. Someone else brought a car around and eased Alice and Shawn into the passenger side, where Shawn was tenderly laid on the front seat—the first awful decision had been whether to attempt to straighten his small body—and Alice crouched on the floor to keep close watch by the light of the dashboard during the slippery 30-mile drive to South Peninsula Hospital in Homer. His translucent toddler skin was dotted with the purple of broken blood vessels just under the surface, his abdomen swollen from the pressure he had endured.

Walter came in from his own five-hour trip on winter roads to be greeted with news of the accident, got back in his vehicle, and headed straight to Homer. By his daughter's telling, "Mom said that was the first and last time she ever saw Dad in tears." Walter says only, "I sat by his bed for two nights."

God bless resilient young bodies. Shawn's recovery from a crushed vertebra and cracked hip was speedy and complete. The doctor merely suggested that in later life he probably should avoid tackle football.

In the early '50s, by Walter's recollection, the state issued permits for the first time for hunting cow moose. Everyone eligible applied, and several of the women at Ninilchik, Alice among them, made the list. A couple of husbands were sure that that meant no moose. The doubters went out the day before the period opened to shoot a moose apiece in advance, with the plan of bringing them in on opening day and presenting them as the women's work. The plan backfired when the women got their own, legally, and the early kills—now extras—had to be brought in somehow under the noses of Fish & Game.

"But not in my case," Walter says. He had confidence, and Alice had grit. He took her to Clam Gulch at exactly 10 o'clock on the big morning and handed her his .300 Magnum. "We saw a nice cow there. Alice shot—and a tree fell down. Finally she did get her moose. But that .300 Magnum left her shoulder black and blue."

Alice had already gotten her first bear, but that was with a .22. Grizzlies were frequent visitors at the Polly Creek fish site across the inlet, a nuisance with the nets and sometimes a hazard in camp. Walter backed her up with a larger gun, but Alice shot the intrusive grizzly herself.

Until the ferry system beckoned in 1962, Walter supported his growing brood with a variety of jobs. When a listener laughs in bewilderment over the sometimes overlapping progression—licensed big game guide for 10 years, lodge owner for eight years, fish trap operator for five years, crabber, set-net fisher, construction worker—he laughs too, then quietly observes, "I'm not telling anything out of the way. That's the facts, whatever I tell you, you know."

He operated a fish trap for the last years of their use in Alaska. When the territory became a state in 1959 fish traps were outlawed. Their contentious history isn't strictly part of Walter's story but makes fascinating, sometimes frustrating, reading. See for instance "Salmon Fish Traps in Alaska: An Economic History Perspective," by Steve Colt, listed in Resources.

"I had a fish trap for five years, right on Ninilchik Point here. Libby, McNeil & Libby [later Wards Cove] had a trap there for years, and gosh, that trap was making big money. I think the year

McKibben [Autumn], Risa and Shawn Jackinsky, c. 1959. Jackinsky family photo.

Risa A. Jackinsky, Designer, Beadworker

The colors and patterns in Risa Jackinsky's designs are beaded reflections of a rich personal history that began on the Kenai Peninsula, a small finger of land jutting from Alaska's southcentral coastline.

Ms. Jackinsky's early childhood summers were spent at the beach site where her family caught the salmon that school in Cook Inlet's treacherous waters. Smooth sand, rough gravel, coastal winds and swirling tides formed a backdrop for her imagination. Lullabies were accompanied by the ever-present rhythm of the surf, washing its influence into her life. Winter's white, frozen silence offered a stark contrast perfect for listening to stories of her heritage, Aleut, Russian, Irish and Mexican ancestors forming a pattern that serves as her template for design. Later Risa and her family moved to Southeast Alaska, a rain forest where towering Sitka spruce anchor the fertile landscape in thick carpets of moss, and mountain peaks jut skyward from glacial waters with little thought to beaches.

Her name suggests an ancestral patchwork: Risa is Spanish for "laughter" as well as the shortened form of "Raisa," Russian for "grace." Her surname was one of the few belongings carried to this country by her paternal grandfather.

Her family tradition and her childhood on Alaska's coastline when life depended on the push and pull of tides and migratory patterns of salmon have given Ms. Jackinsky a deep bond with this country's indigenous people. While living near Tucson, Arizona, she actively developed this connection, introducing the history of that region's native people to the public through her position as community coordinator with the prestigious Amerind Foundation.

Her designs pull together modern fashion trends with traditional native patterns, combining a variety of shapes, textures and found objects, frequently including small faces carved into pieces of cottonwood bark washed up on Alaskan beaches. Her mother's cottonwood carvings inspired that detail, which reflects a weathering of the wood, as well as life itself. . . .

Adapted from a 1990 flyer composed by McKibben Jackinsky, reproduced in Agrafena's Children. *Used by permission of both sisters.*

before I got it, in kings alone they caught 10,000 fish. I went to see the people at Libby's. I said, 'It's pretty close to where my property is. I've lived here all my life. Isn't there a chance that I could have that location?' They said, 'OK, it's yours.'

"Before that they had people from Ballard or somewhere like that to take care of the trap. Then I got it for five years. . . .

"I always had a partner—Elador Resoff was one, and Martin Terezin. Maybe one other. The company had a cabin at the site, and I had a nice tent set up there for the family. Alice would bring McKibben and Shawn and Risa from Jackinsky's Ranch and spend time there on the beach. . . .

"It's a long season—from May 25th to the middle of August, I think. But I didn't do so good. The regulations were changing. For traps you have to have more time to fish—the fish have to have time to get up along their lead and into the trap, you know. And they were limiting our time of fishing.

"Some years it did well. Other years it didn't. It looks like a good thing, but it was just getting too late. . . ."

Overlapping fishing periods made for an intensive summer. While Walter was out drifting with his gillnet boat—first the *Alice J*, then the *Autumn J*—and his partners were minding the fish trap, Alice and the children would set the beach gillnet in the morning and then pick the fish from the loaded nets—on a good day they were loaded nets—when the tide was right, reaching over the end of a dory as it bobbed up and down in the inlet.

Jackinsky's Ranch was the family's business a few miles up the highway from Ninilchik village. "After my dad passed away, 1950, we decided to open up our lodge, a big building right across the highway here. We had it built by a contractor—Mueller Bros., Gene and Don Mueller. They were homesteaders at Deep Creek, and they did a good job. I had a beautiful natural rock fireplace put in there, in the lodge itself. We didn't use it much, but it was attractive.

"People knew there was going to be a big opening, and they came from Kasilof, they came from Homer, you name it. We had a good band. One fellow, a young fellow from Homer, Chuck Carlsen, played a clarinet, and he was just outstanding."

Alice: "We Decided to Tackle the Business Ourselves"

Ours was the only car in the village, and it was soon put to steady use as a "For Hire" vehicle to answer the constant "need" for alcoholic beverages. After considering the prospects of a worn-out Chevy and the revenue flowing toward the liquor stores and bars 40 miles away, we decided to tackle the business ourselves. As the local missionary had earlier petitioned against liquor being sold within two miles of the village, we chose the old family homestead three miles out as our location.

Being completely green to the trade and as nearly broke, we borrowed for our first license and three cases of whiskey. When that was gone, we doubled our order and kept on in this manner until the fishing season approached. Then we knew we were going to have to gamble in a make or break situation. Having built up a good credit rating with the wholesalers by this time, we ordered over $5,000 worth of liquor and chartered a boat to haul it from Anchorage. And when it arrived, the highway construction crew supplied a bulldozer and operator to pull the truck transporting the goods from the village through the mud holes, which were many.

The "highway" was in perfect condition, or so it seemed until the spring thaw when it was revealed that it was only a "rough draft"—a trail without any gravel. And we suspect that there was a very good reason why the three-mile stretch from the village was completed ahead of everything else!

Shortly we realized we would have to take another risk. Toward spring everyone is broke. Trusting the people and the fact that it was to be humpy [pink salmon] year—"10 thousand *gibushay*," as Grandpa used to say—we sold our entire stock on credit.

It was a good season and the payment of liquor bills took precedence that year. We soon hired two young homesteading brothers to erect a building housing a bar (which my husband had promised me we wouldn't have), liquor store and an apartment that was to be our home for eight years.

We had the first refrigerator and propane stove in the area and it was a thrill to see the look on the oldtimers' faces when we would show them how simply a fire could be started or heat from propane could make ice. One word drawn out: "Ay-yi-yi!"

When all was complete, we had a grand opening that caused sister businesses to close down for the night and people came from as far as 140 miles and stayed until the wee hours of the morning—to start all over again by 9 a.m.

And on it went, starting some of the hardest working days of my life. . . .

Kanashka

*Kanashka was my friend—sometimes likeable, some-*times maddening, but my friend. Thinking of him brings smiles. He must have been 40 or 45 years old, thin, slightly stooped, tousled hair.

After a few drinks he was inclined to ramble on—giving the appearance of being much drunker than he was. He always had a can of Copenhagen in his shirt pocket and never seemed to run out of wadded-up dollar bills he would extract as needed from his pants or jacket pockets. Kanashka was always aware of what went on around him. He may not have entered into too many conversations, but no one could trick him into buying them a drink.

One night I was driving home from the village and noticed dogsled tracks ahead of me—obviously the wavering trail of one under the "influence of."

Suspecting who it may be, I was alert. But not as alert as Kanashka. He saw me first and turned his one-dog sled crosswise in the road as I attempted to go around him to the left. His move put him in the place to be hit by my left front fender. He went up in the air, arms extended, like someone missing his hang-glider. And down he fell, to land in the snow bank as I came to a stop. I rolled down the window and frantically called, "Kanashka, are you all right?" He looked up at me and said, "Oh, for goodness sakes, I was just going to your place!"

Much relieved, I got out of the car knowing for sure the dog must be dead. But there he stood, wagging his tail. The sled, unbroken, was hanging on the bumper guards. We moved dog and sled off the highway and headed for the bar, with me seeking reassurance from Kanashka that he was all right. In his usual way, he repeated his words: "I'm fine, I'm fine. Don't tell anybody. Don't tell anybody. Nobody's business!"

When we got to the bar, we went to the back door. I intended telling my husband what had happened and to keep an eye on our friend, but before I could even approach the bar, Kanashka hollered: "Jesus Christ, Vladja [Walter], your wife almost killed me!"

One summer Kanashka's youngest son returned from the service, bringing a bride with him from the East Coast. What an experience for a young woman!

They stayed with Kanashka in the village. One morning he was angry with his son and nailed boards at angles across their door to keep them shut in their room. They heard the hammering and opened the door to a very puzzled-looking Kanashka. He hadn't considered that the door opened inward. Needless to say, the young couple returned to Pittsburgh shortly.

Another time, while in his cups, Kanashka imitated the way a friend with a broken leg walked. He wrapped his leg around a stick, using it as a cane—and fell down and broke his own leg!

. . . Perhaps if the operator of the new bar above the village had followed our practices, Kanashka would still be providing us with stories.

But one New Year's he had his usual drinks while there and was asked to leave. He was very obedient—never belligerent—and he left.

As he turned from the main road to go into the village, he apparently slipped and fell in the snow.

And that's where he was found the next morning, frozen. He went to sleep with one hand holding his can of Copenhagen.

By Alice Lorraine McKibben Jackinsky.

"Then there were several guitar players," Walter says, "and they all played until the wee hours of the morning. Down the road from us was a little place where they were making sandwiches. People ate and started dancing again. It went on till the next day. Not as much, but they were still going all through the next day, next evening, and then everyone gave out because they had as much fun as they could stand, I guess.

"We ran it for about eight years. The first few years we lived on the premises, and then we bought a house at Deep Creek, finished enough to live in. I put on a nice new roof and finished it up.

"We had a big bar and a liquor store, and it was doing good. But when I saw how it affected people around here, that liquor store, I said no, it isn't good, you know, it's got my friends. One of my friends was only 30-some years old when he died, from alcohol. They were spending all their money, you know. It was good for us, but it wasn't good for the families. We gave it up.

"About five years after we sold it, the building burned down. The fellow I sold it to ran it for a while, and he had a fellow helping him and sleeping in the bar room. There was an oil heater in there and something got out of hand. . . .

"There's at least one bar in Ninilchik now, and a liquor store. But alcohol isn't the problem it used to be. For a while, when there wasn't anything else . . . [voice trailing off]. Some people would fish like anything, make big money, and then they'd spend it. Drinking. Kenai was the same. But they're involved in so many things now, you know, that drinking doesn't affect people that much."

Jackinsky's Ranch hosted many evenings of dancing, and visiting musicians could expect to be pressed into service on the spot. But Walter and Alice's children particularly remember their parents gliding through waltzes and foxtrots during the Saturday night movie and dance potlucks at the old American Legion Hall just south of Ninilchik village. "They loved to dance," daughter McKibben says. "And they were beautiful—so smooth."

Melody of Love (Ninilchik Song)

He didn't ask; she told him
Let's get married, it's sink or swim
He said well I was gonna ask you myself
I'll tell you where it all should begin
> Let's go down to Ninilchik
> It's a little slice of heaven above
> When I find myself in Ninilchik
> I'll have my Melody of Love

Let's pack up the rig we'll go truckin'
Down the Seward and the Sterling we'll go
As long as we're goin' I might as well throw in
Our hip boots and fishing poles
Chorus

We'll be down on the harbor at midnight
By mornin' we'll be out on the troll
With a six pack or two watching the sunrise with you
I'll be the happiest man I know
Chorus

Now we're back on the beach, the tide is low
The sea anemones are startin' to show
I'm lookin' real close at a dimple or two
I hope to fill your bucket on our honeymoon
Chorus

We'll gather some driftwood up in a pile
And build us a big bonfire
As we watch the sparks disappear in the dark
We'll fan the flames of desire
> Let's go down to Ninilchik
> It's a little slice of heaven above
> When I find myself in Ninilchik
> I'll have my Melody of Love

Words and music by Butch Leman, © 2003
Published by Sturdy Music–BMI

When news came of openings in the fledgling Alaska Marine Highway System, Walter applied immediately and was hired as an ordinary seaman. "I got a letter from the governor [William A. Egan] himself. He wrote something like, 'You are going to work on the *Malaspina*.' We knew him, you know. Everybody knew him. The population was so small then, everyone knew each other pretty much."

The first "Alaska ferry" had been a military surplus landing craft built to shuttle tanks ashore in World War II. Christened the *Chilkoot*, after the fabled Gold Rush pass near Skagway, it carried up to 13 vehicles and 20 passengers in Southeast Alaska until it was replaced in 1957 by the M/V *Chilkat*. The new ferry, named for Chilkat Glacier northwest of Skagway at the U.S.-Canada border, carried 15 vehicles and 59 passengers on a series of routes and was retired in 1988 after its final assignment in Prince William Sound.

The *Malaspina*, first of the modern Alaska Marine Highway "blue canoes," underwent pre-launch work in Seattle in January 1963. Walter was one of 27 crewmen who spent the second half of the month in Seattle preparing for the trip north. Governor Egan sailed with other dignitaries on that first voyage to Southeast Alaska. Walter eventually served under seven Alaskan governors in nine different administrations. [See Appendix.]

"We spent half a day or longer in Ketchikan—we had open house there, and everybody came aboard. Then it was Wrangell, and through the Wrangell Narrows to Petersburg; then Juneau for over a day, for more celebration. In Juneau we got off and another crew got on. From then we worked one week on, one week off. In a short time I went to AB, able-bodied seaman. I had my certificate from the Merchant Marine and plenty of sea time.

"We covered the regular Southeast run for about four months, and then we took the *Malaspina* up to Anchorage for the celebration there. Anchorage, Homer, Seldovia, Cordova, and then back to Southeast."

After the June 1963 run to Anchorage and points south, Walter and Alice prepared for a family move to Juneau, home port for the ferry fleet. McKibben was a young teenager, Risa and Shawn 6 and 9 years old.

"Malaspina is a Beauty"

Just about everybody in Homer and the surrounding area was out to meet and greet the *Malaspina* on her arrival Sunday morning. As the fine vessel with the gold stars of the Big Dipper painted on her blue funnel came into the Bay, a mighty sigh went up. Pleasure craft sped out to meet the *Malaspina* and airplanes circled overhead dropping streamers. Brightly colored pennants fluttered along the pier to help welcome the visitors arriving aboard the ferry from Anchorage.

The Homer Woman's Club was responsible for organizing the welcome and the Chamber of Commerce and Homer Little Theatre joined them enthusiastically. . . . Even the weather cooperated by being warm and sunny with scarcely a breeze.

The one sour note was that the town's eating places were overtaxed to feed the close to 400 people, and many boarded the plane for home without having eaten.

Homer newspaper article, mid-June 1963,
from McKibben Jackinsky's childhood scrapbook.

A teacher friend lived in the Deep Creek house for five years and finally bought it. Walter and Alice bought a two-bedroom mobile home, former employee housing for the World's Fair in Seattle, and had it shipped to Juneau. "Then I had a good season in Bristol Bay that first summer," Walter says, "and we bought a house, a beautiful house in the Villa de Vista development out Mendenhall Loop Road about five miles from the glacier." Alice had helped run Jackinsky's Ranch at Ninilchik. In Juneau she took community college classes in preparation for an accounting position with the state Department of Health and Social Services.

Juneau was home base for the first 17 years of Walter's ferry service. He was there with the family when the 1964 Good Friday earthquake struck. Southcentral Alaskans tend to date events before and after that horrific quake, which registered 8.3 on the old Richter scale but has since been upgraded to 9.2. The March 27 earthquake and resulting tsunamis killed more than a hundred people in Alaska and 15 people on the Pacific Coast, 11 in Crescent City, Calif., and four in Newport Beach, Ore. Afognak, now a village in memory only, and neighboring communities in the Kodiak area were destroyed by tsunami; Afognak residents resettled in Port Lions, named by grateful villagers for the organization Lions International and the District 49 Lions Clubs in Anchorage, which provided significant aid for the move. Valdez, on Prince William Sound, was destroyed by the triple forces of earthquake, tsunami and fire. "New Valdez" was built nearby at higher elevation and on more stable ground. Tsunami and fire also devastated Whittier and Seward. Juneau and the rest of Southeast were shaken but unscathed by comparison, as was the Ninilchik area, although other peninsula towns were harder hit.

After a year on the *Malaspina* Walter passed his mate's examination and transferred to the *Matanuska* as second mate. He served also on the *Taku* before transferring back to the *Malaspina* as chief mate under Captain Harold Payne and beginning the wait for his own ship. Seven or eight years later—five years as chief mate plus a few seasons as relief captain on the *E.L. Bartlett* and the old *Chilkat*—he and Richard Hofstad took over the *LeConte*, both of them captains, relieving each other in the usual pattern for seven years.

Coast Pilot 9, 1964, "the earthquake edition"

Whittier (1960 population 168; P.O.) is the Alaska Railroad terminus on the south side of Passage Canal, 1.5 miles from the head. In 1964 the port was in caretaker status. The town has a sawmill and a wood-treatment plant.

The March 1964 earthquake caused a bottom subsidence of 5.2 feet at Whittier. Until a complete survey is made of the area, caution is necessary because depths may vary from those charted and mentioned in this Coast Pilot.

Wharves.—There are two main docks at Whittier, both of which are operated by the Alaska Railroad. The 1,100-foot-long marginal wharf with depths of about 30 feet alongside its face handles general cargo and sea trains. DeLong Pier, 425-foot long with 36 feet alongside, is about 550 yards northeastward of the marginal wharf. Gasoline, diesel oil, and water are available in limited quantities at the marginal wharf.

The two oil T-piers westward of the marginal wharf were completely destroyed by the March 1964 earthquake. Submerged ruins may exist in this spoil area ... .

Anchorages.—Large vessels sometimes anchor clear of the 4.5 fathom shoal on Bush Banks about 2 miles northeastward of Whittier or in Pigot Bay.

Routes.—Eastward: From the entrance point to Prince William Sound, 1.5 miles southwest of Cape Hinchinbrook Light, set courses to pass 2 miles east of Smith Island, 1.5 miles north of Point Eleanor Light, 1.5 miles southwest of Perry Island Light, 1 mile northeast of Culross Island Light, 0.5 mile south of Point Pigot Light, 0.5 mile north of Decision Point Light, 0.5 mile north of Trinity Point Light, and thence to Whittier, clearing the south shore by 0.5 mile until up to the waterfront.

Westward: Enter Prince William Sound through Elrington Passage, clear the east side of Evans Island by 1 mile, then pass 0.5 mile east of Pleiades Light, 2 miles east of Crafton Island Light, and follow the route mentioned above. Vessels from Valdez usually use Perry Passage when going to Whittier.

From U.S. Coast Pilot 9: Alaska, Cape Spencer to Beaufort Sea, *Seventh Edition, 1964*

6—The Cordova Times, Cordova, Alaska, Thursday, August 5, 1976

M/V E.L. Bartlett logs in her 1,000th voyage

When the M/V E. L. Bartlett left Valdez last Saturday for Whittier, the captain's log read "ex Valdez en route to Whittier", just as it has countless times before. But the voyage was marked by one ceremonial element—it was the Bartlett's 1,000th voyage.

And a good voyage it was. Capt. Ron Hamrick said the vessel was booked solid—170 passengers and 38 vehicles is the capacity of the 193-foot-long state ferry. With all those passengers, the 24-person crew is kept busy. "It was just another working day for us," Hamrick said.

Commissioned in 1969, the Bartlett made her first voyage from Cordova to Valdez on July 10 of that year. Master Richard T. Hostad was skipper of the vessel, and chief engineer was Hugh McDonald.

In the seven years the Bartlett has been serving Alaska, she has carried 137,692 passengers, and allowed them a spectacular view of Columbia Glacier exactly 1,312 times.

The glacier was missed only once because of fog, the captain said. Hamrick has been master during most of those sightseeing trips—a total of 1,134 times.

The Bartlett has logged in 212,937 miles, and her engines have 16,600 hours on them. "We've never postponed trips due to mechanical failure or weather," Hamrick said, although the ferry's schedule has been juggled to accommodate school ball teams at times.

This summer's ferry traffic shows an increase over last summer's, Hamrick said. Average summer traffic is 21,000 passengers and 5,000 automobiles. The Bartlett continues serving Cordova and Valdez most of the winter, but drops their Whittier voyage in the fall due to the weather and seas.

"I think she's the cleanest ship in the fleet," Hamrick asserted proudly. "I know we have the cleanest engine room in the fleet—that thing sparkles!"

M/V E.L. BARTLETT

Clipping from the collection of Virgil and Dawn Campbell.

Through all this time Walter worked one week on and one week off, until he and Hofstad agreed between them to make that two weeks on and off. Hofstad was commuting from Southern California. Except for annual overhaul runs and time out for schooling, Walter was home in Juneau on alternate shifts. Then came the call for a supposed six-week relief on the *Bartlett*. "They didn't say any more, and I didn't say anything. It was 17 years before I told them, 'I'm going to retire now.'"

Those first six weeks on the *Bartlett* stretched to 14 months aboard ship. No vacation. No "week on, week off." No breaks, period. And Walter remembers it all with gusto.

"They said, 'There's your ship, there's your crew, there's your schedule.' I just lived on the ship.

"Wintertime schedule was easy. We'd get into Cordova about three or four o'clock in the afternoon, and we wouldn't leave until the next morning at nine. We'd leave Cordova and go to Valdez, in the wintertime anyway. We'd lay there all night and come back the next day to Cordova, and stay in Cordova all night. At that time there wasn't much winter traffic for Whittier.

"Summers were something else. There was all kinds of summer traffic for Whittier and Valdez. In the summer, May through August, the longest time we had off was from midnight to six in the morning.

"We made one round trip a day, Valdez to Columbia Glacier to Whittier and back the same way. We always stopped for a good look at Columbia Glacier. Then one or two trips a week between Valdez and Cordova, with maybe a flag stop at Tatitlek. That's an Alutiiq village, about a hundred people, mostly fishermen. Picturesque. They finally put in a dock there about a year before I retired. There's an island on the way in that one of the crew called 'Jackinsky's Island.'

"Cordova to Tatitlek, four hours. Through the Tatitlek Narrows, hour and a half to Valdez. You're in the Gulf for 30 minutes, then the Valdez Narrows.

"When I left Juneau to go on the *Bartlett,* those that had been up there for a short while said, 'You'll never stay.' They said, 'There's just one crew, and the duty's too long.' After the first year,

I thought, 'Gosh, this isn't that bad. What are they talking about?'

"But there in Prince William Sound we ran all the time, except during overhaul. With just one crew. When someone got tired you called for relief from Juneau. After 14 months I said, 'I need a vacation.' They said, 'We don't have anyone to relieve you.' I said, 'I've got a chief mate here, John Klabo, and I think he's qualified.' 'Well, if you recommend him, we'll make him master of the ship while you're gone.' 'OK,' I said, and I took the next couple of months off." [See "Around the World for 20 Years."]

Rules of the Road

Daughter Risa, who left Juneau-Douglas High School without graduating, says Walter told her that if she worked toward the GED credential, he would, too. She passed the examination with no difficulty, and Walter did the same. He also, within a year of hiring on as ordinary seaman, took and passed the test for mate. He's proud of all three milestones, and he and Risa are in good company: Holders of the GED certificate include actor Bill Cosby, Delaware's Governor Ruth Ann Minner and U.S. Senator Ben Nighthorse Campbell of Colorado.

In another year Walter passed the inland master's exam, and then, while figuratively twiddling his thumbs waiting for an assignment as captain, went for the top license, the oceangoing master's license. Any tonnage, any ocean. Or as the U.S. Coast Guard terms it, a bit more prosaically, "any gross tons upon oceans."

The M/V *Malaspina* was lengthened in 1972 by the simple expedient of cutting it in half and adding 56 feet in the middle. That sounds extraordinary to a landlubber but is not an unusual practice in shipbuilding circles. The *Tustumena* was lengthened in 1969, the *Matanuska* in 1977–78. "We went down there [with the *Malaspina*]—got it into the shipyard and had this piece already made for it. Just fit it right in. They cut the ship in half right close to the engine room where it was easy to cut, and put that piece right in. . . . And here's another thing: It made it 50-some feet longer, and it maintained the same speed, didn't lose any speed or anything."

Chief Mate Jackinsky and other crewmembers traveled with the

Malaspina from Seattle to Portland, Ore., where the work was to be done. When the job was well under way he took a three-month leave to study for the unlimited master's exam at Crawford Nautical School in Wilmington, Calif., where he had been based for a time in the Merchant Marine.

"We had a surprise on the way to Portland. Somebody said, 'Hey, there's a stowaway aboard!'

"I said, 'Bring him up here.'

"Here comes a rough-looking guy from the skid row of Seattle. I said, 'What are you doing here?' He said, 'Captain [Ronald] Kutz [pronounced Kootz] told me I could go to Alaska and get a job up there.' I said, 'You're out of luck. We're going to Portland. But you want a job, we'll get you a job. You can help the cook.' He got off in Portland as soon as he could. But before he got off we made a collection, you know. I think I put in $5. He had money enough to get to Seattle and then some. And he was pretty well fed and his clothes were cleaned, so he was happy.

"Anyway, I stayed on until we stripped the ship in Portland and the Willamette Iron and Steel Co. shipyard took it over, and then I headed for Wilmington."

The maritime course at Crawford Nautical School was only one of several Walter has taken. He was glad he had studied bookkeeping and mathematics earlier, in University of Alaska extension classes in Anchorage. "I went twice to Kildall [Nautical School] in Seattle. Once to Wilmington. And then here at AVTech [Alaska Vocational Technical Center in Seward] just for radar endorsement. That's a lot of math."

Masters and mates are required to renew their radar licenses every five years. "You go through a full course, five days of mathematical and navigational problems using radar. The classes are usually six to a dozen people. Once or twice we had women in the class. It's not just masters and mates, but also local people who have their own private boats.

"Parts of AVTech are in the former Seward public grade school. You could board there, and you could eat there, because they were teaching cooks, too. I think we had some cooks aboard ship who graduated from there. I stayed at the Seward Hotel, but I ate one meal, the lunch meal, at AVTech. The last year I renewed my radar, 1996, the instructor was Dennis Lodge. He's an Englishman, a good teacher."

Back in Juneau from Wilmington for his first go at the unlimited license, Walter stayed either with McKibben, who by then was married and in her own apartment, or at a hotel, both places presumably quieter than at home with the younger children. He studied each night till two or three a.m., then rose at six for the day's session.

The first test topic was navigational "Rules of the Road." Thirty-eight of them, to be precise. "You had to get 90 percent on that. Otherwise you flunked. In 30 days you could try it again. That's before you did anything else. You really had to study for that. There were some that missed it and had to wait 30 days. The second time you usually got it. I think the second time you had another try after 30 days, and then it would be six months. It would be a long time before you could take another jab at it."

Walter didn't need another jab. "I got 94 the first time," he says with uncharacteristic modesty. "That wasn't too bad."

The GED, or a high school diploma, wasn't required as far as Walter remembers, but he knows of only one person who became a master with just an eighth-grade education. "Maynard Reeser from Petersburg said, 'I don't know if I can do it, but I'm going to try.' He got the inland, and that was easy. That was really easy. [A moment's reflection.] Well, it isn't easy, but in comparison . . ."

The breadth and depth of knowledge required for the ocean license *is* extraordinary, and not just to a landlubber.

"Rules of the Road took one day. From then on there were more subjects, in eight days. We had the weekend off—five days, then a few more days after the weekend. I didn't go anywhere. I just sat and studied. I wanted to get it over with.

"Navigational rules. Instruments and accessories used in navigation. Aids to navigation. Tides and currents. Celestial navigation. Cargo loading and storage. Ship handling tips and practical maneuvering—single screw and double screw (two propellers or single propeller). Piloting, or pilotage. Lifeboats. Ship construction and repair—you had to know a little about that. In the shipyard where they're repairing your ship, you're right there with them. They give you a hard hat. You can't say much, but you should know what's going on.

"Assistance in towing. Cargo gear testing and inspection. International code of signals—Morse code and flags. A,B,C,D, and so on, with your flags. They had semaphores. You had to know the rules about those. And then you had to know how to flash in code. They gave you a certain time limit. You couldn't be too slow or sloppy about it. You had to be pretty accurate.

("Somebody taps six times: dah dah dah dah dah dah. That's 'emergency.' 'Help.' Even on a whistle. Six blasts on the whistle. You're needing help. Or on the bell, the ship's bell.)

"Stability. That's a big subject of its own. You can roll a ship over, you know. You have to be careful. You've got to start quartering into your waves. The waves are coming, and you start quartering into them. One guy just about rolled the *Bartlett* one time in the Gulf, because the weather was so adverse. He went without even checking with Ketchikan. You start checking with the weather station in Valdez. See, they cover the Gulf pretty much, and they'll give you an idea what it's like. But I guess he didn't think about that, that particular time. They ran out there, and the mate said to him, 'Hey, look here, the barometer has dropped right down. There's a terrible storm somewhere.' And they were really in it, you know. They thought they couldn't turn around because they'd roll the ship. And the barometer just—wham—went right down. Things were going to be pretty bad, but there was nothing they could do. I mean, in big weather you can't turn around so easy."

Big weather?

"That's 30-, 35-foot waves. Maybe more. But those are big. And you get 60-, 65-mile wind. That's enough. In a headwind, you're bucking into it, slowing you down. A real tailwind is good because you can maneuver easier and faster. Except you've got to watch that you hit the waves at the right angle. . . .

"Fire aboard ship. Firefighting. Class of fire." Did he ever have fires on board? "In the galley we did. Nothing very big. It was well taken care of."

"Station bills. That's during our fire drills, we'd have station bills to show what job everybody was assigned to. And there were drills every week.

"Ship's log. First aid and ship sanitation. Ship's business. Business with your office and passengers. Handling money. Most tickets were sold ashore, but some were sold aboard. Meals were sold aboard. And all the money came aboard." Banking is the purser's job, but as always the captain is ultimately responsible. "We had a problem with one purser on the *Bartlett*. He started making use of that money on his own. Somebody in Juneau saw the figures weren't turning out the way they should be, and there was quite an investigation. They had a hearing in Anchorage, and I had to testify. Juneau personnel came up there.

"As far as I know he lost his job, was all. But I think it was thousands that he had taken. Once he started, it was just too easy. He got money he wasn't used to handling. 'I'll take a little more this time.' And he was making his reports so that the state didn't notice until he was taking too much.

"He liked to be the playboy. He had girlfriends everywhere. He even took one of his girlfriends to Seattle with us one time. You weren't supposed to. If they brought somebody aboard they were supposed to pay for them. He had her in his room—nobody knew. Usually the purser would know, but he was the purser.

"He had a good job. He really should have been more careful."

Walter doesn't date his interest in finances to that purser's indiscretion, but at some point he began keeping track of the business side of the *Bartlett* run, just for his own information. "During the tourist season we'd take in about $3 million—that's $3 million, gross, in about four months. I'd tell the crew they'd get two million and the captain gets one. [Crewmembers sent Captain Jackinsky off on one of his vacations with a T-shirt captioned Millionaire In Training.]

"I kept track every day of the summer run, how much we would haul from day to day—everything that came aboard [passengers and vehicles and very occasionally freight]. We ran at capacity so the loads were pretty much the same, but it was interesting. Sometimes we had to leave before the car deck was full because we would get big buses with 45, maybe 50 or 60 passengers, and we'd be over our limit. There were lots of groups that traveled together.

"When I retired I had five or six years of paperwork that I could check against the state's figures—the load and passengers every day, then the total for the season. I left it all there for the others."

One of Walter's former crewmen, AB Virgil Campbell of Moose Pass, remembers the captain's concern for the state's coffers. When the wheel-room carpet on the *Bartlett* needed to be replaced one year, Campbell says, Walter was upset over the size of the commercial estimate for the work. "I said, 'I could do that, Cap'n,'" Campbell says, and he did, with his wife, Dawn, as assistant. "I told Dawn, 'I don't want to mess this up, but you're good with math. Will you give me a hand?' So we took out the old carpet, laid it down on the new one, cut around all the openings and put it in. It fit fine, and Walt was happy. He brought us a jug of rum as a thank you, 'This was the most expensive one,' he said. 'I hope it's good.'" Virgil's overtime pay for the work was considerably less than the original estimate, and the rum from the captain was an unexpected bonus.

Local Knowledge

Back to piloting, or pilotage. Pilotage is "local knowledge." His 1995 master's license specifies these areas of local knowledge for Walter Wallace Jackinsky: "First class pilot of vessels of any gross tons upon the waters of Washington main ship channels between Point Roberts and Alki Point (via Rosario Strait); southeastern Alaska; Prince William Sound, Alaska; Cook Inlet, Alaska; Resurrection Bay, Alaska; [continuing on the reverse] Anchorage, Alaska; also, first class pilot of vessels of any gross tons upon the waters of St. Paul Harbor and the port of Kodiak, Alaska; Marmot Bay and Kupreanof Strait, Alaska; also, radar observer—unlimited." Ships under foreign flags are required to use local pilots in local waters, and with his "local knowledge" of Southeast routes, Walter worked occasionally as a pilot on Italian cruise ships during breaks from the ferry system. He speaks with respect of AMHS Captain Bill Hopkins, who "has pilotage all the way from Seattle to the Aleutians." Captain Hopkins, master of the M/V *Kennicott*, is the son of the late Jack Hopkins, who had served as second mate on the *Tustumena* and then with Walter on the *Bartlett* before going to work for the Southwest Pilots' Association out of Homer. Jack Hopkins died after a helicopter crash in Cook Inlet.

Walter's well-thumbed collection of nautical reference books includes the one he calls "the sailor's bible": a 52-year-old edition of *Captain Farwell's Hansen Handbook*, originally published in 1917, which he credits for guidance in pilotage. "For a while that was the only thing that captains and mates needed. It had everything in there. Right from Seattle, all the buoys, aids, everything. It wasn't as complete as what they use right now. There were a lot of changes. But this was really good. You could go from Seattle all the way to Dutch Harbor and back to Anchorage or anywhere.

"Halibut boats, or any fishing boats, they all had the *Hansen Handbook*, and they didn't even need to have charts. That book did all of it right there. They *had* charts, but that book was a lifesaver."

But there's no handbook available during the examination. "For the pilotage exam they give you just a blank chart that shows the water and the outline of the land. You fill it in and describe the courses, the distances, the depth of water. All the aids and their characteristics. Stationary aids. Buoys and so on.

"You get into fog in Wrangell Narrows, for instance. You have to be good or you're in trouble. You've got to have a good mental picture of what's happening next, what's way ahead of you, you know. You're making your turns before you even see anything. It works pretty good, once you've done it a few times.

"On the examination, the Narrows alone are a tremendous amount. It takes about two days if you're fast, and good. Maybe you'll get the Wrangell Narrows done in two days. And going into Sitka about the same way. Some pretty tight spots."

Walter invited his youngest child along on a trip to Anchorage when he was scheduled for a pilotage exam there. Risa, 13 or so at the time, recalls that her principal interest was in doing some shopping in the big city. At the Coast Guard office where she went to meet Walter for lunch one day, the officer on duty asked if she'd like to come into the observation room to see what her father was doing, and she said, "Oh, sure," without much conviction. "But then I looked through the window and saw him sitting at this great big huge drafting table with a big blank piece of paper, humming a song—he loves to hum—and filling in all this information. . . . It just floored me." Before that, and sometimes even after, she was inclined to feel a bit resentful over the time her father spent away from home, either on duty or studying for yet another examination. "I completely and totally admire everything he's accomplished," she says. "But he was not *present* a lot." The trip to Anchorage "marked a shift in the depth of my appreciation for the effort he was putting into his career."

Besides the periodic retesting on radar and pilotage, the master's license itself must be renewed every five years. But a mariner's responsibility extends beyond data to judgment. Walter cites paragraphs (a) and (b) of the Coast Guard's International Rule 2 (one of the "Rules of the Road"), which he memorized for his original examination and has retained:

"(a) Nothing in these Rules shall exonerate any vessel, or the owner, master or crew thereof, from the consequences of any neglect to comply with these Rules or of the neglect of any precautions which may be required by the ordinary practice of seamen, or by the special circumstances of the case.

"(b) In construing and complying with these Rules due regard shall be had to all dangers of navigation and collision and to any special circumstances, including the limitations of the vessel involved, which may make a departure from these Rules necessary to avoid immediate danger."

"Captains I Have Known"

Walter's designation as senior captain of the Alaska Marine Highway fleet means that at a certain point he had served longer as master than any of his peers. "I had good trainers," he says. "I watched them, and I studied how they did things. Six different captains had different methods, had their own method, you know. And I was just gathering information as much as I could, as fast as I could, from each one of them. That really helped me."

What he calls "my first and only bawling-out" came just a few days into the inaugural trip on the *Malaspina*, when he was in the crew's mess after his first night on watch. "This big old captain stomped in with his big lower lip out and said, 'You were supposed to call the watch and you didn't do it!' That means I didn't wake the next watch—I thought that was the watchman's job. I was in trouble." However, he says with satisfaction, eventually that same captain would say as the ship approached Wrangell Narrows, "Get that Jackinsky up here. I want him to steer through the narrows."

"He was getting a thousand dollars a month and as an ordinary I was getting $360," Walter says. "I thought that was interesting. And by the time I left, a captain made about $7,000 a month. Can you imagine how times changed?"

He recently wrote a candid assessment of the examples set by men he served under before becoming a captain himself. One who shall go unnamed "did a good job but was very temperamental, and not too good in personal habits. At times we didn't agree. I made it a point to do my job and obey the master. But I saw lots of bad faults in work habits and respect. Didn't learn too much from him."

Captain Herb Storey, on the other hand, "was a good friend and did a good job and more or less let the departments take care of their own jobs. I liked him and enjoyed working under him. In personality he was good with friends, crew and passengers. A good boat handler and knew his navigational rules of the road.

"Captain Tillman Dagle was excellent to learn from but very strict and did things by the book. Had many years in Alaskan waters on various boats and ships.

"Captain Jim Sande was a little high-strung and nervous, but still good in doing his job. He came up through the ranks so was still learning. I liked him, and he would listen to good advice. He kept a close and tight rein on what went on aboard ship, to his knowledge. He was respected by officers and crew.

"Captain Harold Payne and I were like brothers. I was willing to give everything I could and had in his behalf. We were a good team and stayed together for five years on the Southeast Alaska to Seattle run. He was a good man. I learned good seamanship from him, and he listened and learned from my experience and knowledge."

Another unnamed captain "was a little ahead of me getting his license, so he became captain before me. Not too responsible and just average ship handler. I felt that I knew and could do as much, so I felt uncomfortable working with him, although we did a good job and all went well, 'shipshape and Bristol fashion.'"

"After working with these various captains," Walter wrote, "I take my hat off to all. I have studied each one for their good and bad qualities, and it certainly made me qualified in all aspects. My job as captain proves that. But I developed my own skills and incorporated what I learned into my skills. That gave me an advantage over those I worked with. It gave me a lot of confidence. And then I was as good as any of them. A little better, maybe."

Strong words, but the record seems to justify them: "In 24 years I didn't have an accident. Nothing. No accident. Nothing at all. In that many years I only got rid of one person. Otherwise I kept every one. The one I got rid of was a cook. The crew were complaining. He wasn't clean. He was doing things they didn't like. And I hated to, you know, but I told him we just can't have you anymore here. It bothered me quite a bit, but I had to do it.

"But from then on, for all those years, everyone stayed on. We had lots of different things that came up, but we always were able to settle it, in our own way."

What kinds of things came up?

"Oh, sometimes they'd come aboard drunk. I'd try to talk to 'em, anyhow. Kinda warn 'em, you know, about doing that. They were pretty careful, but there were occasions when it happened. Gosh, one guy came aboard not just drunk but with most of his teeth hanging after a fight. We were tied in Valdez. So we had to haul him to Whittier and have him get to Anchorage and get taken care of. But he came back. He came back and went to work.

"Some of them—they'd bring girls aboard. I told them it really wasn't fair. It was OK to bring them aboard if we were laying in port. But then they'd sometimes keep 'em aboard [in their own cabins] if we were making a trip, you know, without me knowing it. I said, gosh, at least pay for their fare. They'd bring 'em aboard and not even pay for their fare. But I didn't do anything about it. I just talked to them and told them they shouldn't do it, it wasn't fair. 'OK, we won't do it any more.' And they didn't. Not that I know of, anyhow."

Regarding a captain's discretion on when to break the rules, Walter remembers a man he served under in the early years who refused even to bend them. "Sometimes they'd let us know [from shore] that passengers were going to be maybe 15 minutes late. This guy would say, 'Ohhh, no! The schedule says we leave at six o'clock. We're going to leave at six.' And he would.

"Here's this bunch of school kids hurrying to get on from Wrangell to Petersburg, and he was taking the lines in. I said, 'Gosh, there's a bunch of kids there waiting.' 'Oh, no,' he said. 'I'm going by the schedule.' They ran up on the dock with their pop bottles, the school kids did, and threw them at him. He's on the wing, ducking and swearing, maneuvering away from the dock, and they're yelling and throwing pop bottles. And he took off! I don't know what they did—probably had to charter a plane."

(Times do change. A February 2003 press release from the Alaska Marine Highway System alerted travelers to "two schedule changes for Southeast Alaska vessels to accommodate the travel of basketball teams and spectators who will be returning from the All Native Basketball tournament in Prince Rupert, B.C., this weekend. The M/V *Taku* will depart from Prince Rupert three hours early on Sunday, February 16, to enable passengers to connect with the Inter-Island Ferry, M/V *Prince of Wales*, sailing from Ketchikan to Hollis. On Sunday evening the M/V *LeConte* will depart one hour 15 minutes late from Ketchikan to Metlakatla.")

SOS!

Chief Mate Jackinsky was on duty aboard the *Malaspina* when a predawn SOS came from the *Meteor*, a passenger ship ablaze in Canadian waters several miles away.

"We headed right there—I got the captain out, and we headed full bore right for it. We were loaded full, out of Seattle, going to Ketchikan.

Seattle Post-Intelligencer Sat., July 17, 1971 S★ 3

Two Ferry Officers Cited

Their Boat Saved 70 on Burning Ship in B.C.

BY GEORGE FOSTER

Master and first mate of the Alaska State ferry M-V Malaspina stood before the brass telegraph in the ship's wheelhouse yesterday while Capt. Frank Huxtable of the U.S. Maritime Administration read the citation.

"It is my privilege to commend you and the crew of the Malaspina for competence and fine seamanship directed to the rescue of 70 survivors of the burning M-V Meteor in the Georgia Strait," the document started.

The fire that broke out on board the Meteor off the British Columbia mainland the morning of May 22 eventually claimed the lives of 33 crew members.

The streamlined ferry was on her way from Seattle to Ketchikan when the distress call was received.

First Mate Walt Jackinsky of the Malaspina made this notation in the ship's log that morning:

"0326 hours received Mayday of MV Meteor 10 miles north of Sister Islands (Georgia Strait) ... Proceeding 0347, MV Meteor one mile ahead ..."

The Maritime Administration's citation to the ferry's skipper, Capt. Harold Payne of Seattle, told the rest of the story:

"You raced to the given position, called the c... prepare lifeboats i... diate launching... the scene in ... utes and f...

HAROLD PAYNE

Captain of the Malaspina

WALT JACKINSKY

First mate on ferry

—P-I Photos.

...rs of the stricken vessel ...ifeboats in the water. ...our crew, in a state of readiness, quickly lowered the lifeboats which were still on the falls, and safely

hoisted them aboard in a matter of minutes ..."

"This rescue operation was successfully accomplished with no injuries within two hours of receiving the SOS."

Capt. Huxtable read the last paragraph of the citation, making reference to "the highest traditions of the United States Merchant Marine" and he and the master and first mate exchanged the customary handshakes.

Passengers, campers and freight trucks were boarding the Malispina as the brief ceremony came to a close. Within an hour the vessel steamed out of Pier 48 into Elliot Bay on another weekly run to points north.

Seattle Post-Intelligencer article, July 17, 1971, from the childhood scrapbook of McKibben Autumn Jackinsky.

"You could see the smoke coming out through the portholes. Some of the guys were sticking their heads out, trying to get some air. I guess they couldn't get above deck.

"We got our lifeboats out and got as close as we could, and gosh, the passengers came in their nightgowns. Some of them were elderly—the sailors carried them off the lifeboats. They had elderly people in their arms.

"They came aboard in nightgowns, and we had coffee and doughnuts for them. The stewards gave them their little white jackets to put on. That's what they wore when they went ashore in Vancouver. I asked one of the officers, maybe it was the captain, how serious was the damage. He said, "We lost 33 crew members." They got asphyxiated in the fo'c's'le. That many. They couldn't get out. And it was just a darn mattress fire to start with.

"Those sailors [aboard the *Malaspina*] worked like anything. They went out there with their lifeboats, picked them all up, put them on our hoist. Run them all up aboard and started feeding them. We changed our course and headed for Vancouver to take them there.

"By that time a tugboat had answered the SOS and was alongside the *Meteor*. I think they towed it into Vancouver when the fire was out. We didn't stay—we had Coast Guard orders to take care of the passengers. The first one there was the one that had the responsibility. We were the first one there."

"And who might you be?"

As of this writing it is seven years since Walter retired, but he often reverts to present tense in talking about his ship:

"Things are happening pretty fast when we load. I'd be busy on the bridge—get things ready, get the engines started. I didn't have much time to greet people. . . .

"I'll call the engine room, tell them to start warming up 15 minutes ahead. I get the radar ready. The mate comes up to the bridge [from the car deck] when the loading is finished. When we're ready, I call out, 'Let her go fore and aft,' and they start letting the lines go. I maneuver the ship away from the dock and turn it over to the mate. I'll be with the mate for a while until we're clear of any close quarters or any danger, and then the mate's on his own pretty much. He has a sailor to do the steering.

"There are engine controls on either wing, port and starboard. Sometimes we dock port, sometimes starboard. As soon as the lines are let go I use whatever speed I want and we get away. When I've got everything going the way I want it, I call to the mate to take over and we transfer power to the bridge." When the ship docks the captain is at the controls again.

The first time he took the controls as captain of his own ship, Walter says, he felt the way he did soloing for the first time in a plane. A little shaky. But confidence built quickly, along with his own routine.

"The captain has the purser and a mate to oversee the loading, but if they're having problems I'll go down and help a little. I sometimes even go down in the engine room. See how things are down there.

"Sometimes we'd be loaded right down to the maximum [on the car deck], and we'd find some tanks that were leaking gas. That could be very dangerous. The engine room is below the car deck. One little spark down in the engine room and it's hard to say what would happen.

"We'd get an engineer down to the car deck to stop the leak or drain the tank. Find the passenger the vehicle belongs to.

"I'm pretty strict for safety, you know. The chief is usually in charge of all that, but he can make mistakes so I go over him sometimes. Look to see if the lifeboats are tied down safe. If the lifesaving equipment is OK. . . .

"There's a lot of other things. I'll go visit with the chief steward to see how his crew is coming along. Maybe talk to the cook. Talk to the dishwasher once in a while to see how everything's going with him. I like to go in the galley to see what kind of food they're serving. At first they said, 'You just tell us what you'd like and we'll fix it for you.' I said, 'No, I want to eat the same as the crew.' Because it's always good, you know—everything's good. Pastas. Always a big pot of beans or some kind of stew. Meatloaf is a big thing. Salmon was a big thing. During the summer we had a lot of salmon. And halibut. That was big. The purser would make arrangements with some fishermen and buy it from them, in Cordova mostly.

"They had a good variety of things. We had a Mexican night maybe once a week, a Chinese night maybe every other week. Lots of fresh stuff, salad stuff. Trucks came to Valdez from Anchorage with our fresh stuff. . . .

"During lunch hour I could greet people. My table was in the same room except it was in a corner and had a sign that said Officers. Usually one of the mates was there with me, and the purser, and we talked to passengers who were close by. Sometimes I had a guest. The state of Alaska had fellows traveling with us who were working on their pilotage. They had to make quite a few trips to Tatitlek, through the narrows there, and we were the ones that were making all those trips so we were the ones they used pretty much. They were already licensed, so they were qualified. They were on the bridge most of the time, but they'd come down and eat with us."

In *Alaska's Ocean Highways*, author Sherry Simpson notes the work-as-long-as-you-can-stand-it schedule for the *Bartlett* crew and says, "Perhaps the *Bartlett* has a homey, comfortable feeling because people do live on it. The sign announcing hours for the dining room reads: 'Breakfast, 7:30 a.m. 'til fed. Lunch, 12:00 'til fed. Dinner, 5:30 'til fed.' Unlike other ferries, passengers are allowed on the bridge wings; only a rope separates them from the wheelhouse crew."

Captain Jackinsky was on the bridge wing of the *Bartlett* one day in about 1983, preparing to take off from Whittier, when a young fisherman who was headed Outside from Bristol Bay spoke to him: "Hello, Grandfather."

Walter remembers the day well. So does the young fisherman, who is now a law school graduate and a writer.

"He shook my hand with a curious expression on his face and asked me, 'And who might you be?'" says Tom Peterson, Vonnie Jackinsky's eldest child.

"I told him I was his oldest grandson, and he politely showed me the whole ship and introduced me to the entire crew. He said he could perform every function of every crewmember aboard the 193-foot *E.L. Bartlett*. . . . He showed me his Rolex watch. Ashore in Cordova he let me shoot his .44 Magnum. . . .

"He told me something I remember clearly. He said, 'I know you will be able to do whatever it is that you want to do. You will be successful at whatever you try.' It was good to hear him say that to me. I think he said it twice."

Captain and Crew

For all his frankness about seeking the status of master mariner, and the exhaustive effort he put into attaining it, Walter seems not to have leaned on his rank except in the practical, day-to-day sense of running a 933-ton operation. No "romance of the sea" talk from him. But his love affair with his ship and with the *challenge* of the sea is an open secret. Richard Henry Dana Jr.'s *Two Years Before the Mast* had him wide-eyed as a boy, he says, and intentionally or not, it shows. The man who is so proud of having "come up through the fo'c's'le"—Navy parlance says "through the hawsepipe," and both mean working one's way up from the lowest rank—identifies with his crew. AMHS Captain John Klabo, who first served under Walter as second mate on the *Bartlett* and eventually succeeded him as master, credits what he calls Walter's "give everyone a fair chance" style of leadership. "When it came to deck officers he was an especially good teacher and very generous with the piloting and ship handling of the *Bartlett*," Klabo says.

Walter's own description of the master's role is modest enough. "The captain's there, whenever he's needed," he says. "For anything. But lots of times he sits in his room and waits for an hour or two. He's not at the helm [except for docking and undocking]. He doesn't even navigate. He's got officers to navigate his ship, and an AB, able-bodied seaman, steering. The mate does the navigating and gives commands to the sailors. You can maybe come up there once in a while and see how everything's going. If you're in fog, then you're in charge, period. Otherwise everything's pretty normal. You read, play a little music. There's always so much paperwork. But I had good pursers. They'd do all the paperwork for me,

From left, AB Mark Sawyer (at the wheel), Captain Walter Jackinsky and Chief Mate Jim Soucie on the bridge of the M/V E.L. Bartlett, *April 1991. Photo © Alissa Crandall / www.alaskacalendars.com.*

any I wanted. On the bigger ships they have two, an assistant purser to take care of the money, and loading, traffic, stuff like that. Staterooms.

"Mates had it pretty good—they work six hours on, six hours off. But [recalling his own time as mate] sometimes a captain would say, 'Come on in my room when your shift is over—I've got some people I want you to meet.' And before you know it your six hours that you're supposed to sleep are up and it's time to go back to work. Of course, you're young, and it's fine. [Note: Walter was almost 50 when he became a mate.] You look forward to your week off. But as captain, you sleep for an hour, they call you for something, you sleep for two hours, they call you for something. . . . If there's any course change or change in speed you wake up right away.

"One of the new captains—I think he's fairly new—hit a rock in Wrangell Narrows not too long ago. He got suspended. I don't know whether he'll go back to work for the state or not. Years ago a captain on the *Matanuska* docked at Petersburg on his way to Juneau. They were only going to be there a short while so he left all the controls on the bridge alive, and then he was called off somewhere. In that short time a couple of young boys got in there on the bridge and grabbed those controls and shoved them up forward. The engines were alive, and the power of the engines and the movement of the *Matanuska* itself tore the whole dock down. For three or four months until they got it repaired we had to use tugs and barges to haul our freight from Wrangell into Petersburg.

"But unless it's a mechanical error, it's your fault. If you're in your cabin and one of your officers hits a rock, that's your responsibility. You've got to answer to the charges. The deck officer is supposed to call—he's got a notice right where he works: Be sure and call the captain for anything you're not sure of, at any time. And the captain's right there, right close by, waiting for him. . . .

"The deck officers I had were pretty much with me the whole time I was there [on the *Bartlett*]. I had an attorney from Anchorage, Dave Dawson, who gave up his practice to come and work with me. He got his second mate's license.

"Deck officers are the chief mate—first officer or first mate—

and second mate. Then there's the bosun. He's in charge of the deck crew. He has six sailors who work under him. There are three engine room officers: chief engineer, with first assistant and second assistant, plus two oilers and two wipers.

"Wiper—that's the beginning of the 'black gang,' the old name for the engine room crew. Then you move up to oiler, then deck engineer—some of them do, taking care of machinery on deck. If you want to move up any further you have to go for a license [an engineer's license].

"The chief steward is in charge of the whole galley operation, the dining room. . . . Under him are the cooks, the waiters, dishwashers. . . ."

Besides the licenses for mates and masters, everyone working on the ship is required to have Coast Guard certification—an identification "Z-card," plus a lifeboat ticket. Licensed crewmembers come aboard with lifeboat training already on their record. The others have to pass muster with the Coast Guard as one of their job requirements. Walter taught a lifeboat class through the University of Alaska Southeast and is pleased to say that his 20-some students all performed well. In the classroom they had to be able to diagram a lifeboat and be familiar with all its parts. When he felt they were ready, the class went out to Auke Bay to demonstrate rowing skill and take turns giving commands, with Captain Jackinsky and a Coast Guard officer watching.

As to the Z-card, "They take your history, your driver's license information—they take more now than they used to. And they always test for drugs, by urinalysis. On our ship, every time a fellow went on vacation he had to take a drug test before he came back. I did. Everyone did."

Published mention of Captain Walter Jackinsky usually begins as in Alissa Crandall's *Along the Alaska Marine Highway*: "Born in Ninilchik of Aleut heritage . . ." Was it unusual for someone who identifies himself as an Alaska Native to be an officer on a ferry crew? Walter's response to that question may be as interesting for what it doesn't say (*Yes, it was unusual!*) as for what it does.

"There were lots of Southeast Natives, Tlingits mostly. Half, quarter Tlingit. I don't believe there were any mates that were part

Native. Lots of deck crew, stewards department, engine department. The stewards department had other nationalities, too—Filipinos, African Americans, Mexicans. There weren't any other Native captains that I know of.

"Most, maybe all, of the captains are new since I retired. All the ones I was with are pretty much gone. The only other Alaskan captain I can think of was Dick Hofstad. He and I worked opposite each other on the *LeConte*. And both his parents were Norwegian. He came from Petersburg, and he had a little bit of Norwegian accent himself. He told us he would always say to the flight attendant when he got on Alaska Airlines for Seattle, or coming back, 'Turn on the blowtorches!' That meant the jet engines.

"He was a good dancer. I saw him a few times at a place in Seward. . . .

"Most captains came from around Seattle—worked for the ferry system there. Hofstad and I both went and got licenses that were unlimited. Way better licenses than the bunch in Seattle—they had inland master's licenses and we got our unlimited ocean license. We were good for anything."

The cooks wielded authority along with their ladles. "I walked in the galley once, early morning, and the cook was standing there waving a big knife. The watchman had gotten in there and stolen some doughnuts he just made. I said, 'Holy smokes, you better look out.' That watchman weighed 340 pounds.

"One steward would break the rules and come up on the bridge. No one's allowed on the bridge unless they're invited. The chief mate was navigating, and he'd say, 'Get out of here!' I said, 'You shouldn't be that strict with him,' but he chased that steward out of the room. The steward said, 'I'm going to fix that guy. I'm going to piss in his coffee.' And he did it, I think. I said, 'You better not.' But he was really mad.

No Whistling

Walter has a printed list of "Superstitions Among Sailors" culled from United Kingdom Admiralty sources. Never whistle on board a sailing craft (it not only angers the winds and gets on other crewmen's nerves but can signal mutinous plotting). Never mention the word "rabbit" on board, and avoid sailing if you see one of these animals on the way to the ship. Don't coil a rope or stir a cooking pot counter-clockwise, or "widdershins," against the direction in which the sun travels. Serving split-pea soup is a sign of an impending storm. And one ancient prohibition that went by the boards in Walter's time: No women on the ship.

"When they first started this equal opportunity on the ferries there were staterooms just for men. Suddenly there are women, and sometimes they have to share a stateroom with a man. Fine, no problem. Well, there was one teacher who came aboard in June for a summer job, and when she saw that, she said, 'Oh, no, I'm not going to share a room with a man.' But in most cases women were pretty good. I was surprised. We were all a little surprised that they would do that [make the rooms unisex], you know, but the state said, 'They're declaring equal opportunity, so we've got to do it.'

"I was kind of worried, too, on my ship, how things would happen when we got the first woman. She was a sailor, an ordinary seaman. She said, 'Don't worry about it. We'll take care of it and everything will go good.' This was the *LeConte*, maybe the late '60s. And everything did go good.

"It wasn't very long before there were more. There were always women in the steward crew, but they had a room to themselves, or two women to a room. But now, with women in the deck crew, a man steward and a woman steward shared a room, too, when necessary. That's all there was to it.

"On the *Bartlett* I had women crew members right from the beginning. Women sailors. I had women cooks, women pursers— that's a junior officer. Most of my pursers were women. They were good. And in the engine room one time we had a first assistant engineer who was a woman. She was an engineer right under the chief. She did fine. She fell in love with the chief steward, and I got a card from them on vacation in Yakutat, I think it was: 'The sun is shining, we're on the beach just having a good time . . .' That was the end of it, though. Things finally cooled down."

Walter likes to say that he had to fire only the one crew member in all his time as captain on the *LeConte* and the *Bartlett*, and in the discretionary sense he means it, that's true. But some matters are out of the captain's hands, and he tells of two such cases. Equal opportunity law enforcement.

"On the *Bartlett* we had just gotten to Valdez and tied up when one of the stewards came to my room and asked if she could talk to me. She said, 'I hate to say this, but I believe my roommate has drugs aboard the ship.' So I had the first mate check, and sure enough, there was a pretty good amount of marijuana in the room. 'Well, you'd better call the troopers, Alaska State troopers,' so we did. First we called the Coast Guard, then the troopers. The nearest ones were 120-some miles away—they were at Glenallen then. They drove all the way down. I called the roommate to my stateroom and talked to her. She admitted that it was hers. A nice young gal—good worker and everything. I said, 'You've got to get off. We can't have that.' We gave the purser the marijuana and he turned it over to the troopers. She had to get off. I don't know what the troopers did about it.

"Then just before leaving Cordova one time, they called me to come down to the purser's counter. Here's a guy with a pistol—an able seaman—and another guy, Joe Dymesich, an oiler. They were having an argument and the seaman was pointing the pistol at Dymesich. I said, 'Hey, you better knock that off. Give me that pistol.' And he was good, he gave me the pistol. Of course, he had to leave the ship. I gave the pistol to the purser. The purser handles any firearms on the ship."

At Home on the Bartlett

Oiler Joe Dymesich was just one longtime member of Walter's crew on the *Bartlett*. Historian Diane Olthuis, who served aboard the *Bartlett* and the *Tustamena* as a nature interpreter for the Chugach National Forest during Walter's last year as captain, is still impressed by the crew's camaraderie.

"The *Bartlett* was the more challenging boat to be a crew member on," she says. "It was built with just the tiniest quarters for the crew, because it had been assumed that the ship would always

Aboard the M/V E.L. Bartlett, *1974.*

Officers, standing, *from left: Captain Walter Jackinsky (on temporary assignment); Ron Hamrick, chief mate; Bill Barry, purser; John Klabo, second mate.*

Front row, *from left: Rusty Noll, waiter; Homer Herndon, chief cook; Dave Pelch, oiler; Bill Cronin, AB or OS; Del Hunter, chief engineer; [name not recalled]; Alce Smith, chief steward.*

Back row, *from left: Chad Dixon, OS; John (the Baron) Van Tasler, first asst. engineer; Jerry Huey, AB; Ralph Osborne, second asst. engineer; Virgil Campbell, steward; Rod Shockey, steward utility [?]; Joe Dymesich, oiler (in profile); Ron Myking (in Alaska cap); Don Nelson, oiler (with glasses); George Chambers, AB; Jim Soucie (half hidden), AB; Hank Paski, watchman.*

overnight in port. When I was on board, the ship was in motion most of the time. As Forest Service interpreter, I either slept on the floor or on the cot in the infirmary. I loved my two-day stints on the *Bartlett* but always needed to catch up on my sleep when I got home. I was amazed that the crew could keep up the pace without looking tired.

"The whole crew was very chummy and stayed in good spirits. They took great pride in their work. . . . [And] they still got excited every time they saw the Columbia Glacier."

The "infirmary" Diane Olthuis recalls was an innovation on the *Bartlett* under Walter's command. First he brought exercise equipment aboard, starting with a rowing machine. "I had that in the auxiliary engine room. That's all we had for a while. For one or two or three years. Finally we started getting more—bench press, Nordic ski machine, stationary bicycle—and we made a space for it. There's an area there in the lower passenger lounge—we blocked a certain amount of it off, and made a good exercise room.

"That was just for the crew. But we did make a good sick bay, too, with a bed in it and all the equipment that was necessary, and we used that sometimes as a passenger room, if passengers weren't too well. They'd use the sick bay to relax."

As a part of his own exercise regimen, Walter enjoyed swimming at school facilities in Valdez and Cordova. "I'd usually go in the early morning, get there before six. They'd open the pool at six o'clock. Early morning was good because the longest you could be in the pool during the day would be 45 minutes, or maybe an hour. In the morning you could be in there maybe an hour and 45 minutes. I liked that.

"I swim on my back—I'm good for 30-some meters."

And, he said, "in Cordova or Valdez there are a lot of places to go. I could walk on the shore and find places to explore. . . ."

Diane Olthuis recalls Walter as "a fine gentleman of the old school. He appeared to be loved and respected by all of his crew. Everyone was amazed by his age, as he appeared much younger. There were jokes the next year of trying to reach his record of working to age 81."

AB Virgil Campbell, who also served as shipboard union delegate for the unlicensed personnel (stewards, deck and engine departments), served aboard the *Bartlett* for 13 years all told, with time out for a union post ashore. He says it's still a wonder to him that someone could work as long in a job as Walter did, and with as many people, and not be spoken ill of by anyone.

"He was a prince to work for," Campbell says. "He said a lot without saying much." As an example, he tells of a time when one of the mates on the *Bartlett* "cut this one point pretty close coming out of Columbia Bay near Valdez. Iceberg Point, I think it's called. Walt wasn't even on the bridge. He was in his room. But he could feel what had happened just by the way the ship was acting. He came up and said quietly, 'We're a little tight on that point, aren't we, mate?'"

"The mate said something like 'Oh no, we're fine,'" Campbell continues. "And Walt said again, 'We're a little tight on that point, aren't we?' The mate had to admit it. When Walt turned and went back to his room the mate said to me, 'Damn! How does he do it?'"

Larry Edwards, who served as both ordinary and able-bodied seaman—OS and AB—on the *Bartlett*, says Walter merely had "a slightly different tone of voice from his usual tone of voice" when he was upset about something. "But if you knew him, you'd hear that and you'd know something wasn't right, and you'd look for an exit."

Virgil Campbell also describes Walter as one of the better ship handlers of all the masters he worked with. "Some couldn't hit the dock with both hands," he says. At the other extreme was the skipper known to all as Captain Crunch.

Campbell's office "on the beach" for the Inlandboatmen's Union of the Pacific was run out of his home in Moose Pass. "We also covered longshoremen in the ports of Valdez, Kodiak, Homer, Kenai and Dutch Harbor, and any towing vessel covered by our contracts," he says. "I spent most of my time on the road." After the second stint aboard the *Bartlett* he returned to Moose Pass, to his family's landmark I.R.B.I. Knife Shop on the Seward Highway. Those long spans of duty on the *Bartlett* were grueling, he says—he saw more of his fellow crewmembers than he did of his wife. He

Larry Edwards, Virgil Campbell, and Virgil's father, Irvin Campbell, on the deck of the Bartlett. *Photo courtesy of Larry Edwards.*

138

doesn't miss the shipboard work. But he misses the shipboard family.

Bosun Tom Faulkner served on the *Bartlett* for 28 years, 1970 to 1998, until his knees "went out" and he retired. He has a virtual sea chest full of Jackinsky memories. "I was there when Mr. Jackinsky came on as chief mate," he says. "He had all the credentials, but he had to come on and work for three weeks under the captain whose job he was assigned to take, and the captain would then become his first mate. It was three weeks of hell. But Walter Jackinsky handled it. He is the most honorable 'young old guy' I've ever met in my life. [Despite Tom Faulkner's having retired as senior bosun of the AMHS fleet, he is almost 30 years Walter's junior.]

"The only time I ever saw him get mad had to do with a young ordinary seaman, Doug Privett. They were sitting at the captain's table and talking about catching red salmon. Doug says, 'Well, I caught a 12-pound red salmon.'

"Mr. Jackinsky says, 'I caught a 22-pound red salmon.'

"Doug says, 'But Walter, it couldn't be that big.'"

"And he stood up," says Faulkner, referring to Walter, "and he said, 'You can call me Mr. Jackinsky. You can call me Captain. You can call me Walter Jackinsky. But don't you ever call me Walter.' The poor kid was sitting there stammering.

"But that's the only time I ever saw that man upset. You met him, you instantly respected him."

Tom Faulkner had a bit of trouble of his own one night, however. "Mr. Jackinsky got a totem pole from Valdez as an honorary type thing," he recalls. "It was about 10 inches tall by 12 inches wide at the wings. He wanted it mounted by the captain's table, and I decided I'm going to put it up with contact cement because he didn't want to drill into the steel. I didn't bother to read the instructions for the contact cement, but I got it up there all right.

"I was on the 8-to-12 watch that night and he comes up to see me. Seems the totem took a header into his plate of food, where he was sitting having dinner with some visitors. He wasn't what you'd call happy.

"The next time, I read the instructions. The totem wasn't quite straight, but it stayed there. It stayed there till the day he left, and it's probably still there. You'd have to use a jackhammer to get it off the wall."

The honorary totem is a bird of a different feather from the ornamental "concrete chickens," as the crew called them, that Captain Jackinsky acquired in Seattle from a ship under renovation—"kind of like a bird totem, with a beak."

"They weighed about 80 pounds each," Faulkner says, sounding like something of a fish-story-teller himself. "They could change the draft of the ship, they were so heavy." He says the crew contrived to hide them for about eight months, moving them from place to place on the ship in hopes they'd be forgotten. "But the captain had his mind set on those chickens, and he finally got them. Between the engine room guys and the rest of us, we managed to get them mounted, one in the forward lounge and the other in the dining room."

Walter wasn't above a little deviousness of his own, according to Virgil Campbell.

"I hadn't been working on the ship very long at the time so didn't know his sense of humor," Campbell recalls. "The chief steward, Mike Anderson, and the captain and I went duck hunting out of Cordova. We didn't see too many birds, but Mike made one hell of a shot on a high-flying bird and dropped it. When we got to where it had landed and he picked it up, I saw it was a common merganser, or sawbill.

"'What kind of duck is this?' Mike asked, because the merganser doesn't have a bill like a duck. I was just about to say it would taste like an old boot when Walter tells him, 'They're delicious. We eat them all the time.' I'm thinking, man, it must be pretty grim in Ninilchik if they eat sawbills, so I just keep my mouth shut.

"When we got back to the ship I went back to the galley, and Walter was kind of staying out of Mike's sight. Mike was trying to pluck the sawbill and not having any luck. It was not only tough as nails but a little smelly, too. Walter calls me over and quietly says, 'Look at Mike, trying to skin that old sawbill.'

"I think Mike finally threw it overboard, but Walter and I got a pretty good chuckle out of it. I was just glad to hear they didn't really eat them in Ninilchik!"

Tom Faulkner turns serious for his favorite recollection, of a trip his father made on the *Bartlett*. "He was a farmer from Montana," he says, "and Mr. Jackinsky took him and showed him every bit of hospitality. My dad tried to eat with the crew, but Mr. Jackinsky wouldn't have it. My dad ate at the captain's table. He and Mr. Jackinsky were meeting people from Japan and Germany and everywhere in the world, and he treated my dad like royalty. He made his trip totally wonderful."

Walter's sense of hospitality extended to the crew, Faulkner says. "When he first came on the ship as captain we were getting into Cordova around 1:30 in the afternoon. We'd tie up, and then the captain had happy hour. You put one guy on watch and everybody else better be at Captain Jackinsky's happy hour at the Cordova House or the Reluctant Fisherman, that fancy place down by the beach. He'd buy one round and then he'd get up and go.

"He liked to walk, you know. My wife Janet [then Janet Perley, cook on the *Bartlett*] was in good shape, and sometimes she'd go ashore to walk with him. But she couldn't keep up with him. He'd walk one block, then run two blocks. He'd meet her on his way back when she was only halfway there."

According to Captain John Klabo, "the fancy place down by the beach" was owned by banker Dick Boer, whose wife, Margie Johnson, was mayor of Cordova for several terms.

Finally, Tom Faulkner says, there were the Rolex watches. "Mr. Jackinsky came back from a trip with a Rolex Oyster Mariner, I think it was called, the top-of-the-line Rolex watch, and he was so proud. He showed all of us that watch."

"Then we had some guys who went over to Taiwan," Faulkner says innocently, forgetting to mention that he was one. "He paid who knows how much for this watch, maybe $3,000, and a month later here are all these deckhands going around with our $10 'Rolexes.' . . .

"He was a wonderful man. We just loved to fool with him."

Walter in turn speaks of his longtime crew with affectionate familiarity. "Jim Soucie and Homer Herndon were on the *Bartlett* all the time I was there, and they were there when I left. They both lived in Cordova. Homer Herndon started as a cook. Then he decided to be a sailor, and then he became a mate. It was [first mate] Jim Soucie who named that island on the way in to Tatitlek 'Jackinsky's Island.'

"Johann Sorensen, cook on the *Bartlett*. Tom Faulkner, bosun. He married Janet Perley, also a cook on the *Bartlett*. AB Larry Edwards—retired Coast Guard, a real good fellow. I think he finally retired to Lake Havasu, Arizona. AB Joe Amon. One time he stayed on the ship for a whole year straight. AB James Swartz—we had a nickname for him. What was it? Doug Privett. He came to work for us as an ordinary seaman when he was just 17, I think. Worked with us, went to the *Tustumena*, then left and started doing something else. Mike Croft, chief engineer, all the time I was there. He's retired, too.

"That cook, Johann Sorensen, lived in Petersburg, but he was from Iceland. He was a fancy dancer! He danced, and he played the accordion, and he'd dress nice—put on a suit. He fell in love with a Greek lady in Seattle and they decided to get married. He asked me to be his best man, but the marriage didn't last very long.

"In the summertime when we were hauling tourists, we served dinner between six and eight o'clock. When everything was cleared in the dining room, Johann would take his accordion in the dining room and gosh, he'd play and those Germans would get up there and dance like anything. He knew a lot of German songs. . . .

"Robert Ganaway was another one in the stewards department. They called him 'Popcorn Man.' He sold his special popcorn in Seward, and sometimes he brought some aboard.

"Pursers came and went, but Les Shepherd was on longest as purser. He typed out my log from that trip around the world. Did a real good job of it. I had just a rough copy.

"Nancy Wolford was one of the longest ones as purser. Her husband also worked for the ferry system, as a marine architect. She got a call from Juneau one day saying, 'Your husband died.' He was in his late 50s, hadn't been ill that I know of. She went straight to Juneau and didn't come back to the ship. Just lately I tried to get hold of her through some of the other people I knew. They said she was living on an island she owns near Juneau. She was good—knew what I needed, what I wanted done. She did all the work even without me asking.

"Janet Baron came on the *Bartlett* as a steward—wanted to be a purser. She went to school and became a purser on the *Tustumena* till she retired. She married the relief chief engineer on the *Bartlett*, Dennis Leponas. They got to know each other and got married and now they have a home in Anchorage.

"When they were courting they'd have dinner together, toast each other with a glass of wine. They sat there eating their dinner, enjoying each other. They were right next to my table, but I pretended like I didn't know what they were doing. There's a bar on the ship for the passengers, but we don't approve of the crew drinking. . . .

"And John Klabo. He was first an ordinary, then mate, then got his inland master's license. I talked him into being assistant captain, and he was on the *Bartlett* after I left till it was sold. [See Epilog.] He's on vacation now until next season."

Fish Story

"In the winter in Cordova, some of the fellows would hang fishing lines off the stern. Gosh, one time they caught a hundred-and-some-pound halibut. Another time they caught this monster. They said, 'Man oh man, we've got something here. You better come on down.' They said, 'Take this pole!' I couldn't do it. The pole was shaking, the line was going, you know. I said, 'I can't do it!'

"The cook came out, Johann Sorensen, and he said, 'I know what that is—one of those big kings that they catch in Petersburg in the wintertime.'

"Then out comes this big guy, Virgil Campbell—'You take it!' He took it, and then Bugsy and I ran up on the bridge and put a searchlight on. And pretty soon we see this doggone sea otter stick his head out of the water. We couldn't stop him, and down he went. He kept on pulling and pulling until the line went out, and he broke the line.

"They were using herring for bait—whole herring. And down

Robert (Bugsy) Giachino on the Bartlett, *docked at Valdez. Photo courtesy of Larry Edwards*

at the bottom where they were fishing, sea otters usually don't feed. Must have been hungry. . . . They wanted a halibut. With herring we caught mostly halibut. . . .

"This was Virgil Campbell from Moose Pass, not Virgil the watchman on the *Malaspina*—I think he was from Oregon. And there was one more, Virgil Ward, chief steward on the *LeConte*. This Virgil Campbell married a woman named Dawn Burch in Cordova and worked with us on the *Bartlett*.

"It was Bugsy's outfit over the side. He loved fishing. His real name was Bob Giachino."

(AB Giachino may have loved fishing, but it was Captain Jackinsky who made the most unusual over-the-side catch. Thanks to his crew on the *LeConte*, he hauled in his line at Auke Bay one day to find he had hooked a can of tuna.)

Foxy Beauty

Walter remembers when the ferry brought Foxy Beauty to Juneau, but daughter Risa remembers the details.

Seems she was one of those 10-year-olds in love with horses. She and a slew of other Juneau kids spent all their free time out at Thunder Mountain trailer park, where owner "Grandpa" Reed kept a herd of horses. Originally from New Mexico, Grandpa Reed was "a lanky old cowboy guy" who besides his horses had a collection of antique riding gear, nickel-plated bridles and so on, that he spun stories about for the kids. He was, in short, Risa's hero.

Walter and Alice asked Risa one day if she was serious about wanting a horse. They'd heard of a man in Skagway who was giving one away. Risa was ecstatic.

"With his big old wooden paneled truck that he hauled horses in, Grandpa Reed and I went to Skagway on the ferry and brought Foxy Beauty home. She was 24 years old, with one brown eye and one blue eye and a big roman nose. She wasn't beautiful. But she was tough! In Skagway people turned the horses out in the winter. If they made it to spring, they were tough. And she was tough.

"When my mother took me to visit her the first time at Grandpa Reed's, Beauty was out in the middle of the corral. I crawled under the fence with a bunch of carrots in my hand and walked toward her. She put her nose to the ground—I remember steam coming out of her nose—and she chased me all over that corral. I was running and crying and saying, 'But I *love* you!' And Mom was telling me, 'Get back in there. You can do it.'"

They made friends sooner rather than later, but Foxy Beauty was always a trickster, Risa says. "Sometimes I used a western saddle, but mostly I rode bareback. I'd make the jump to get on her back and she'd quietly move over a foot or so. Clunk. Or we'd be out riding, me feeling free and one with my horse, and she'd decide all of a sudden to change direction. Of course I kept going in the *other* direction, and we were no longer one.

"When she was 26 or 27 we gave her to the Williamson family [developer of the Villa de Vista area where the Jackinsky house was built]. They had about seven children, the youngest a little girl around 3 years old. . . . And I had another horse by then."

Over the years in Juneau Risa had five or six horses, but only one was a Foxy Beauty.

Dry Dock

Walter again: "Most of the sailors are kept on the ship in dry dock. Some stay there on watch during the night. There's always maintenance work—shipboard maintenance. There's lots of work for them besides the shipyard work. Except for the stewards department—everything is torn down there. A van comes around with lunches, sandwiches, whatever you want. Some of the crew sleep aboard, and [as captain] sometimes I did. But mostly I slept ashore.

"There was one year the M/V *Tustumena* was sent to Seattle for maintenance and overhaul repairs in one of the shipyards there—Lockheed, or one of the dry docks anyway. When they first got there, they docked at the regular pier, I think Pier 42, and unloaded, and naturally the sailors had to go on a little party for a couple of days. A little fun after being in Alaska for a year. Then in the morning when they were just getting ready to go back to work, the bosun said, 'Wait a minute, I've got to go to the head.' He went into the head, and they heard him sneeze. They heard him sneeze a second time. When he didn't come out they looked in there and he had died, after his second sneeze. That was it. That was the end of the bosun. He was only maybe in his 50s."

The annual overhaul might be performed in Seattle or in Seward or in Ketchikan, where the *Bartlett* was the first to use the city's new floating dry dock brought by tug from Korea—and where, according to Virgil Campbell, the crew decided the terms "dry dock" and "Ketchikan," with its record rainfalls, were mutually exclusive. "Ketchikan is beautiful," Campbell says, "but imagine doing the outside painting there! And it always had to be winter—it was either too wet to paint, or too cold."

Much of the annual dry dock work is preventive maintenance, with the captain and chief engineer in hard hats observing the condition of the ship while it's out of water. The ship's crew of sailors is responsible for work above the waterline—washing down and degreasing the surface, painting below decks as well as outside, sand-blasting and painting the "knight's-hood" bow, in the case of the *Bartlett*. The dry dock crew does the necessary work below waterline. Special paint keeps barnacles to a minimum now, and modern-day vacuum equipment has replaced the ages-old job of scraping barnacles.

In a conversation with Walter in 2004, Virgil Campbell laughed, but a bit apprehensively, reminiscing about the one time he saw the captain of the *Bartlett* truly angry: the time some mischievous member of the overhaul crew yielded to grade-school-kid temptation and painted a big F in place of the big B on the side of the ship in dry dock. Walter, usually so genial, gave Campbell a stony stare after all those years, and Campbell said again what he had said at the time, "It wasn't me, Cap'n. I didn't do it." ("I was so relieved it wasn't me," he said in an aside. "And really, everybody took a lot of pride in the ship. It ran really smooth. We took good care of it.")

"When we had the *Malaspina* in Seattle for the very first annual maintenance," Walter recalled on another occasion, thinking of his own time as sailor, "I stood night watch, midnight to eight a.m., and then went to school to study for my mate's examination—the

The M/V E.L. Bartlett *in dry dock at Seattle, above, and Seward.*
Seattle photo courtesy of Virgil and Dawn Campbell; Seward photo from the Jackinsky family collection.

Virgil Campbell in "mummy gear" for dry dock painting, below decks on the Bartlett. *Photo courtesy of Virgil and Dawn Campbell.*

Kildall school at the YMCA on Fourth Avenue. The class was supposed to last a month, but I didn't want to wait that long. 'I'm going to take that exam!' My teacher tried to talk me out of it. When he saw I was going to do it no matter what, he said, 'OK. But try to remember some of the questions they ask you!' "

Crossing the Gulf

In a reflective mood shortly before his retirement, Walter wrote: "Every dedicated captain has been humbled by the ocean's power and beauty. . . . When you sail in violent storms and hurricane force winds, you take all necessary precautions. [But] in some cases, it is even exciting and beautiful to experience stormy seas. The amazing part is that usually the next day the storm has subsided and the ocean is calm and resembles the doldrums or Misty Fjords. . . ." His latter-day reminiscences are more pragmatic but still full of zest.

"The worst part of the *Bartlett* run was taking the ship down from Cordova to either Seattle or Ketchikan for annual maintenance," he says. "These ships are built for inland waters. Except for the *Kennicott* and the *Columbia*, they're not built for open ocean.

"The Gulf of Alaska is bad in the winter, southwest wind coming up from the Aleutians. You've got to watch that weather. I'd check with the U.S. weather station in Valdez, and they'd give me a prognosis three days ahead of time. But they can't always be certain.

"You're 50 miles offshore, you know, as you're going across. When you get into the Gulf you're pretty much on your own. There are no harbors to go into or anything. You have to take whatever there is. We'd constantly get into a snowstorm, and the radars won't work, and it's blowing, and it's snowing, and it's dark on top of that.

"It's about 24 hours to cross the gulf, if everything is good. If we have to slow because of weather then it takes longer. Maybe another five hours. Maybe 10 hours. Maybe even longer. But you can't slow down too much, either. You see what the ship can take, how much beating it will take. If it starts pitching too much, you've got to slow her down.

"One time I waited 11 days to leave Cordova because there was no end to storms—storm after storm. They wanted us down there [in dry dock] because everything was ready for us. We were getting late. But there was nothing I could do, you know, because of the weather. Larry Edwards, AB who used to be with the Coast Guard, was keeping an eye on it. It could really do some damage. I told Juneau that. It's the captain's decision. They said, 'Don't.' I said, 'OK.'

"We were on the ship for 11 days, getting weather reports, and the last report was that there were two storms, one ahead of us and one behind us, about 18 hours apart. If we could get between those two storms we might make it. So I said, 'Le-e-et's go!' [Not surprisingly, a favorite expression.] Everybody was anxious to get going anyhow. We just kind of stayed in that one little area there between the storms. It was still rough in there, but the big storms were ahead of us and behind us. And we went right across the Gulf between them. Larry Edwards didn't like the Gulf, but he said with me in charge he'd go."

Larry Edwards confirms that. "The captain would say, 'We've got a window of several hours—if we're gonna go, we've gotta go.' And if he felt it was OK, then it was OK with me. We had a saying: 'The weather god has blessed Captain Jackinsky again.'"

"He and I worried more about that weather than anybody else on the ship," Edwards says. "The big concern, the stuff we watched for, was when we were making the trip down to Ketchikan or Seattle [later Bellingham] for overhaul. I'd go up on the bridge and see him or he'd come and look me up, and we'd swap information. 'What's the last you heard?' We'd get the long-range forecast in the evening and go from there. They could pretty well predict a lot of that stuff coming across the gulf, all the way over from Japan. But he was the man to make the decisions, and he never made a bad one. Oh, maybe we had some bumpy rides, but it wasn't our decision to go down for overhaul in January instead of in the middle of the summer!"

As a 20-year Coast Guard man, Larry Edwards had seen plenty of storms, mostly on the Oregon and Washington coasts. But those were far different craft. "You could roll those things over and then

Prince William Sound on a peaceful day, with Bartlett *kite fliers John Lam and Homer Herndon, above, and Brian Spurling with Homer, below. The kites were constructed during the annual trip to dry dock with "sticks and paper we found on the car deck," Virgil Campbell says. Photos courtesy of Virgil and Dawn Campbell.*

you could get back up. You wouldn't want to do that on the ferries."

"When we made those trips," Walter says, "I told everybody, 'Stay in your bunk until we get across. Don't bother getting out of bed, or cooking, or anything.' I was up and down in my room, trying to stay in my bed, if I could, but also be ready in case the mate needed help. It might even be that he's seasick. Sailors, officers up on the bridge—if they can't do it, if they're sick and it's bad, they better get someone to help.

"Maybe that's why I like it. Of all the years and years that I've spent on the water, it's never bothered me. . . ." (In a separate reminiscence, Bosun Tom Faulkner wonders whether there might have been just one uncomfortable time. "We were coming from Whittier to Cordova on a summer afternoon and ran into the worst storm in my 28 years on the *Bartlett*," Faulkner says. "Everybody on the ship was sick except the mate and me, and he had to pull me out of my bunk. I was too scared to get sick. We had 18- to 24-foot seas head-on—a freak storm. The mate went back and knocked on Mr. Jackinsky's door, but the captain didn't get up. 'I wasn't sick,' he said when he came out. 'I just kept getting thrown back in my bunk!'")

Walter continues, "On the way back to Cordova one time, about three o'clock in the morning, I put the searchlight on and all I could see was white water all the way around me. I said, 'Turn that searchlight off.' If you don't see anything, then it doesn't bother you that much.

"When we got into heavy snow, wet snow sticking to our radar antennas, then the radars weren't any good. Before one trip south I told the port captain in Juneau, 'We've got two radars and they both have been giving us trouble all winter. I don't want to take any chances with poor radar through the Inside Passage.' He said, 'What are you going to do?' I said, 'There's a radar technician in Seward we can hire. He can travel with us and see if the radars work, or he can repair them on the way.' He said, 'OK, get him if you want him, but come on down. We've been waiting for you.' So we got him. He got paid real good for the four or five days that he was on. And he earned it. That was Pat Mars. He has a radio shop in Seward, Communications North.

"It's four or five days to Seattle [from Cordova] if you didn't stop in Ketchikan for water. Several times I'd ask our engineers, 'How's our water?' They'd say, 'Pretty low. We're going to be just about out when we get there.' I'd say, 'Le-e-et's go! Let's not stop. Conserve on the water [for crew use] as much as you can.' One of those times we got into Canadian waters—Milbank Sound. That's open to the ocean, crossing that sound. There's about 20-some miles of open ocean. There was a real awful storm, and there's a tug out there with a barge, and they're broke down. The Coast Guard said, 'You have to go on assistance, if you can.' So we went out there. We couldn't do much except maybe pick up the passengers or crew if we had to. The engine room hollered, 'Hey, don't let it roll!' The engine wasn't getting the oil it should because of the heavy pitching.

"So we stood by until the Coast Guard came and relieved us. We went a little farther and there's a doggone fishing boat having problems and we had to assist that for a while. . . ."

One November when the dock at Petersburg was under repair, the *LeConte* was sent down to shuttle cargo from Ketchikan to Wrangell and then pick up its regular run. Come Thanksgiving Day, Captain Jackinsky and his crew were eager to get home to Juneau. "So we took off, and we got to Wrangell Narrows, and Wrangell Narrows was just socked in solid with fog. What in the heck are we gonna do? The wives are calling, 'We've got turkeys, we've got all kinds of food ready, you're going to get here just in time.' They were expecting us in six hours.

"'Well,' I said, 'to heck with it. Let's give it a try. Let's go.' Everybody was all for it, and they did everything they could to help me. And we somehow made it through.

"It's really, really dangerous, you know—treacherous—to go through Wrangell Narrows in fog. There are aids coming up, lights coming up, and you just barely saw them, you know. This time the chief mate, Harold Nevers, was looking in the radar. (We called him 'Blue Water' Nevers because he had an unlimited mate's license, an ocean-going license.)

"You'd Better Pull Over and Let Us By"

*I was running a load of salmon to a Petersburg can-*nery one inky night in the fog, when the radio suddenly spoke, "This is the Alaska ferry *Matanuska*, southbound in Wrangell Narrows at buoy 10. Northbound traffic, please advise."

"Buoy 10?" I thought. "I'm almost there." Quickly I flipped my radar up to a longer range and felt my throat start to constrict—a very large target was bearing down on me rapidly and I was in one of the narrowest parts of the channel.

"Ahh, Matanuska . . . this is the tender *Emily Jane*, just passing buoy 3A."

"*Matanuska* back," the radio snapped. "Yeah, I can see you there on radar. You'd better pull over and let us by. It's pretty damned tight here." I could feel the tension in that skipper's voice as the tide pushed him down the narrowing channel with only eerie green glowing images on a radar screen to guide him.

I slowed right down, idling into the current, easing over to the side and peering out into the black, trying to see him. We were so close his target on radar had disappeared into the sea clutter in the middle of the screen. I was bracing myself to either hit him or slide onto the gravel beach—we were that close.

Then I saw him—just a row of lighted portholes rushing by in the black. I don't know how those fellows do it, but I wouldn't have wanted to be that skipper that night.

By Joe Upton, on www.cruisealaska.com.

"He could only see the aids when they were right up just about against us. In my mind I had to have a good picture of everything.

"Sometimes you'd get caught in that fog. You'd get in halfway and then you've got to do something. Some captains get leery, and they find a place where they can anchor, but that's no good because there isn't much room to anchor.

"It would be so easy to go aground, or get tangled up with a navigational aid. They're built out of concrete, you know. You could hit an island. But darned if we didn't get through there. We got those supplies unloaded and got to Juneau in time for Thanksgiving dinner. . . ."

The passengers and the crew and the Thanksgiving chefs weren't the only ones hoping the *LeConte* would make its schedule. Walter's son Shawn remembers the thrill of waking up mornings to the fragrance of Hills Bros. coffee perking, "because that meant my dad was home!" Alice drank tea.

Unknowingly, Shawn echoes Risa when he says, "I'm extremely proud of my father and all he has accomplished. He came up through the ranks, and it wasn't that easy a go for him. But he was gone a large percentage of my life, either fishing in Bristol Bay or on a ship somewhere, and it was hard for us, too. I remember as a small boy wishing he was there at night to keep the bogeyman away. When he was there the house just seemed more secure."

After high school Shawn had a taste of the ferry system himself, working as a messman and waiter on the *Malaspina*, the *Tustumena*, and the short-lived *Wickersham*, a Norwegian ship that serviced Alaska for about six years, from 1968 to 1974, before being sold back to another Scandinavian company.

Life and Death and Love

"In '68 or '69 we had a pregnant woman aboard the *Malaspina* out of Seattle. She checked with her doctor—'Am I going to be safe to make this trip?'—and he said sure. She was going to Ketchikan, just 50-some hours. In about 30 hours she started getting what you call contractions. We made several announcements to see if there

156

was a doctor aboard, or a nurse, but there wasn't anyone. So our crew had to take care of her.

"The women waiters were good. They were right there with her. And we had a special stateroom for her—blankets, sheets, water, everything she wanted.

"I was in and out of there quite a bit. But everything went good. It was her first baby.

"Whenever there's a child born on a ship you stop at the first port you can. It's in the regulations. The first one was Prince Rupert. We went in there, in Canada, and the doctor checked her and said everything was good. So the child got Canadian citizenship because she was born in Canadian waters.

"From there we went on to Ketchikan."

The baby's name? Malaspina, of course.

"On another trip, heading south from Skagway, an elderly couple came aboard. They were from New Zealand, retired, on their first trip. After we stopped in Haines I was making the rounds on the outer walkway and happened to look through an open porthole, and there's this fellow sitting with his shirt off, his undershirt halfway off, resting like this [gesture of head leaning on one hand]—pretty normal. I didn't think anything of it. But it began to kind of bother me so I came back again after maybe 15 minutes and looked, and he's *still* there. So I told the purser, go in there and find out—it doesn't look right. And that was it. He wasn't living. It was fortunate that the porthole was partially open so I could see through there, instead of his wife finding him.

"We called Juneau. They had a coroner there when we docked and took him off the ship, right there in Auke Bay."

Walter was first mate on the *Malaspina* when the namesake was born and when the elderly New Zealander died. And again:

"This was also leaving Haines. We took on a big load there. Everybody was in a hurry. We were late, and there were sailors running around, and the captain was screaming at them. After we let all the lines go, a sailor who was supposed to be up on the bridge ran through one of the lounges and up the stairs and just keeled over and fell down. He died right there. We went back to Haines and delivered his body there.

"He was an AB who lived in Wrangell, I believe. He was in his middle forties, but he did have some kind of heart condition. Afterwards we found out about that."

An eerie sight aboard the *Malaspina* on another trip caused some agitation.

"We were hauling a hearse with a body from Sitka to Wrangell. Around midnight the watchman made the rounds on the car deck and saw somebody sitting up on the coffin in the hearse, moving around. He was a big guy, this watchman—Virgil, a big strong logger from Oregon. I asked him once and he told me he had a 54-inch waist. But he got all shook up. His hair was standing up, and he's sweating. He came and told me, 'That dead pioneer we're taking back home—that person came to life!' We had a Polish bosun, Ray Volski. He and a Tlingit guy from Ketchikan named Dickie John went down to check it out. (Dickie John's nickname was Broken Arrow. I think he was from Craig originally.) Dickie John said Ray Volski was crossing himself for protection. But it turned out to be the driver of the hearse. There wasn't supposed to be anybody down there—we had the barrier chain across—but somebody in the stewards department told him he could go down. He said he was trying to secure the hearse so it wouldn't tip when he went over the ramp at Wrangell."

Captains, mates and pursers were required to have some emergency medical training, but that didn't apply to the crew in general. As first mate, Walter was in the officers' mess one afternoon with the captain and others while the *Malaspina* was unloading at Juneau. Suddenly the second mate burst in.

"Ken Mayo came running in, grabbed a couple of teaspoons, and ran out again. Someone was having an epileptic seizure on the car deck. I ran down with him, and there was Virgil [the watchman], 340 pounds, wrestling this guy to hold him and keep him from hurting himself. That was Virgil's idea, but you're not supposed to do that. . . .

"He had already passed the critical stage. The purser called the ambulance—we were still at the dock—and they got him on a litter and took care of him. He was traveling by himself, but he wore something on his wrist that identified his condition."

The first wedding ceremony performed by Captain Jackinsky was a spontaneous affair on the *LeConte*, between Juneau/Auke Bay and Haines.

"A young couple came up and asked me if they could be married before we got to port. She was a teacher in Skagway. She came up here by herself and spent a year. He wasn't going to come up and see her. They had agreed that he would stay away. But he came anyhow, and within a couple of hours of being together they wanted to get married right now.

"The purser had to call the magistrate and get his OK because we were in inland waters. Then we got 'em up on the bridge. I was there, the purser was there, the chief steward and chief engineer and a few other officers. That's all there was to it. I married them right there on the bridge. This was '74, maybe '75. Once they got on the ferry things just started happening."

Another couple who boarded the *Bartlett* in Valdez had everything planned. "They had all the papers they needed. They wanted to be married right in among the icebergs, right against Columbia Glacier. We took them in there and went out on the bridge. The purser was announcing. We had a load of passengers, maybe 170 or 200 passengers, and they all listened and watched while this was going on. We did it right on the wing of the bridge, at the glacier. There were a lot of pictures taken, and a lot of flowers."

Walter smiles at the recollection of attending a friend's wedding at Cordova's Million Dollar Bridge, with the couple's big malamute husky as best man. The Million Dollar Bridge, which actually cost $1.5 million to build in 1909-10 [see Appendix], hasn't carried any traffic since it lost a span in the 1964 Good Friday earthquake. A retrofitting project now under way could make it the Fifteen Million Dollar Bridge.

He officiated at another Cordova wedding, on the *Bartlett*. "We were tied up there, and they wanted to get married right on the ship. The husband-to-be was an AB, Al Fuller. He was on duty and we couldn't let him go. His fiancée and her mother and some of the other relatives flew to Cordova from Anchorage. There were quite a few of them.

Coast Pilot 9, 1964, "the earthquake edition"

Cordova *(1960 population 1,128; P.O.) is on the east-* ern shore of Orca Inlet opposite Spike Island, which is wooded. Cordova is 1,221 miles from Seattle via the ocean route and 1,363 miles via inside passages through British Columbia and Southeast Alaska to Cape Spencer. It is one of the most important towns in southwestern Alaska and is the supply and distribution point for numerous outlying fishing localities.

The March 1964 earthquake caused a bottom uplift of 6.3 feet at Cordova. Shoaling and new dangers may exist requiring extreme caution until a complete survey is made of the area.

Prominent features.—Mt. Eyak, 2,498 feet, and Mt. Eccles, 2,680 feet, dominate the approach, the town nesting at the foot of Mt. Eyak.

Channels.—The deepest channel, and the one used by larger vessels, leads north of North Island and then follows the eastern shore southward to Orca and Cordova. The buoyed channel had a controlling depth of 22 feet in April 1964. . . .

Routes.—Eastward: From the entrance point to Prince William Solund, 1.5 miles southwest of Cape Hinchinbrook Light, clear the western side of Hinchinbrook Island by 1.5 miles then follow the marked passage through Orca Bay and Orca Inlet to Cordova.

Westward: Enter Prince William Sound through Elrington Passage, pass 1 mile eastward of Point Helen Light, 1.5 miles westward and northward of Seal Island Light, and set a course to enter the marked passage in Orca Bay.

Fishing vessels sometimes approach Cordova through Orca Inlet from the south by one of the unmarked channels.

Pilotage.—Vessels may obtain a pilot at Seattle, Ketchikan, Juneau, or on advance notice from Anchorage. A local pilot for Cordova may be obtained by calling AKO-44 Cordova on 2134 kc; pilot will board vessel off the buoy at Sheep Point on advance notice.

From U.S. Coast Pilot 9: Alaska, Cape Spencer to Beaufort Sea, *Seventh Edition, 1964*

"Al and Karen wanted the wedding on the bow of the ship, so we made room there up on the bow. The guys put the oars together just like an archway. And the cook had a nice buffet for them.

"I think Karen traveled up and back with us. And we let him have all the time he wanted. . . ."

Bosun Tom Faulkner says Captains Jackinsky and Hofstad were disappointed when he and his wife-to-be "ran away" to Washington state to be married. "They said they wanted to take the *Bartlett* and the *Tustumena* into Valdez and go bow to bow and have the ceremony there. That was too much for us. We ran away and got married down here [on Whidbey Island, their present home]."

The wedding Walter remembers best took place at Auke Bay on the *LeConte*, but Captain Jackinsky didn't officiate. He gave the bride away.

"My youngest daughter, Risa, wanted to get married on the ship. They had a minister, and a good crowd. And I sent [the newlyweds] to Hawaii for a week."

Some people designate the ships for a final passage. Several families arranged for the ashes of loved ones to be scattered from the *Malaspina* while Walter was first mate. "One man's family wanted his ashes spread on Lynn Canal, so we slowed down and stopped there. That's maybe seven, eight miles out of Haines on the way to Juneau. There was another coming out of Sitka. One in Juneau. Usually there would be flowers—we'd throw over some flowers—and a little reception after that.

"And then the prayer, the 23rd Psalm, the same as on ships for many years back, even in sailing days when they had regular burials at sea. 'The Lord is my shepherd; I shall not want. He maketh me to lie down in green pastures. He leadeth me beside the still waters. He restoreth my soul. . . .'"

Home Port

". . . An avant-garde artist would have a field day in Prince William Sound, where surrealistic icebergs sail past near Columbia Glacier, and kelp, like the draped clocks and telephones in a Salvador Dali painting, waves sinuous arms in the deep. By night the

Oiler Joe Dymesich with Jilian and Hunter Campbell, aboard the Bartlett *at Columbia Glacier. Photo courtesy of Virgil and Dawn Campbell.*

boat trails phosphorescent wake and one feels altogether in a different world. . . ."

Walter might not put it quite as poetically as Lone Janson did in 1967 for the Cordova Chamber of Commerce publication *Discover Alaska First at Cordova*. But then again he might. After all those hundreds of circuits with the *Bartlett* he is as enthralled by Prince William Sound as any first-time passenger, or Chamber member. Two of his favorite views, he says, are the black-legged kittiwake rookery on the approach to Whittier, with its neighboring colony of literally thousands of glaucous-winged gulls, and massive Columbia Glacier, the largest tidewater glacier in Prince William Sound and second largest in the state. (Like glaciers elsewhere it is now receding at what many consider an alarming rate.)

In the thoughtful piece Walter wrote while still aboard the *Bartlett* he speaks of "the clear and beautiful waters that prevail in Prince William Sound, and also Columbia Glacier Bay, where we usually encounter large icebergs and harbor seals riding the smaller ice floes, orcas ['sea wolves,' or as they used to be called, killer whales], humpback whales, sea lions, and sea otters. . . . Further, there is a great variety of gulls, and sea and shore birds. From the bridge we have an especially good view in sighting migrating and feeding whales spouting, or their flukes or tails coming out of the water. We have occasionally even seen bear roaming the shores and beaches, and mountain goats on the hillsides. . . ."

AB Larry Edwards has a slightly different take on the glories of Prince William Sound. For the crew there's a tendency to start taking it all for granted, he says. "Day after day after day you're riding the *Bartlett* from Cordova to Valdez to Whittier. The crew's quarters are right under the main deck, and you're trying to sleep. Let's say we're coming into Columbia Glacier. All of a sudden the engine would slow down and we'd wake up. Then you could hear the passengers running on those steel decks and you knew damn well there was a killer whale up there, or a seal pup on a hunk of ice or something. You'd get so mad: 'Why do those people have to *run?*'

"Then you're home for a while and you get to thinking: Here I am working a job that people pay thousands of dollars for, just to pass through those waters one time on a cruise ship. Once in a life-time—they'll never be back again."

When he was first assigned to the *Bartlett* after a couple of ferry assignments in Southeast and was told to report to Whittier, Edwards says, his response was, "Where's Whittier?"

"I was brand new to the system," he says. "You had to take what they gave you if you wanted to work. I flew up to Anchorage the next morning, took the bus down to Girdwood and got on the train to Whittier, went wandering down to the ship. Here it is, the whole bow open [the 'knight's-hood' bow unique to the *Bartlett*], and I thought, 'What have I gotten into?' I called the wife from Valdez: 'I'll be home tomorrow if I have to fake a heart attack.'"

It was six months before Larry Edwards saw home again.

"It was just so much fun," he says. "That crew was unreal. Even the food was great. One thing I loved: The captain made sure we had fish at least once a day. And by golly, if there was fresh fish in Cordova then you had fresh fish. He didn't want any of that stuff that came out of a box." Edwards had a few other assignments before he got a permanent job on the *Bartlett*. "I knew one of the dispatchers," he says. "She was married to a Coast Guard guy whose boss I used to be. I had to butter her up to get back to the *Bartlett*. I spent 20 years in the Coast Guard, but the time I spent on the *Bartlett* was the best of my life."

Toni Bocci, ferry terminal agent at Cordova, remembers Larry Edwards as the *Bartlett* crewmember who was almost as fond of her dog Tom Tom as she was. "Tom Tom was a 'mixed breed,' i.e., mutt," she says. "He didn't stand over 18 inches high, but he didn't know that. He would tie up the ferry with me, being careful to just sit and watch and never get in the way. However, untying the ferry he would follow me line by line from stern to bow. . . . He was almost wider than he was tall, and I have to blame that on his diet—thank you, Larry Edwards!" Tom Tom was loyal to Toni—"this was a dog that would follow me anywhere"—but he also knew which end of the ship his bread was buttered on. "I always handled the stern line at Cordova," Larry Edwards says, "and I always had a snack for Tom Tom. Sometimes he would come roaring down the ramp even before we got tied up. He wouldn't even take

The "knight's-hood" bow of the Bartlett *open to receive vehicles at Whittier, 1996. Photo courtesy of Diane Olthuis.*

Ria Bocci with Tom Tom in Cordova, 1993. Photo courtesy of Toni Bocci.

a steak from anybody else. I'd sneak into the galley when the cook wasn't looking. Make him a little sack lunch and give it to Toni." The day that Toni Bocci came down alone to tie up the ship, crying, Larry knew immediately what had happened. He still feels sad talking about it. Toni says, "Tom Tom was put to rest on the cliff overlooking the ferry dock nine years ago. We think and speak of him often."

Larry Edwards and his wife, Joan, left Alaska for Arizona after Joan had lung surgery and they were advised that she should have a warmer, dryer climate. She is now well recovered and they both have fallen in love with the community of Lake Havasu City. But when Arizona temperatures start climbing past 100 degrees each spring, Larry says, he starts thinking wistfully of Prince William Sound.

In another branch of the extended *"Bartlett* family," Cordova author Lone Janson turns out to be the aunt of AB Virgil Campbell's wife, Dawn. The Campbells' children, Jilian and Hunter, grew up considering the ship their second home, Dawn Campbell says, because they made the trip back to Cordova so often after moving to Moose Pass. The year Hunter turned three, ship's cook Tomás Delgadillo baked him a birthday cake and the crew sang "Happy Birthday."

Walter remembers other occasions, too. Residents of the Harborview facility for the developmentally disabled in Valdez (since closed) were invited for a winter cruise on the ship each year. "We'd offer them a trip for nothing. 'We'll take you guys out and give you a good treat. Go on a trip with us right around the bay.' The stewards would have ice cream cones for them. Then the big, strong, burly bosun would put a cap on and dress up like Santa Claus. 'Oh, Santa, Santa,' they cried, and would put their arms around him. . . .

"Once when we were tied up in Cordova we invited the local people for a party on the *Bartlett.* Fixed a lot of prime rib—we had at least two seatings, at least 70 or 80 people for this party.

"Another time we decided, 'Let's give them a little trip out of Cordova. Let's go on a little cruise.' So we invited anyone who wanted to come. First we cleared the forward lounge, so they could gamble. If they wanted to gamble aboard the ship, they had gam-

Jennifer and Emily Long in Grandpa Jackinsky's chair on the LeConte, *c. 1980. Photo courtesy of Emily Long Aley.*

bling tables set up. And we took off for about four hours, cruised around Cordova, around the bays, and brought them all back. I don't remember if they paid something. I don't think so. Of course, we cleared this with Juneau. They were good about it.

"Cordova felt like the *Bartlett* was their ship, you know. And it was."

For Walter's own birthday one May, three generations of Jackinskys got off the train in Whittier wearing party hats and carrying a banner and a big cake to take aboard the *Bartlett* for the round trip to Valdez. Alice and Risa and McKibben and her two girls and Shawn and his family crowded around the captain's table in the dining room and serenaded the birthday man, to the delight of the other passengers, then spent the night on deck chairs and returned the next day to Whittier.

"We all got on the ferry whenever we could, just to see him," McKibben says. "The girls and I would take trips on the *LeConte* when they were two and three and four, to spend time with Grandpa. We'd board with our little backpacks, and at bedtime they'd troop up to Grandpa's stateroom so they could put on their snap-together pajamas. When they were settled in their sleeping bags on the deck, Grandpa would come down and tuck them in."

"Something sacred had been defiled"

Oil tankers began plying the waters of Prince William Sound in the 1970s, after the Alaska Native Claims Settlement Act of 1971 cleared the way for oil exploration in the interior and the TransAlaska Pipeline was constructed. Tanker traffic added a hazard to navigation, particularly in the Valdez Narrows. But Walter says, "We had good communication and we knew their schedule, so we could slow down and give them the chance to get through. We'd wait a mile or so away because it's harder for them—they're bigger. We didn't have to wait very much."

Walter happened to be on a two-week break from the *Bartlett* in March 1989 when the tanker *Exxon Valdez* went aground on Bligh Reef beyond the Valdez Narrows and spewed 10.8 million gallons of crude oil into Prince William Sound—and eventually onto more than a thousand miles of beach in Southcentral Alaska—with consequences even more far-reaching than the effects of the Good Friday earthquake almost exactly 25 years before.

As the Alaska Oil Spill Commission said in its final report in February 1990, "No human lives were lost as a direct result of the disaster, though four deaths were associated with the cleanup effort. Indirectly, however, the human and natural losses were immense—to fisheries, subsistence livelihoods, tourism, wildlife. The most important loss for many who will never visit Prince William Sound was the aesthetic sense that something sacred in the relatively unspoiled land and waters of Alaska had been defiled. . . . A spill that ranked 34th on a list of the world's largest oil spills in the past 25 years came to be seen as the nation's biggest environmental disaster since Three Mile Island."

Many of the points raised in the commission's report hark back to the basic "rules of the road" that Walter and every master mariner must commit to memory and understanding. " . . . The grounding at Bligh Reef represents much more than the error of a possibly drunken skipper," the report concludes. "It was the result of the gradual degradation of oversight and safety practices that had been intended . . . to safeguard and backstop the inevitable mistakes of human beings."

Short staffing on the tankers operated by Exxon Shipping Co. may have been a factor in the spill, the report says, citing research that belies the company's claims of uncompromised safety levels despite dramatically reduced crew levels over the years. (" . . . Automation does not replace humans in systems, rather, it places the human in a different, more demanding role.") The commission recommended "that crew levels be set high enough not only to permit safe operations during ordinary conditions—which, in the Gulf of Alaska, can be highly demanding—but also to provide enough crew backups and rest periods that crisis situations can be confronted by a fresh, well-supported crew."

The Exxon Shipping Co. is no more. It was renamed the Sea River Shipping Co. The former *Exxon Valdez*, now the *Sea River Mediterranean*, is used to haul oil across the Atlantic. It is prohibited by law from returning to Prince William Sound.

Coast Pilot 9, 1964, "the earthquake edition"

Valdez (1960 population 555; P.O.), at the head of Port Valdez, is at the southern end of Richardson Highway, which connects with Fairbanks, 374 miles distant. Open all year, the highway also serves Anchorage and Seward and links with the Alaska Highway.

Valdez is 1,234 miles from Seattle via the outside route through Strait of Juan de Fuca and 1,376 miles via the inside passages to Cape Spencer.

Prominent features.—The stack of the large asphalt and steam plant, painted in red and white horizontal bands, and the yellow water tank at the eastern edge of the city are prominent landmarks when approaching Valdez. Port Valdez Light, 15 feet above the water, is shown from a white square day-mark on a dolphin on the edge of the shoal about 0.4 mile northwestward of the Valdez City Wharf.

The approach to Valdez is deep and clear of dangers once through Valdez Narrows. There are no safe anchorages at Valdez except for a narrow shelf 100 yards off the wharves in 13 to 20 fathoms. Convenient anchorages in the approaches in Valdez Arm and Port Valdez have been described. . . .

Routes.—Eastward: From the entrance point to Prince William Sound, 1.5 miles southwest of Cape Hinchinbrook Light, pass 3 miles westward of Porpoise Rocks and enter Valdez Arm 1.5 miles westward of Bligh Reef, thence through Valdez Narrows and Port Valdez to Valdez.

Westward: Enter Prince William Sound through Elrington Passage, pass 1 mile eastward of Point Helen Light, 1.5 miles westward of Seal Island Light, 2 miles eastward of Smith Island, and enter Valdez Arm 1.5 miles westward of Bligh Reef.

From U.S. Coast Pilot 9: Alaska, Cape Spencer to Beaufort Sea, *Seventh Edition, 1964*

"American Heart"

For two days in the late 1980s the *Bartlett* was a movie set.

"We got to Bellingham [for winter overhaul] and they were doing a movie in Seattle. They wanted to rent the *Bartlett* and the crew. So for two days we worked out of Seattle. 'American Heart' is the name of the movie. Jeff Bridges was the star.

"They were good to work for. I told them 'Do whatever you want. Just stay clear of the navigational areas.' They were building structures all over the bridge and everywhere else, and running the power plant on board the ship. They had a big dining room set up—not on the ship, though. Ashore. They said, 'You guys can eat there with us.' But we didn't do that. We had our meals on the ship.

"Sometimes there would be maybe 20 people on the bridge, you know. They'd say, 'OK, take off this way, and head for the sunset.' 'Now head for Mount Rainier.' 'OK, let's go back to the dock again.' I think I did that 11 times in one day. Tie up, and off we'd go again. Back and forth. They had to rehearse a lot of things a lot of times. You do it—no, that isn't right, let's do it again.

"They all knew in Seattle. The Elliott Bay traffic knew what we were doing, so they tried to stay out of our way as much as they could with their ferries and their tugs and everything else. The film company had to pay the Port of Seattle, too.

"They had at least 50 or more people, ordinary people, that they hired every day as extras, you know, to be passengers. There were Alaskans coming with big packs, snowshoes and long coats, parkas, women in long dresses, you name it. They had them dressed pretty good.

"It's a good movie. I saw it on video but I forgot pretty much about it. It was so many years ago. . . .

[Anyone who has not yet seen "American Heart," released in 1992, might want to skip the next three paragraphs. Suffice it to say here that the credits include "The captain and crew of the M/V *Bartlett*."]

"There was a fellow, Jeff Bridges, involved in drugs or something like that, and he was in prison. Walla Walla. He got out of there and said he was going to go straight. He always had Alaska in his mind, so he came to Seattle. But there were people that knew him and wanted to get rid of him. They said, 'He's going to maybe cause trouble for us. Let's kill him. Get rid of him.'

"He stayed somewhere in Seattle and hid, and then one morning the ferry was there and he took a run—he ran as fast as he could just before we left. He jumped to get on the ferry and they shot at him. They hit him, wounded him. But he came aboard and we took off and he ran into his son. He had a son from a former marriage, a 10-year-old son, on the *Bartlett* also.

"So they got together. It was very emotional. I was on the bridge, I saw it, and I had a movie camera. I was taking pictures of what was going on. He was dying and trying to tell his son. His son was trying to hold him up. There were several scenes. He didn't know whether the dying scene was any good or maybe use another one—jumping over the side, I guess, or something. That was the story.

"They had it arranged for the son where he'd go to school right there on the ship or wherever they were, you know, besides doing his work with the movie.

"While they worked, Jeff Bridges would come up to the bridge sometimes, play his ukulele.

"Seattle must have made about $8 million or $9 million on that movie. I don't know what the state got. The state got a pretty good chunk for the two days, I know that."

Appearance and Disappearance

From the log of the M/V *Malaspina*, February 1973:

The ship's position when sighting was abeam of Twin Island, Revillagigedo Channel. The time was 0655 hours Pacific Standard Time. The weather was clear with unlimited visibility. Wind Northeast 10 knots, temperature 28 degrees, and the barometer pressure was 30.71.

Standing watch on the bridge was Chief Mate Walter Jackinsky and two sailors—one at the helm and one lookout. A huge vessel was seen approximately eight miles dead ahead, broadside and dead in the water. This vessel resembled very much the Flying Dutchman. The color was all gray—similar to vapor or clouds. It was seen distinctly for

about 10 minutes. It looked so exact, natural and real that when seen
through binoculars sailors could be seen moving on board. Within
seconds it disappeared into oblivion.

This is the first such sighting to any of these present, all of whom
were in full agreement.

Walter has never forgotten that sighting, noted in Sheila Nickerson's *Disappearance: A Map*. The *Flying Dutchman* legend often includes accounts of a violent death suffered as a consequence of
having seen the ghostly ship. But Walter and his fellow crewmen
didn't know that, and they were merely thrilled with their experience. "We thought it was the other way around," Walter says. "We
thought we were really fortunate that we were able to witness
something like that. We told everybody about it—it was in the
Juneau paper and everything.

"We saw it, just a beautiful sight, and broadsides. We were
heading right towards that bay. We couldn't get it on radar—but I
guess we wouldn't be able to, would we? Because there wasn't anything there! But the formation, or clouds, or whatever it was, was
just beautiful—billows, and men on the ship, and everything else.
Then the closer we got, pretty soon everything was gone. But we
were excited for a while there, the three of us."

Nickerson's *Meditation on Death & Loss in the High Latitudes*, the
subtitle of her book, does say that a month before the *Flying Dutchman* presented itself to the *Malaspina*, "a woman employee on the
Malaspina had jumped to her death . . . about 190 miles south of
the sighting." Walter well recalls that brooding day, also.

"We didn't know anything until one or two hours afterwards.
We had to assume she had jumped. The captain said, 'There's no
possibility of doing anything.' We just went on."

Family Matters

When he took over the *Bartlett*, Walter bought a condo in
Valdez, "but I never stayed there. I thought it would be good to
have a place to relax even for a few hours. But it didn't work out. I
just stayed on the ship. . . .

"Alice and I kind of went our separate ways when our children were grown. But we were always good friends. When I did have time off from the *Bartlett* I usually headed for Juneau. Alice's job with the state was going good, and she had her apartment there—we sold the house when it got too big for us, with the kids gone. McKibben and Shawn had apartments in Juneau. Risa was in Anchorage for several years.

"Finally Alice decided to come to Ninilchik and build, and we all started moving up here. She retired. Or semi-retired. In the winter she'd work a while in Juneau and then come back. . . ."

Alice's "retirement" included a contract with the state to work during the legislative session in Juneau each winter. She would travel to Southeast via highway and ferry and stay in Juneau for the season, then head back to Ninilchik. Daughter Risa remembers hearing about one wild commute, when Alice's car hit an icy spot on the Haines Pass. "She flew off the road in her car, shearing off treetops as she kept hitting the brake—in mid-air!—before landing 30 feet or more down an embankment. [Risa's sister McKibben says the tow truck operator needed 100 feet of cable to reach the car.] All the doors popped open, and she gathered up her two mini-dachshunds and climbed back up to the road to try to find help.

"She walked for five or six miles until she came upon a dog-sledder's parked truck and climbed in back to curl up. She said her two little dogs were going stiff with the cold and she had just finished saying mental good-byes when she saw headlights and got out in time to flag down a car. The two men inside—professional river guides, I think—helped thaw her and the dogs and got her to safety."

McKibben and her Jennifer and Emily, pre-teens by this time, were in Juneau awaiting Alice's arrival ("Grandma's coming! Grandma's coming!") when they got a phone call from Haines: "I'm fine, but there's a problem with the car. Could you have a tow truck waiting at the dock?"

And, says Risa, "that was just one of Mom's adventures."

Son Shawn, busy with his own family by then, remembers stopping by on occasional summer evenings at the house Alice built on the homestead. "My dad moved right across from my mother's

Alice Jackinsky on a hike at the Grand Canyon. Jackinsky family photo.

place," he says. "I'd go by and find those two having dinner together and giggling—and then they'd straighten up because they had company. . . . They loved each other a lot."

In the late 1980s Alice developed symptoms of thrombocythemia, a blood disorder characterized by the production of too many platelets in the bone marrow. In 1994 she and Risa rented a small apartment in Anchorage for three months so she could be near the hospital for observation and treatment. Four years later, on the way to a gathering of the family in Las Vegas for the wedding of her granddaughter Emily, McKibben's younger daughter, Alice stopped over with Risa in Phoenix. Severe abdominal pain sent her to the emergency room of a Phoenix hospital on St. Patrick's Day, March 17. She was readmitted several times over the next several days, with no relief. Finally she refused further treatment and insisted that she was going to the wedding. Risa rented a van so Alice could lie down as they traveled. The evening before the wedding her condition worsened, and Risa and McKibben took her to the hospital in Las Vegas. She died the day after the wedding, March 29, with her daughters nearby. Shawn and his wife were partway home but returned to Las Vegas when they got the news.

On Mother's Day 1998 the family gathered again at Ninilchik, to scatter Alice's ashes from Walter's boat, the *Jaco*, on the inlet directly below the homestead.

Walter retired from the ferry service in January 1997, the year before Alice died. His family and friends did him proud, with toasts and tributes and a fine spread of food—and music for dancing, of course—at the American Legion Hall in Seward. He was presented with a ship's clock "from the officers and crew of the M/V *E.L. Bartlett*, in recognition of 34 years of service with the Alaska Marine Highway System," and calipers hand-forged by AB Al Fuller that hang on a wooden plaque engraved "with appreciation and esteem, for all are better sailors for having served with you." AB Virgil Campbell gave him a specially made filleting knife "because you shouldn't be keeping an eye on the clock anymore."

The captain relishes the recollection of a splendid day.

"The whole family was there, and the crew from the *Bartlett* who could make it. Some from the *Tustumena*. Officials from

Juneau. Legislators came. People from around here. . . ." One of the dignitaries was then-senator, now Lieutenant Governor Loren Leman of Ninilchik. Singer-songwriter-recording artist-fisherman Butch Leman, Loren Leman's cousin, provided the music. AMHS Captain Karl Schoeppe, who attended Juneau-Douglas High School with McKibben, then served under Walter as a young maritime academy graduate and is now master of the M/V *Columbia* and considering retirement himself, was "on the road" but telephoned with congratulations from himself and his crew.

There is no doubt that Walter also relished every moment of his 34 years on the Alaska Marine Highway. He's appreciative of the healthy pensions he earned as a state employee and a member of a storied union, the International Organization of Masters, Mates and Pilots, and he is everlastingly proud of his hard-won captain's insignia. But he didn't look back.

The honorary commodore and some of his crew at the American Legion Hall in Seward, January 1997. **Front row,** *from left: Homer Herndon, first mate (former cook); Gail Lowell, first engineer; Captain Jackinsky; Tom Faulkner, bosun.*

Back row, *from left: Al "Sweetwater" Fuller, OS; Billy Sullivan, deck crew; Mike Croft, chief engineer (black cap in profile); Nancy Wolford, purser; Bruce Erkenbrack Jr., oiler; Captain John Klabo; Dan Gagnon, then chief cook (forehead visible behind Captain Klabo); [visitor, in dark cap]; Bill Little, retired AB; Bill Whitmore, second mate; Jeff Lamb, AB; Larry Edwards, AB; Virgil Campbell, AB; Katie Haven, second engineer; Dan Knocker, AB. Photo courtesy of Tom Faulkner, who says it was taken by Mary Ann Little.*

Walter Jackinsky on a street in Moscow, 1980s. Jackinsky family photo.

KALEIDOSCOPE
AROUND THE WORLD FOR 20 YEARS
5

On December 11, 1980, I took the early morning Pan Am bus from downtown London office to Heathrow West Airport about 24 miles away, departing Heathrow Airport at approximately 1000 hours. Flew across the English Channel, and the first stop was Hamburg, Germany. Everyone had to disembark and go through the airport terminal at Fuhlsbuttel Airport for strict security check, including customs, passport, and immigration. After nearly one hour, we reboarded and continued on the same flight to Berlin, Germany; ETA 1400 hours at Tegal Airport in Berlin: strict security check again. I made reservations previously by telex from London at the Penta Hotel. . . . ETA West Berlin and hotel at approximately 1500 hours. After checking in at the hotel, I made a short walking tour of downtown Berlin. Back at the Penta Hotel, I drank excellent German beer and then had dinner. The food was very good. I had hocks, vegetables, sauerkraut and delicious dark bread.

Excerpt from Day 8, round-the-world travel log of Captain Walter Jackinsky Jr., Dec. 4, 1980–Feb. 2, 1981.

Walter Jackinsky Sr. hoped after World War II to travel to his home country in Europe for a reunion with his brother Adolph and a sister, Eusepha. He had never returned after leaving as a boy. But visas were hard to come by, and he reluctantly gave up that dream. His children have traveled for him, in particular his namesake son.

"Let's see. We made a few trips to Hawaii. But my first big trip must have been around the world. Pan American had a special offer there, around the world for $3,000 or something like that, and it sounded good.

"I stayed on the ship [the Bartlett] for quite a while, more than a year, but then I had time to travel. The kids were grown. And I felt I wanted to travel to see what the rest of the world was like. I was quite interested to know what other people were doing. . . ."

Day 9. December 12, 1980. In the morning I made a bus tour to East Berlin, inside the Berlin Wall, which extends 100 miles and divides Berlin in half. The wall is fortified and well guarded. East Berlin is the German Democratic Republic, and they call it GDR for short. All checkpoints are with very strict and tight security control. Armed guards take over, and they are all business with no pretense or foolishness. We transferred to a different bus and entered the Berlin Wall through "Checkpoint Charlie." Atmosphere here is most depressing. Many armed guards wearing a red star are everywhere, and there is strong Communist control and rule. We were escorted by a Russian-speaking tour guide at all times. . . .

Then a bus sightseeing and lecture tour in the afternoon of West Berlin. Saw many business and residential areas as well as great prisons where Nazi war crimes trials took place. Passed by a prison where the Nazi war criminal Rudolf Hess is kept in captivity. West Berlin is all newly built, and very impressive. . . . The city is well decorated for the Christmas holidays. There is occasional light snow falling. . . . The rate of exchange in West Berlin is the "Mark" O.R. US$.5660. East Berlin is "Ostmark"; O.R. is also US$.5660.

"After that Pan Am deal was a trip to Russia. I'd always wanted to go there, to Moscow. My brother Ed went first. He took two of his girls, Joann and Sara, in 1975. ["But You Can't Dance in Lenin Square," a *Homer Weekly News* article reproduced in *Agrafena's Children*, tells about that trip.]

"All the Russians are pretty close. If you speak Russian, and you're a Jackinsky, well, gosh, you're part of the family. . . .

Day 13. December 16, 1980: Swiss monetary unit is the "Franc"; O.R. is US$.6135. Departed by Eurail at 0800 for Innsbruck, Austria. Traveled for many miles along Lake Geneva. Beautiful residential and recreational areas. Also numerous farms along the way. Snow on the

Walter and Sergei, Moscow. "If you speak Russian, and you're a Jackinsky, you're part of the family." Jackinsky family photo.

mountains in all areas and much skiing activity. . . . ETA Innsbruck approximately 1200 hours. Snow here. . . . I did a casual walking tour of the city for several hours. It's beautiful and surrounded by mountains. There are many ski enthusiasts from all of Europe and various parts of the world. Austria exchange is the "shilling"; O.R. is US$.0796.

Departed Innsbruck by Eurail in the afternoon and on a direct route through Italy to lower Italy to port city of Brindisi. Passengers were extremely crowded. Even most of the aisles were occupied and utilized. The majority were Italians and Sicilians. There also were many children, families, lots of baggage, food and wine. You were lucky to find a place to sit down and to be able to hold on to. It resembled a cattle car and the smell of food and wine was strong. Lower part of Italy had beautiful farm lands and many orchards. The train ride was approximately twenty hours from Innsbruck to Brindisi.

"In Moscow I told the clerk in a shop, an old lady—I said in Russian, 'Do you take American Express card?' She said, 'Let me go and ask the manager.' And he came out and said, 'Hey, that guy's a millionaire. Sell him anything he wants!' American Express card, gold. Yeah!

"This was with a group from Seattle to Helsinki. Twenty-six of us got on a bus and toured Russia. We went all the way from Helsinki to St. Petersburg to Moscow down to Yalta and the Black Sea. Swam in the Black Sea. Nothing but jellyfish in there. Flew back to Moscow and then I joined another group and toured the Scandinavian countries. From Copenhagen to Norway, Sweden, where else? Finland. And then another group, a small group, to Lapland.

"'*Kan ni prata svenska?*' That's 'do you speak Swedish?' I speak broken Swedish. '*Kan du snakke norsk?*'"

Day 15. December 18, 1980: There is a large demonstration in the morning in the downtown area of Brindisi involving teenagers and high school students. I located a tour company and arranged for passage on a Greek car and passenger ferry to Patos, Greece. There is a quiet, casual atmosphere in the city. I enjoyed walking along the waterfront, docks, taking pictures and watching fishermen come in. . . . Departed from Brindisi at approximately 2300 hours on the M/V *Expresso Greece*, a fairly nice passenger and vehicle ship approximately 400 feet in length. It carried a good deck load of vans and cars and some 600 passengers. . . . The schedule included two stops in Greek ports . . . crossing the Adriatic and Ionian Seas. I got a berth in a four-berth stateroom. All beds were occupied. Mine being an upper one was uncomfortably hot. After several hours en route we encountered a severe, violent tropical rain and wind storm. There were many passengers who were seasick during the duration of the storm. Operation of the ship was most casual, baggage being scattered and strewn everywhere, and dogs were not restricted to any particular areas. Lots of good Greek food was served aboard, although it was strong in garlic and greasy. The trip was certainly most interesting and relaxing, in a way.

"Then around 1991 Alaska Airlines was just starting their flight to Siberia, so McKibben and I went. We were just about on the inaugural flight. Not quite, but close to it. . . . Father Simeon, my cousin, traced our grandfather Gregory Oskolkoff's family back two generations to the capital city of Siberia, Irkutsk. I've made three trips to Irkutsk. Lake Baikal is right there close by, about 30 miles from Irkutsk. It's the deepest lake in the world—more than a mile deep. I have a bottle of water that they said they got from the very bottom of Lake Baikal. Hand-carried it home."

Day 22. December 25, 1980: Christmas Day. Took a taxi from the hotel early to the Vatican and Mass at the St. Peter's Cathedral. At approximately 0830 people are already streaming in like a pilgrimage to the pope's (John Paul II) Christmas Mass . . . . I was fortunate to be able to get good seating in the church and close to the front. Everything understood, super vision, order, control; well organized and guarded. There were many high priests attending the pope during Mass. He was exceptionally impressive during the service. The president and his aides sat in the balcony above and close to the front, and many VIPs also. After Mass I walked out on the square, and there

185

Mongolian yurts, and Walter on a visit to a yurt, 1990s. Jackinsky family photo.

were wave after wave of people crowded as far as I could see; they were on rooftops and balconies. . . . His message and blessing were carried out in a strong voice. People cheered. I would estimate possibly 500,000 people were there. The population of Rome is over 4 million. There was a large group of Polskas with a beautiful red and white banner. . . .

After the pope's messages the large cathedral bell started ringing, and people slowly dispersed and scattered, each going their way. . . . All this was most impressive to me. . . .

I walked leisurely to the hotel, which was some four miles away. The weather continued to be the very nicest. Romans (Italians) say that the pope had ordered it to be so. At the hotel I had Tom and Jerrys and also got a large basket of fresh fruit in my room, compliments of the Hilton Hotel on Christmas. Had a nice dinner at the hotel, and there was excellent live organ music in the lobby most of the evening. . . . I made a couple of overseas calls—Christmas greetings and tidings to loved ones—and then retired early.

"I took Risa to Siberia about five years ago. And then to China. And I went there by myself, to Mongolia. A separate trip. Gobi Desert, Mongolia. I have a video of that . . .

"I also took a walking trip in Kamchatka. That's what they called it, a walking trip, but it was really some pretty good hiking. McKibben thought it sounded like too much hiking for me, but I did OK.

"I stayed—not in a home, but in a *dacha* with a family for about two weeks. The father of the family and I went mushroom picking with one of his dogs. He gave the dog directions in Russian, and the dog understood! That seemed strange to me until I thought about it. . . .

"They've got the biggest bears in the world on the Kamchatka Peninsula. We always thought Kodiak bears and the brown bears on the Alaska Peninsula were big, but they say theirs are bigger."

Day 23. December 26, 1980: In the morning I made arrangements to fly with Iberia Airlines to Madrid, Spain. Departed around noon, and all I could get was first class passage; possibly the last ticket on

Walter Jackinsky and Andre Sokoloff, who with his wife, Larissa, was Walter's host in Kamchatka. Below, a traveler's fine bed in the Sokoloffs' dacha.

Walter skinny-dipping in a Kamchatkan hot spring, and right at home with a couple of Kamchatkan bear hunters. All Jackinsky family photos.

that flight. Certainly was treated like a VIP, and sure got the first-class service. . . . Served all the various drinks right after we boarded, and plenty of good food with a white tablecloth. Departed Da Vinci Airport and flew over the Mediterranean Sea. Visibility was clear. . . . Saw various islands and the port city of Barcelona. Landed at the Bajaras Airport, Madrid, and took a taxi to the city. It is somewhat cooler and windy here. Got a room at the El Colosa Hotel in a good section of the city. . . . This being December 26, Madrid continues in celebration of Christmas. Businesses are closed during the holiday and many people are in the city. Currency here is "peseta" and O.R. is US$.01427. . . . I went on a night bus tour of the city and then continued to a dinner party and live entertainment, which was Spanish flamenco dancing. Unexpectedly ran into a black nurse from Capetown, South Africa, whom I had met previously during one of my bus tours in London. A surprise.

"Maybe I'm ahead of myself now. The years go by so doggone fast. Let's see. . . . Eight years ago, I believe it was, I went to Fiji and Australia. First I went twice to New Zealand, and then a couple of years after that I went to Australia. Saw the Great Barrier Reef, and swam there. I had to do that.

"Didn't quite see enough of New Zealand the first year. I was only there about 10 days, and that wasn't enough. So I had to go back and see more of it. Lots more of it. I stayed with a family on their farm."

Day 27. December 30, 1980: Took a subway (DeGaulle) to mid center of Paris. Had difficulty in finding my way out, but help was available. An incident occurred. A young passenger had his pocket picked, but he was able to catch the culprit. . . . An argument took place and a fight occurred and within minutes the young Algerian had his throat cut and was dead. . . . It happened so fast that no one had time to realize or do much but to start shouting, "assassin, assassin!" and to my knowledge the old pickpocket got away fast and was engulfed in the crowd.

Made a double-decker bus tour of the city. . . . Also walked along the River Seine. There were numerous barges, tugs and water craft

Around the world in two photos: Walter at Uluru *(Ayers Rock) in Australia and McKibben in Israel. Jackinsky family photos.*

191

traveling up and down the river. . . . The river and the Eiffel Tower were quite impressive. I saw many women dressed in beautiful fur coats of fashion. Everyone seemed to enjoy walking their dogs on a leash at leisure. Currency is "franc": O.R. US$.2440. Population of Paris is approximately 8 million.

"Four years ago McKibben and her teacher from grade school Ilene Adams and I went to Egypt and Israel with a group from Soldotna. November 1999. I'm sure of that because McKibben wrote about it ["Israel trip changes traveler in many ways," *Peninsula Clarion*]. She wrote a good article on it. We went all over Israel, West Bank, Egypt. The Wailing Wall. The pyramids. Swam in the Dead Sea and gosh, you don't even have to swim there. You just float, you know. Because of the salt content.

"I was baptized in the Jordan River. Jesus was baptized right there in that spot. And we walked on his path, where he carried his cross. . . ."

Day 32. January 4, 1981: . . . Made another city tour by bus and covered both Old and New Delhi. I made a night Indian dinner and local dance and show tour. An interesting performance where a girl dancer balanced seven jugs on her head and then got up on three saber blades, sharp edges up in a rack, and barefoot walked on them. . . . It seemed that the food that night wasn't too clean, as I ended up with what they call "Delhi Belly." Had cramps all night until I got medicine for relief, and it cured it. I took a day's bus tour to Agra . . . where the Taj Mahal, the wonder of the world was built and stands. . . . The traffic was extremely heavy from oxen-drawn carts and camels loaded and carrying heavy loads, to people pushing carts. Also numerous bicycles all over. It seemed that driving regulations are lax. The sight of the Taj Mahal was very exciting. It is simply a wonder of architecture and beauty. . . . Weather continued fair to nice. India water is very bad, in most places, for drinking purposes. . . . A popular dish, traditional and the national dish, is rice and curry. If done right, it's delicious. Beer is fair. . . .

"Risa and I made a trip to Tahiti and Maurea. I went there twice, in fact. I took Risa there, and I also went with a friend from the ship. Oh, we went down to Bora Bora, too [laughing now, perhaps in sympathy with the note-taker]. Bora Bora was interesting. That's where the Tahitians left to discover the Hawaiian Islands, you know.

"Those Tahitians had certain navigating instruments—maybe you read about that. They navigated with certain instruments. But a lot of times the porpoises would come and play around the boat, you know. The Tahitians said, 'Hey, they're showing us where to go.' And then once in a while one of those big albatrosses would come. They had a big mast and the yardarm, and the albatross would sit on the yardarm, and once in a while he'd just raise one foot and hold it like this, balance with it up in the air. 'Hey, he's showing us how to go, he's showing us the direction.'

"And they did find the Hawaiian Islands."

Day 42. January 14, 1980: I made a three-day bus trip to Chiang-Mai City, some 500 miles north [of Bangkok] and close to Burma. Chiang-Mai was the original capital city at one time, a beautiful place with extremely friendly people that love to smile. Made a minibus tour out into the country from Chiang-Mai and watched how the elephants are used to work at logging. Had a chance to get on one and ride on an elephant. Made another tour to some of the remote and real native villages and tribes. (They also grow marijuana.) We had to watch for snakes and other predators. Went to a "Thai" dinner and dance show. They are very exotic dances. I was asked or picked to go on stage and dance with a "Thai" partner. There were a lot of others chosen, so it all added to the fun. After that, went to a city public market with lots of activity there until nearly midnight. Also visited many factories, where cloth, silk, furniture, pottery and local silver-smithing were done.

"Oh—20 years ago, early '80s, I traveled around in South America. Chile, Peru. Macchu Pichu. Flew to Rio, spent some time there. Stayed at the Intercontinental Rio. They were getting ready for their big Carnaval. You could see bands and groups on the beach practicing at night. From there, from Rio, we flew to Buenos Aires and toured there. I visited the grave of Luis Ferpo, the world-famous boxer. Went on the intercontinental highway, that big highway that runs through South America, then up through the country where the big cattle ranches were, and where gambling was. You could gamble if you wanted to. I gamble a little bit. Not too much. Just for fun. I'm surprised how lucky I usually am."

Day 52. January 24, 1981: Made a bus tour of Hong Kong, Victoria City, Aberdeen City. Took a sampan water tour in Aberdeen to a tour of people living their entire lives making their home on boats and junks. Boat people. It's very congested and unclean. The children go to school on boats that are assigned as schoolhouses. . . . Visited the Victoria Peak. The view is magnificent. Also saw where the refugees have built houses and are living. It's mostly on a face of a rocky hillside. Unbelievable that anyone is able to build in such a location. Also refugees live under bridges in cardboard shelters. . . . In the afternoon I made a bus tour of Kowloon area and the New Territories to the China border. Saw lots of agriculture and various farmland with rice fields, fish-raising ponds, and numerous domestic duck farms. Most of Hong Kong's drinking water is brought in from mainland China. Was able to walk up to the border wire fence, which is quite high and constructed with heavy barbed wire in a roll on top. The fence is approximately 85 miles long, starting from the coastline in the South China Sea. It is also well guarded and patrolled. Hong Kong is under lease to Britain for seventeen more years, then Peking, capital of China, will have to decide what they want to do with it. People are beginning to show some concern over the situation.

"My children all like to travel. A few years ago I took my youngest daughter on a tour out of Fort Lauderdale, Florida. We cruised the Caribbean, a 14-day cruise. There were a lot of stops. Panama. Went into Maracaibo, Venezuela. Caracas. Back to Fort Lauderdale. . . .

"Before the trip a doctor in Anchorage checked me [after an earlier angiogram at Virginia Mason Hospital in Seattle]. I told him I had a trip already lined up, a cruise, and he said, 'Go ahead, and we can do something afterwards.' When we got back to Phoenix, Arizona, where Risa was living, I just didn't feel—I felt like I should

Risa Jackinsky at the Dolphin Research Center in the Florida Keys, where Walter swam with a dolphin. Jackinsky family photos.

go and see a doctor again. I had kind of a touch of the flu or a cold that I picked up somewhere. We were in the Florida Keys and I went swimming several times, and I must have caught a cold or something. . . .

"They got all the records from here, and they said, 'I think we should do it. You're getting up to the age [84] where we kind of hesitate to do heart surgery, but . . .'

"I said, 'Let's get it over with.' So on the way home from the cruise I had a double bypass in Phoenix. . . ."

Day 60. February 1, 1981: Mount Fuji bus tour consisted of a full day. The countryside was beautiful and clean. Well-kept farms, and people are industrious. Was able to get to the 8,000 foot level on Mount Fuji, then encountered snow and was unable to go further. The height of Mt. Fuji is 12,000 feet. It was visible and distinct all day due to a clear and sunny day. Then to a lodge and restaurant for lunch, and from there drove to a large lake, where all boarded a boat for a cruise on a catamaran for several miles. Then picked up by the bus again and to a train terminal station, and transferred over onto the Bullet train and rode back on it to Tokyo via Nagoya and Yokohama. The Bullet is the fastest train in the world, traveling at 130 mph. We were picked up by bus again and brought back to the various hotels. The New Otani Hotel had a large, beautiful dining room and cocktail bar that overlooked a Japanese garden. During various hours starting in the afternoon, a twelve-piece orchestra, Ohara and his group, would entertain and play in this lounge. I occasionally stopped and would have salmon snacks and sake. Spent a leisurely day around the hotel and then a night bus tour to a live dance show, then teriyaki steak dinner and to a geisha house for entertainment and dancing. (Japanese food with rice is delicious.) Weather continues fair and nice.

"My boy and his wife and I went to Hawaii last year, 2002, a 15-day trip to Hawaii. Stayed at the Marine Surf at Waikiki. A lot of Alaskans stay there.

"I told Shawn here just the other day, I said, 'I'd like to take a trip around Cape Horn at the southern part of South America next winter. Do you want to go?' We'd fly to either Valparaiso, Chile, or to Rio. I've been to Rio. And then take a ship from there around the Horn to Valparaiso, or Valparaiso to Rio. Between the Pacific and the Atlantic.

"I'm not sure if Shawn can make it, but it would be nice to spend some time together. . . . Otherwise I'll probably go by myself.

"'The Roaring Forties'—that's what they call those latitudes."

Day 61. February 2, 1981: I made a short walking tour and then several hours in a Japanese garden and barbecue garden combined. Had lunch in the Otani Hotel and departed for Narita Airport via airport bus. Japanese exchange is "yen" O.R. US$.00465. Departed for Honolulu at 2100, Pan Am airlines 747. . . . A wonderful night flight with a tailwind of 190 to 240 mph and a completely full load of passengers. It was beginning to turn into daylight before we knew what was happening. We were catching up with the sun. Like the song, "East of the Sun, West of the Moon." The time was moved ahead, or advanced five hours, and we gained a day as well, as we crossed the international date line, going from west to east. ETA Honolulu at 0730, a very fast flight with such a strong, favorable wind. Flew nearly 4,000 miles in 5.5 hours. We were fortunate to get into Honolulu early, as there were seven other flights coming in to land very close behind us. Honolulu weather is beautiful and in the 80s. Proceeded to customs and immigration. It is certainly a wonderful feeling to be back in the USA. . . . I had reservations at the Princess Kaiulani Sheraton Hotel. . . . Light breakfast . . . quick shopping . . . immediately headed for Waikiki Beach. . . . I was on "R&R" for fifteen days in Hawaii, reminiscing about my trip around the world and all the adventures. Aloha and sayonara!

Motherland of the Spirit

On the Trans-Siberia Railway—The swaying of the train nudged me awake. Inches away, on a matching narrow bench seat, my 75-year-old father still lay sleeping. Our makeshift beds were softened only by the sheets and blankets we were given when we boarded the train the day before.

Through the window of our tiny compartment I gained first impressions of the countryside. Birch trees glowed silver in the light of dawn. Dew-laden wildflowers filled the space between forest and train track. In the brief moment that touched both night and day, so familiar was the scene sliding past my window that I believed it to be the country around my family's homestead in Ninilchik, on Alaska's Kenai Peninsula.

But this was not Alaska; it was the Soviet Far East. My father and I were on the Trans-Siberian Railway, heading 2,000 miles inland to Irkutsk from Khabarovsk.

My father was born in Ninilchik. His mother was Aleut. His father came from what is today Lithuania. As a young boy Dad fished and hunted the country around his Ninilchik home. He helped with the family's huge vegetable garden. He harvested wild hay that fed the livestock through Alaska's long, harsh winters. His first language was Russian, the language of his father.

In 1985 my father made his first trip to the Soviet Union. He traveled with a group from the Pacific Northwest to Europe, then Moscow and Leningrad (now St. Petersburg). He returned with caviar, vodka—and a new light in his smiling blue eyes. He had set foot in the country where his father was born. There was a wholeness about him that we had never seen.

Shortly after Alaska Airlines announced plans to fly to the Soviet Far East in the summer of 1991, Dad asked me to go with him as he returned to what he laughingly called "the mother-land." We would travel first to the Far East and then to Siberia.

It was easy for me to decide. With Alaska's history so closely linked to Russia, it would be a thrill to see what had been only pictures in museums and books. But to share this trip with my father was even more appealing.

And so, in the quiet early morning, while he slept, I felt my excitement flicker. Looking at countryside thousands of miles from all that is familiar, I was momentarily confused, thinking this to be home.

For the next two days we jostled through tiny villages. We passed farmers herding cows. Children swam in clear streams, enjoying summer's hot, cloudless days. We watched fields of wild hay being cut with scythes much like the one hanging in our shed.

Watching the harvest, my father recalled when he, too, pitched forks full of hay onto a growing stack, his shirt off. The hot Alaska summer sun warmed his bare skin. Dry hay spilled down his back. In my mind I saw the young man he tells about, strong arms reaching overhead, straining with the weight of hay.

The houses we glided past were old. These, too, were like many in the older Russian settlements of Alaska. The hand-hewn logs, their dovetailed corners fitting perfectly, reminded us of the log home my father was raised in.

There were others in our group who shared a Russian heritage. They visited with each other and with villagers when our train made its occasional stops, thrilled to speak a language they seldom use. The light I have seen in my father's blue eyes shone also in theirs. It was a celebration of heritage, of one another.

Our discussions sparked other memories. The retelling of long-forgotten moments filled the miles. We drew closer, not just father and daughter, but all who shared this adventure.

On our last morning in Siberia a small group of us innocently walked into a scene that is anchored in my memory. We had toured the city of Irkutsk, museums, houses and the marketplace. It was raining and hot. We were tired. Our bus pulled up in front of one of several "active" Russian Orthodox churches.

The guide led us around the grounds, pointing out the many monuments. Then he invited us inside the church. Most of the tourists continued taking pictures outside or returned to the bus. Only a few of us accepted his offer.

As we stepped into the church, a service was in progress. From windows high above, the gray light of day filtered down through the darkness, illuminating icon-covered walls. Candles surrounded the altar, their light flickering across the faces of the worshipers. A thick cloud of incense hung in the dusty air.

In a room on the right, new members of the faith—adults, not infants—were being baptized. They stood in a circle, leaving us on the outside.

Peasant voices joined in a chant of faith, a hymn of devotion and strength. Older men and women, poorly dressed, joints gnarled from hard work and severe temperatures, leaned on canes. Some knelt on the worn wooden floor. Deep lines in their faces matched the depth of their conviction. It was an intensely intimate moment.

Our small, voyeuristic group stood quietly, anxious to go unnoticed. We were deeply touched by what we saw.

And then my father began to sing—first quietly, then more strongly—the same responses those around us were singing. The words flooded across the forgotten years out of the depths of his memory, his voice blending with those around us.

It was impossible to see his eyes, but I knew the ember had found its flint. The spark was in full flame. In that moment, my father had stepped across a bridge long empty.

"The motherland," he'd called it. And so it was—a motherland of the human spirit. By this unexpected expression of a common heritage, he had traveled to a place where foreign is familiar and local is global. Walls crumbled and strangers became friends.

The sleep-induced confusion from days before became crystal clear. There was no mistake. This was a journey home.

By McKibben A. Jackinsky, from "We Alaskans,"
Anchorage Daily News, *Feb. 16, 1992.*

THE SALMON TSAR

6

The Homer Spit, located in Kachemak Bay, is the site of an ongoing stocking program of early-run chinook and coho salmon smolt. Fish are stocked at a small inlet on the Spit, formally called the Enhancement Lagoon but commonly known as the "Fishing Hole," and most of the sport fishing effort on these stocked fish is directed here. The major goal of the program is to meet the summer demand for more sport fishing opportunities along the Kenai Peninsula road system. The majority of the return is harvested by recreational anglers. This is a terminal harvest fishery; salmon returning here will not naturally reproduce because there is no spawning area available. Regulations protect salmon from snagging while they are susceptible to being caught using conventional angling methods, but allow a snag fishery when salmon become sexually mature and cannot longer be caught by non-snagging methods. Snagging is permitted for an abbreviated period of time, permitting the harvest of surplus fish. After this harvest is achieved, snagging is again prohibited. . . .

When this program was first initiated, chinook salmon smolt were artificially imprinted to a chemical at the Elmendorf Hatchery. This same chemical was dispensed from several drip stations anchored along the Spit to attract imprinted adult chinook salmon returning from previous years' releases. The majority of the returning chinook salmon, however, imprinted to the Enhancement Lagoon were held in pens prior to release. As no fresh water is present, the fish apparently imprint to some unique characteristic of the inlet salt water and the use of drip stations was discontinued. . . .

The success of this fishery resulted from the team efforts of the Alaska Department of Fish and Game, the City of Homer, and the South Peninsula Sportsmen's Association to promote the idea, improve the Lagoon itself, implement the fishery and promote the fishery. These three entities were co-recipients of the American League of Anglers and Boaters Sport Fish Management Award for best project in the nation for 1990.

From "Recreational Fisheries in the Lower Cook Inlet Management Area 1995-2000," a report to the Alaska Board of Fisheries by Nicky Szarzi and Robert Begich, October 2001.

Coast Pilot 9, 1964, "the earthquake edition"

Homer Spit, *on the north side of Kachemak Bay, is a* low gravel and shingle spit, covered with grass and some trees. It is about 4 miles long and from 100 to 500 yards wide. It is described as the longest inhabited spit in the world.

The March 1964 earthquake caused a bottom subsidence of 5.7 feet at Homer. Until a complete survey is made of the area, caution is necessary because depths may vary from those charted and mentioned in the Coast Pilot.

The pilot station for Anchorage and Nikiski Wharf is at Homer Spit. The pilot usually boards incoming vessels about 2 miles southwestward of Coal Point.

Coal Point, the outer end of Homer Spit, is marked by Homer Spit Light (59°36.1′ N., 151°24.5′ W.), 34 feet above the water. An aero light is at Homer airport, about 3.5 miles northwestward of Coal Point.

On the northeast side of Coal Point is a wharf used by deep-draft vessels. The northeast face is 126 feet long, with a depth of about 18 feet alongside; the southeast face is about 60 feet long, with a depth of about 24 feet alongside. Petroleum products and fresh water in limited amounts are available. The Sterling Highway leads from the wharf to Homer and thence connects with the highway system to other points in the state. The city wharfinger has an office at the head of the dock.

The small-boat basin just northwestward of the wharf was heavily damaged during the March 1964 earthquake. The outer part of the northeast breakwater was destroyed during the quake. The basin is only partially usable, but offers no protection; depths in the basin are about 12 feet.

Excellent anchorage can be had 0.8 mile or more northward of Homer Spit Light, in 10 or 15 fathoms, soft bottom. Coal Bay, the bight northeast of Homer Spit, is shoal but there are no outlying dangers.

From U.S. Coast Pilot 9: Alaska, Cape Spencer to Beaufort Sea, *Seventh Edition, 1964*

Some people's idea of nirvana is a grilled halibut sandwich at Boardwalk Fish & Chips on the Homer Spit. But don't bother to use the h word with Walter. To him "fish" means salmon. King (chinook), silver (coho), red (sockeye), pink (humpies). Legal, illegal. Salmon.

September 2003: "I caught 40-some fish at the Fishing Hole this season. . . .

"These aren't farmed fish, you know. They're wild fish. 'Enhanced.' Farming is where they're fed throughout their whole life. They're kept in one location.

"But with these enhanced fish, Fish & Game people come in with a big tank and a hose and just blow those fingerlings right into the doggone lake or pond or wherever they want to plant 'em, you know. They're big enough to survive and go to sea, and once they get out there they're on their own. They know what to do, I guess, because they come back full-grown. Beautiful fish. Ready for the fisherman.

"They hit the Pacific Ocean, they get into this current—it runs clockwise, clean around the Pacific Ocean—and it takes them four years. They're feeding and growing, feeding and growing, until they come back. In four years they're back to the same river—the same river, or hole, or wherever they're from—to spawn. And then they get caught.

"At the Fishing Hole they don't spawn. They can't. It isn't the right habitat for spawning. They've got a lot of beautiful eggs in them. They're coming there to spawn, but they have no place to spawn. . . .

"There's first a period when you can fish. Then when the fish are not biting anymore, they know they've got to get rid of them, they say, 'Open to snagging,' and the snaggers clear everything out.

"That's being done pretty much all over Alaska. Kodiak, and everywhere else, for the sports fishing. In one Cordova area they have a fishing hole that was just kind of dredged out for gravel, and there's a big old culvert that emptied the water coming out of this hole. They enhanced fish in the gravel pit, in that water, and the fish came right on back, through that culvert right into where they were first planted. Back up in there, and that's as far as they could go.

"A lot of families depend on that, families that can't go out and fish anywhere else. There'll be the husband doing the fishing, in a chair. Here comes a fish! He reels it in and she's there on the bank with a club to hit it over the head.

"I was surprised this year. Usually I catch most of my fish with a net, you know, a subsistence net. If you come back in May I'll set that net and show you. But this year it was so much fun fishing in that hole in Homer, and I was doing so good, I forgot all about the net. And I caught at least 40-some, I think, 46, 49. [The limit is six per day.] I have a new fiberglass pole I got in Deep Creek. . . .

"One Russian came by and said, 'Can I have a fish?' and I said, 'Sure, take one.' He said, 'I'll club your fish.' I was bringing one in, the fish was fighting, and he grabbed it, clubbed it, took the hook out, and I said, 'Well, help yourself.' I gave him a fish, two or three times. He said, 'I'm going to smoke it, make some kippered salmon.' . . ."

Russian Orthodox "Old Believers" have established several communities on the southern Kenai Peninsula in the past 40 years. Signs in Homer shops are routinely posted in Russian as well as English, and the luxuriant beards of the men and modest caps and long skirts of the women are a familiar sight. In Nikolaevsk, Voznesenka, Razdolna and Kachemak-Selo, the traditional ways carried from Russia when the Old Believer odyssey began generations ago are the foundation of daily life. "At the Fishing Hole the other day a Russian lady said, 'I'll clean your fish for the eggs.' I said, 'Help yourself. Take all the eggs you want.' I caught six, I think, that day, and she cleaned them for me. She got all the eggs I had. She was going to make *ikra*—caviar—just like they did in Kamchatka when I was there."

Fishhead Soup

When it comes to teaching culture, food tells a powerful story. A pot of spaghetti sauce simmering over a wood stove transforms any remote Alaskan cabin into an Italian villa. Pronouncing "tortilla" correctly is an important lesson in Spanish. A loaf of freshly baked *kulich* turns the calendar to Russian Orthodox Easter.

But step into my dad's kitchen for a bowl of fishhead soup and you've stepped into Ninilchik village, where settlers of mixed Alaskan Native and Russian descent first arrived in the 1800s. Where the sounds of Russian being spoken were once the first sounds to greet infants' ears. Where everything that was eaten was either hunted, caught in Cook Inlet or the Ninilchik River, or grown and gathered. Where bread was baked in ovens of coal-fired stoves, the two heavy aromas soaking into hand-hewn logs of village homes and hanging heavy in the air outside. Where subsistence was a lifestyle, not a hot potato. Where everything was used and nothing was thrown away.

I understand that in households in other parts of the country, family gatherings center around charcoal grilled steaks some dads cook. Other fathers are even known for preparing elaborate Sunday morning breakfasts. But in my family, it was always an event when Dad put a carefully carved salmon head in a pot with homegrown potatoes, carrots and onions, and cooked it to "perfection."

This isn't the only way to eat salmon. Thick-sliced salmon steaks are perfect when cooked shortly after the fish is caught or kept in the freezer to be eaten during the winter with a side dish of rice. Even thicker chunks can be set aside for roasting in the oven or in the glowing coals of a driftwood fire, where slow cooking allows the flavor of salmon to mix with the accompanying tastes of onion and bacon. Letting carefully trimmed strips hang in a cold smoke takes days from start to finish, but the mouth-watering results are well worth the wait. Pickling small, bite-sized pieces produces an irresistible snack. Canning may be time-consuming, but the sandwiches, patties, or loaf are a prize worth the effort.

But no salmon recipe says "Ninilchik" like a bowl of fishhead soup.

When I was a kid, seeing that steaming mixture put on the table produced my own internal soup of bubbling reactions. Pride in my heritage. Awe of my father. Waves of nausea. Fear that I wouldn't be able to keep the soup down. And the anticipated shame of disappointing my father and my ancestors if I couldn't get through the meal.

I don't remember the first time my brother and sister and I tasted Dad's fishhead soup, but our children and our children's children have been introduced to it since our own childhood days. Every summer, when the fish start running, we know it's only a matter of time until he gets out the soup pot. And every summer, no matter what my age, I've been victim to the same internal reactions.

This last summer, I was away from the family homestead for a couple of months. Far away, where no one had ever heard of fishhead soup. In September I came home. Birch leaves were turning from green to gold. Fall temperatures were whispering that snow wasn't far away. The smell of high-bush cranberries was beginning to fill the air. Fishing season was over.

One morning shortly after my return, my dad telephoned to say that he and I were invited to his 86-year-old brother's house for lunch.

For fishhead soup.

My reaction was as strong as ever. Pride. Awe. Nausea. Fear.

There was no way to gracefully excuse myself from the invitation.

Tucking a still-warm loaf of homemade bread under my arm helped settle my nerves. Not only was I taking something to put on the table, I was also giving myself something to eat that would hopefully settle my stomach.

Being in Uncle Ed's kitchen transported me back to my childhood. The familiar view from the kitchen window of Cook Inlet and the snowcapped mountains beyond. The table and chairs worn from years of use. The faded school photos of my cousins lining the walls. And the simmering soup.

I sliced the bread. Dad uncorked some wine. Our friend Faith, who was about to sample this Ninilchik delicacy for the first time, got out bowls and spoons, eager to see what all the fuss was about. Uncle Ed set the pot on the counter beside the table.

Eagerly, Dad and his brother filled their bowls. Laughing, they dished out fins and eyes along with vegetables and small pieces of meat. Faith and I stood back while they picked out the "choicest" parts, each of them making sure Faith and I saw what juicy tidbits they had selected.

Faith bravely followed suit.

Lacking Faith's bravery, I picked out some potatoes, a few chunks of salmon and some broth. Just enough so I could say I'd had some.

Not enough, I hoped, to shame myself. A couple of carefully placed slices of bread on the edge of my bowl gave the finishing touch to what I hoped conveyed enthusiasm.

Hearing Dad and Uncle Ed slurp and smack was almost more than my stomach could stand. Faith squealed and winced, her enthusiasm impressive for a rookie. Long before they were ready to quit, I came to the bottom of my bowl and finished my bread.

"Eat some more," Uncle Ed laughed, stripping gelatin-like goop off a fin with his teeth.

"She did pretty good," my dad answered, hypnotized by the intricacies of cleaning every morsel from a jawbone.

Faith focused on extracting tiny little salmon teeth from her mouth.

And then the richness of the scene overcame my longing to leave the table. The laughter. The familiarity. The good-natured teasing. The afternoon shared between two white-haired brothers who have seen the world change around them but find continuity at the family table with a pot of fishhead soup. . . .

By McKibben A. Jackinsky,
excerpted from the Trading Post,
Volume I, Issue 2, November 2000.

Walter skirts discussion of the "hot potato" issues: subsistence fishing, commercial vs. sports fishing. He is not a crusader. He is also not a catch-and-release man. He wants to *fish*.

"My first couple of years with the ferry system I took the summer off to go fishing in Bristol Bay, but then they said no. That's a really busy time for them, you know. I was able to do it twice, but that was it.

"Other years I'd come back here on my vacation and see how my brother was doing. Spend a little time with him on the beach and help him fish. I helped him two or three summers, I guess, just to be doing something.

"Ed had my dad's set-net sites, and he had his family there. He liked it. For years the price of fish was high, you know. He would even hire people to work. He said, 'I can hire a person for a hundred dollars a day, and here I'm making thousands by hiring him.'"

Commercial fishing has always been one of the most hazardous of occupations, and it has not always been the most profitable. Nevertheless, Walter's exuberant recollections of fishing Bristol Bay and Cook Inlet and Aleutian waters are topped only by his stories of the most recent Fishing Hole visit. Even if that means snagging, for which he has been known to profess scant regard.

From a conversation after the first day of the snagging period in September 2003:

"Things were really going strong [at the Fishing Hole] yesterday. There were a lot of people. And I lost three hooks. Maybe you saw the snagging hooks, big triple hooks.

"I got some kind of snag on the bottom of the pond, and I had to tear it off, to get it loose. And then one just got lost while I was working with my gear. Then I put a third one on, and my line broke. The fish took off with my hook and line. That was the sixth fish. I would have had my limit.

"The one I gave you was pretty good, wasn't it? This one was about like that, I think. I'd say 12 to 14 pounds. It fought like anything. It was a good fighting fish. . . .

"And the people. Oh man, in certain areas where the fish were heavy, they were all over. People were just everywhere. You had a place, and you didn't leave it, or you would lose it, you know. Stay right there.

"Hooks were flying like anything. Everybody was anxious to get in on the school of fish that was there. That's the quickest, easiest and surest way, if a school comes through. They were coming in schools. If a school comes through, then your chances are good to get one right away. The fellow next to me, from Kasilof, he got six within maybe an hour, while I was still poking around there, getting one or two, you know. . . .

"He got his real fast. But the ones that he got were—I was really glad that I waited. I got this nice big one to start with, the one I gave you. I said that made up for the time that I lost. His were kind of scraggly ones, most of them. . . .

"It's supposed to open at 12 noon, but there was a crowd there

Sam Moore of Sutherlin, Ore., took two telephoto shots of Walter Jackinsky at work at the Fishing Hole in Homer ...

... then changed cameras for the classic triumphant pose, August 2003.
Photos courtesy of Sam Moore.

at 10:30, when I got there. I was walking around and talking and looking and getting excited. I told them seven minutes before 12, then six minutes, then five. Before I said 12, the hooks were flying already. People couldn't wait till 12. . . .

"But they were pretty good. I was getting excited myself, when it got to about four or five minutes. The hooks started flying then. And I threw mine, but the guy next to me wouldn't do it until exactly 12 o'clock. . . .

"He got those six fast. He said, 'I think I'll throw this away.' I said, 'No, I don't think you can throw any away.' You know, if you catch them, you've got to keep them. In that case, he kept six. They weren't even worth keeping. I think one there, especially, that he hooked, he was going to throw back.

"But then the purpose is to clean the Fishing Hole out. Get rid of the good ones *and* the bad ones. . . .

"I was getting my hook right out where the big school was. I'd get just as far as I could, and that's where the good big ones were. The smaller ones were pushed ashore. They were easy to catch. But I was getting my line out there where the more fresh fish were. . . .

"I've got a nice glass pole. You can bend it but never break it. Man, when you put the pressure on it, it's way bent over. That one, the one I like the best, I just got about a month ago. I've got two others that I used before, but this is really as good as I could find. . . .

"I don't remember the brand. Or the weight. But I've never seen one broken in half! I'll get it. It's in my car right now. Two of them, in fact, are in there. . . .

"For the snagging I use 20-pound line, because you're putting a lot of pressure and you're bringing a fish in sideways. Sometimes you get right on the back, you know, and he's fighting. . . . Other fishing, I use 12-pound. Some of the Russians said they use as light as eight-pound because that line is invisible down there in the water. The fish can't see it at all.

Angler Ethics

– Don't pollute—please haul trash out of the field and dispose of it properly. Remember that discarded fishing line can be lethal to birds and other wildlife.

– Obey fishing regulations.

– Respect private property. Native allotments and other private land holdings are common along Alaska's waterways—seek permission before using private land.

– Think about your needs and take only the fish you require. Preserve your fish appropriately.

– If you plan to kill fish, do so quickly and humanely. If you plan to release fish, handle them gently and do not remove them from the water.

– Minimize stream bank erosion.

Caring for Your Catch

Landing your catch is only half the battle when it comes to putting good tasting fish on the dinner table. How you handle your catch afield will determine how much your family and friends appreciate it.

The flesh of fish not quickly killed, cleaned, and chilled will rapidly deteriorate. It is illegal to keep your catch alive on a stringer. A blow to its head usually kills the fish quickly, and breaking a gill will cause the heart to pump much of the blood from the flesh. Blood breaks down very fast and shortens the time preserved fish will last.

Avoid storing your dead fish in water. Clean and ice your fish in the field, so you can remove the kidneys and additional blood from the backbone and rib cage. Packing the body cavity with ice will speed chilling of the flesh and retard spoilage. Distribute your catch in the ice chest or refrigerator so that fish touch the ice or are packed in it. Fish should not touch one another or rest in melted ice water.

From Sport Fishing Regulations Summary, 2003, Southcentral Alaska, *Alaska Department of Fish & Game (Homer office).*

"They lose fish like anything, but then the chance to catch them, too, is that much easier. I use a 12, because you can bring in a pretty good fish with a 12, by letting it play a little bit, tiring it out a little. . . .

"And then you usually have a club on the beach, or alongside of you. The Russians call it *kalatushka*. You bring in the fish, the fish is frightened, and you grab that little *kalatushka* and whack it over the head.

"There was another fellow next to me who came to fish, and he caught one right away. He brought it in, and I said, 'Here. Do you want to use this club to kill it?' He said, 'No, I have a different method. I don't hit them in the head with a club.'

"I tried to look and see what he was doing. He had the fish's mouth open, and he was sticking something in its mouth. But I don't know what else he did there. He said, 'No, I don't hit them at all.' He didn't like the idea of clubbing them over the head.

"He caught that one fish, and he and his girlfriend left. It would be interesting to know what he did. I was trying to look, but then I was busy fishing anyhow. I saw where he had the fish's mouth open. Whatever he did then, I don't know. . . .

"Lots of them will bleed their fish. They'll put a knife right where the gills are, you know. I don't do that. They'll bleed them, but I just leave them like they are and leave them whole. . . . It's a mess when you bleed them. They're all bloody. You've got to either wash them in the pond there or set them in a plastic bag, and they're still bloody and messy when you bring them home. I don't know whether it even does much good or not. . . . I should have asked somebody what the purpose is for bleeding them. . . .

"You'd have gotten a kick out of it. [!] You could stay farther back where there wasn't any danger. I tell you, it is a little danger-ous. You've got that big hook, and you fling it out there, a big triple hook, pretty good-sized one, and they're flying out there, and many of them aren't looking behind them to see who's there, you know. . . ."

So snagging season at the Fishing Hole is either carnival or car-nage, whichever end of a 12-pound line you're on. In any case,

Walter doesn't participate after Day 1, when he feels there's less fi-
nesse involved.

"But we also have—the Natives, anyhow—we have the educational fisheries. I've got two nets. I can use either one, whenever I
put my name on the list, or McKibben's name, whoever we decide
wants to fish. [McKibben has mentioned that this decision is rarely
left to her.] I take the net out there and only fish for maybe six
hours. Put the net out at the right time, check the tide. And then
the tide's coming in and the fish are getting caught in this net. You
pull it in—the net's on blocks, so you pull it any time you
want. . . ."

"Educational" refers to an informal program for teaching the
young people of the community the traditional ways. "For instance, I'd show them how to open the head up, you know, clean
the head out if they want to use that. . . . We get together right on
the beach, where the net is. They observe what goes on. And you
show them as much as you can, so they can learn. . . ." McKibben
painted a word-picture of that scene in an essay titled *"Súgucihpet—
Our Way of Living,"* for *Looking Both Ways: Heritage and Identity of
the Alutiiq People.* A white-haired Elder kneeling on a rocky beach.
The fresh-caught salmon. Excited youngsters ("their heads of
black, brown and blonde hair . . . a testimony of cultural blending") pressing close to see and hear over the raucous call of waiting
gulls. "Alutiiq people reclaim their identity through hunting and
gathering," she wrote. "The sustaining of life encompasses the
physical, the mental and the spiritual."

Walter enjoys the role of educator. But he exults in the "hunting and gathering."

"Anytime I fish [with the set gillnet], McKibben is usually
there. And then we have maybe two or three other friends who are
interested in it and want to come down. Once the netting is out
the net is doing the fishing, and you can build a big fire and have
hotdogs or something like that and watch as the fish are hitting the
net. You know, they're splashing in the net like crazy. 'There's another one.' 'Hey, there's one more.' 'Hey, this one's a king salmon.'
'Look at the corks going down.' 'There's a seal coming!' Seals come
right to the net sometimes, start eating, or looting. They go right

Walter Jackinsky, picking salmon from the subsistence net on the beach just north of Ninilchik. Jackinsky family photo.

for the gills. Tear off a big bunch of fish, right around there. We even threw rocks at some. They were that close. Now I carry a gun, and I'll scare them. I have a gun that I got in Russia. I'll show you. A gun that was used—not that particular gun, but that style of gun was used when they killed Nicholas IV and his family. . . ."

Steelhead (sea-run rainbow trout) seem to be the exception to Walter's personal "fish = salmon" preference, but the Cook Inlet limit for steelhead now is two fish. That's two fish per year. Ninilchik River, Deep Creek and Anchor River are among the exceptions. Their annual limit is zero. (Steelhead "may not be removed from the water" is the language in the regulations. Catch-and-release is a hot potato of its own.)

Long gone are the days of a dory full of steelhead on their way home to Ninilchik under a moose-hide sail. Walter's wistful, convoluted account of almost catching a steelhead in Deep Creek "by mistake" last year bears repeating only as a cautionary tale.

"What if I'm fishing and a steelhead takes my hook? That's kind of like a mistake. . . .

"I was really trying to get a silver, [but] this doggone big steelhead was putting on a good show, you know. Also, after a certain time you can't use triple hooks. And I had triple hooks on without even realizing it. . . ."

Without even realizing it?

"I didn't know for sure whether you could use a triple hook or maybe you weren't supposed to. And then, behind me—here's that goldarn Fish & Game. She said, 'You're doing a good job of bringing that in.' And I was. But then it broke the line, and gee, I was glad. . . .

"I could always say that it looked like a silver. It could be a silver. They look an awful lot like silver."

Hard to believe that a Ninilchik boy can't tell the difference.

"Oh, I can tell the difference pretty well, but a lot of people couldn't, you know, because when steelhead come in from the sea they look a lot like silver, except they have that beautiful red stripe along the side. Maybe you've seen them, haven't you? They're a little different, but they're still a lot alike, a silver and a steelhead. . . .

"Anyhow, that was one time that made me think I should watch

"That's a 70-pound salmon. Maybe 80 pounds." Jackinsky family photo, c. 1997.

those laws closer. I have never had any kind of offense, you know, with the state or anybody."

That may be at least partly thanks to the vigilance of the children who played lookout one night almost 50 years ago on the hill above the Ninilchik River while a few illegal nets were spread below. At least one lookout says she still can feel her heart pounding with the fear and excitement of standing between father and the Fish & Game. (On the other hand, she says, it may well be that there was no chance of a confrontation and the fathers merely wanted to keep the children occupied.)

Walter looks a bit nostalgic, hearing that account. But ask him directly for a fish tale and you get this, straightfaced:

Seems a pair of friends [insert nationality] were fishing in waters about 10 miles out of Juneau and hit upon a spot so productive they knew they had to mark it somehow, so they could find it again the next day. A buoy wouldn't do—someone else would surely notice. They pondered and conferred and came up with a sly idea: Paint an X on the side of their boat. Yeah!

NINILCHIK, 2003

7

Via e-mail, Sept. 13, 2003: Hey, everybody: Let's squeeze in one more cookout before the frost hits. Food is potluck, although there'll be the usual hotdogs and potato salad. There are a lot of birthdays this time of year, so there'll also be a cake, candles and balloons. Weather is potluck, too. Keep your fingers crossed that we can enjoy the outdoors and a campfire—and wear something warm. Where: At McKibben's, Mile 132.2 Sterling Highway. When: 2 p.m., Saturday, Sept. 20. . . .

The September birthdays were celebrated on the last day of my two weeks of "conversations with a resolute Alaskan." My heart was torn, as always when it's time to leave home in Alaska for home in California, and my mind was dizzy with stories and statistics and impressions. The statistics were in a jumble of Alaska references from River City Books in Soldotna and the Homer Bookstore; the stories were mostly cached on audiotape. Together they filled a big canvas Homer Farmers Market bag that was beginning to weigh as heavy on my mind as on my shoulder. Three valiant transcribers would attempt to deal with those tapes before I could attempt to turn them into narrative. But the impressions are still whirling like uncharted planets around my head.

Almost every day I drove the 30 miles to Ninilchik from my lodging above Homer, where childhood friend Eileen Mullen, commercial fisher and owner of Island Watch Bed & Breakfast, took good care of me—and of the salmon, whole or steaks or fillets, that Walter sent with me at the end of each day in misplaced confidence that I could turn them into something sumptuous in my miniature microwave oven. It was Eileen who told me of Walter's open-heart surgery in Phoenix on his way home from the Caribbean, or rather she told me what she had heard of his lengthy convalescence. Daughter Risa, his companion on the Caribbean trip

"Going Up the Beach"

Ninilchik Native Descendants First Annual Beach Walk

Walk the 74 miles (the distance on the beach between
Homer and Kenai) that Ninilchik Villagers used to take
to get to town, to buy supplies or go to a dance.

Walk between August 10 and October 10, 2003.
All finishers will receive a 2003 "Going Up the Beach" T-shirt.
Entry fee: $25 per person.

WALK ANYWHERE YOU LIVE!
ANYBODY CAN JOIN IN THE FUN.

Walk, run, crawl, or swim the distance between Homer
and Kenai following the beach. When you sign up you will
receive a log to chart your miles as well as historical tidbits about
the beach from Kenai to Homer. Get some exercise, get in
shape, walk the dog, push a stroller or a wheelchair, and relive
a little bit of history along the way. Walk in groups or walk
alone. Walk around the block, on a treadmill, swim laps in the
pool, climb a mountain, or walk the beach! Just log your miles
and send them to us postmarked by Oct. 15, 2003.

All proceeds will go to the NND Historical
Documentation Project.

and during six months of alternating recovery and rehospitalization in Phoenix, told me a little more. Among her professional roles is that of personal trainer, and she and Walter worked together to meet his goal of getting back to Alaska under his own steam, so to speak. After those six anxious months in Phoenix and a week or two on the Kenai they took off again, on a trip to Hawaii that had been planned before his surgery, so Risa could run the 2001 Kona Marathon.

Walter apparently hadn't thought any of his heart history worth mentioning. For that matter, Risa didn't mention that she finished 12th of 120 women in her 40-49 age group, and in the top quarter of 983 runners overall, women and men, all ages. I found that information on the Kona Marathon website. "Thanks for telling me," she said. "I actually didn't know. I'd been having some hip problems, and I think I *walked* the last six miles. I was just focused on finishing." It must be genetic.

Watching Walter demonstrate the rowing machine and the bicycling apparatus that he uses for an hour or so every morning, one day rowing, the next pedaling, I certainly wouldn't have known of his ordeal.

"I do this about 500 times," he says, pedaling briskly. "Usually every morning at six o'clock I'm in here watching the news and either rowing or on this machine. It's a health exerciser, like a bicycling and rowing combination, which is really good. You want to try it?"

"No," says the person 20 years his junior, forthrightly.

"Let's go over there, and you can try that one. I'll just show you what it's like, so you can."

"Well, you show me what it's like. I'm always nervous about my back. I don't try any machines. I walk."

"That's good. Walking is the best exercise you can get," he says generously. "But rowing is good, good for your vascular and everything. . . ." On the other machine now, he leans back with the oars, then in at a deep slant and back again. "The first news comes on at six o'clock, so I'm here just before then. Tells me Alaska news and world news and everything. Sometimes the president is making a speech. Six forty-five I go back to bed, sleep for about an hour. . . .

"My pressure is terrific, my blood pressure. I have an instrument that I can take it with. I think last time it was 117 over 77, something like that. And before, it was up to 140-something. Or maybe 150. . . .

"Anyway, that's the story. It took me, what, maybe a year to really recover good from the surgery, you know. And I'm still not—I'm fully recovered but I'm not—well, I couldn't be like I was before, because I'm older. But I've got lots of energy."

I tended to head straight for the kitchen each time I arrived at Walter's place, partly because we had agreed to work at the table there, maybe partly because he usually offered some sweet or savory leftover from his and McKibben's supper the night before. If she's not on assignment or otherwise engaged McKibben generally walks over from her corner of the homestead for a communal evening meal. "When I'm cooking I tell her not to bring anything, there's plenty here," Walter says, "but she always has fresh bread she bakes, or corn muffins or a salad or cookies. When she's cooking, gosh, it's a roast, or spaghetti, with everything. . . ." He had had a porcupine cooking for their supper one recent day—"like dark turkey meat," he suggested this time, a more useful description for non-woodchuck-eaters.

The day he demonstrated his exercise machines, which I had passed half a dozen times without noticing on my beeline to the kitchen, I realized that the cabin is larger than I had thought. To the left as you enter from the porch is Walter's office, with a desk and a computer on which he declines to do e-mail, and a small bedroom off that. The room directly ahead of the porch does triple duty as foyer and parlor and workout station. On the wall above the bicycling machine are the ship's clock and the calipers from his crew on the *Bartlett*. Virgil Campbell's knife is kept with Walter's fishing poles in his car, for all those times of not watching the clock.

A few steps to the right of the door from the porch is the doorway to the kitchen, with a small bathroom including shower just ahead and the working area of the kitchen again to the right. A

Walter Jackinsky at the "conversation table" in the old fox farm cabin, September 2003. Photo by J.R.B. Pels.

heavy door behind you as you face the kitchen sink leads to a storage loft. Our "conversation" area, with sofa and easy chair in addition to the table where we sat with the tape recorder, is to the right again, so that the entire layout has the feel of a spiral.

Tacked to the walls in each room and draped on sofa backs and arms are colorful, finely woven scarves that Walter has collected on his travels—here Colombia, there Russia and Maracaibo. In the place of honor on the wall behind the conversation area sofa is a huge quilt in patterned blocks of ocean blues and grays made for his birthday one year by "the women on the *Bartlett*": purser Nancy Wolford, steward Renee Pettingill, a steward named Dorothy, and others. "Dorothy was from a family of six daughters," he says. "She was a steward, but we needed a cook one summer and I said, 'Dorothy's real good. Why don't we upgrade her?' The chief steward agreed, so we did. I wish I could remember her last name."

In 2003 the cabin was 85 years old, or 16, depending on how its history is told. Walter Jackinsky Sr. built it around 1919, and his granddaughter McKibben rebuilt it in 1987—took it apart, numbered each log, and with the help of Alice and friends reassembled it on a new foundation, in a new location, with a new roof. They added a porch, so the original 20′ by 16′ structure became 20′ by 20′.

In the spring of 1979 McKibben and her two girls moved in. Two years later came another assembly job: An ancient warehouse on the homestead was moved to the cabin site, again log by log, and placed on a foundation dug adjacent to the cabin. Now the structure was its present cozy layout and size.

Somewhere along the line Walter had decided he wouldn't be returning to Ninilchik, but as happens with many of us the old home site started calling to him. He had helped with parts of the rebuilding, and he has wintry tales of working with Shawn on the new roof for the warehouse. He began borrowing the cabin from time to time when McKibben was working on the North Slope. Some of the homestead acreage had been sold over the years, and Walter had divided the remainder among Alice and their three children. When Risa decided she would stay Outside he bought her share. Eventually he and McKibben traded lots, and he kept the old/new cabin. Today, as you face east from the inlet, first comes Alice's lot on the bluff, spread north to south. In east-west wedges abutting her lot are McKibben's piece, to the north, then Walter's, then Shawn's, to the south. A sufficient distance behind them runs the highway.

Alice's move back to Ninilchik was the impetus for the rest of the family. Determined to settle in on her own terms, she lived in an aluminum storage shed while she planned a cabin. She put in a cookstove and a cot and built herself some shelving. The shed had little ventilation and was always damp inside with condensation; Alice routinely encased her sleeping bag in plastic garbage bags to try to keep it dry. There was no road in to the place at the time, no electricity.

She began her 14′ by 16′ cabin with help from the children, but as McKibben says, "We went down there [from Anchorage] as often as possible, but none of us knew what we were doing." However, a structure gradually emerged, and Alice installed a Franklin stove and a couple of windows and moved in. When she decided to add on, Risa and McKibben got the job of ripping the roof off the original, "a good assignment for our carpentry skills," McKibben says. Shawn helped Alice raise the new walls. Alice had the enlarged cabin put on a basement, and she never did stop working on the place. The year she died, she and Shawn had been making plans to trade lots, and Alice was full of ideas for redoing Shawn's house.

McKibben's own cabin was the last to be built. She and daughters Jennifer and Emily lived for a time with Alice in her place, an adventure in camaraderie. At first, as in the homesteading days of 40 years before, the only "plumbing" was an outhouse. A trip to the Laundromat for family-rate showers was a thrill. After other moves, and with the girls through school, McKibben started planning for her place—by leaving town. Her work on the TransAlaska Pipeline helped underwrite her homebuilding. The architectural and spiritual saga of her copper-and-brass-domed sanctuary among the birches is a story waiting to be set down by the poet herself. Her Uncle George Jackinsky shared her vision and was a bulwark through the sometimes overwhelming process, she says. The contractors she chose—Batir Construction of Kenai—were empathetic

From start to finish: *The old fox farm cabin before its move; refitting the warehouse logs for the addition—from left, Jennifer Long, Walter Jackinsky, Emily Long; the addition nearing completion; and Walter at home, 2003. Jackinsky family photos, 2003 photo by J.R.B. Pels.*

as well as innovative. And friends gathered for a housewarming as they have gathered frequently since.

Meanwhile, Walter is pleased to be at the center of the family compound. Everyone agrees that the cabin reassembled from Walter Sr.'s old structures has its own personality, as befits its lineage. When Walter's sisters Margaret and Cora visit, McKibben says, "they feel embraced by their family history." And on one of the logs in the warehouse adjunct is carved in a boyish hand the name of Adolph Jackinsky, their forever-young brother.

A colorful homemade sign above Walter's porch greets visitors: "Buenos Airs." When I asked him why of all the places in the world he's traveled he chose that name, he studied the sign for a minute and said, "I spelled that wrong, didn't I?" I assured him that my interest was not in proofreading, and he gestured generally south-north and said, "Especially in the summer there's a pretty good breeze through here. Good air. That made me think of Buenos Aires. . . ."

We leaned on Walter's porch rail and gazed at the inlet beyond Alice's house as we talked. (Her cabin is out of the family now but remains "Alice's house.") The view reminded me to ask about Alice's travels. Did she share Walter's wanderlust? "Not too much," he said. "I sent her to Jerusalem when the nuns out of Anchorage were going there. I heard about it and asked her, and she went. She enjoyed it. They went for about 15 days, on a tour. That's about the only trip she made, I think, except for Hawaii."

Walter may well have forgotten, but I'm told there was at least one more. Alice took third place in a big salmon derby in Juneau around 1970 and chose as her prize a round trip for two to Acapulco. According to their fond but amused elder daughter, fisherman Walter agreed to the trip only after Alice promised not to tell anyone they met how they happened to be there.

In fact, Alice had two or three fishing boats at different times in Southeast, including a couple of Bayliners. She entered one derby with a 16-foot skiff, and, says McKibben, "I thought we were going to die that day, Mom and my ex-husband Steve Long and Mom's friend Leigh Galinski and I. She took us for a wild ride."

As to the nuns, Alice joined the Catholic Church when the family lived in Juneau, and the children had been baptized in Catholic ceremonies even earlier. Walter tells of four baptisms in his own life. The first, of course, was in grandfather Gregory Oskolkoff's hand-crafted tub at the Transfiguration of Our Lord Russian Orthodox church overlooking Ninilchik. Then, with what was probably a provisional baptism, he was welcomed into the Roman Catholic Church in a ceremony in Juneau. Alice was his godmother. And then twice, he says, with the group in Israel. "We went on a boardwalk and right into the Jordan River up to our waists. We had big white robes on—I'll show you some pictures. They took us and said a prayer for us. . . . Then the two guys grabbed me and submerged me, and they said, 'We didn't submerge you enough. We'll do it again.' They submerged me again.

"That was another really important part of my life, when I think about it—the Jordan River. . . ."

Nowadays when Walter attends church it's in the Roman Catholic parish of Our Lady of Perpetual Help in Soldotna, 30 miles north on the way to Kenai. "It's a good church," he says. "An active church. The pastor is Father Frank Reitter. Sister Joyce Ross takes care of things when he has to be gone. They're both good." He says he understands the services in English better than he does Orthodox services conducted in Slavonic. "In Russia they were in Russian, and I enjoyed going to church there. But here they had the Slavonic books, what's called Church Russian. There's quite a bit of difference, from what I know. I don't even understand it. I can sing their songs and their prayers, but I understand Russian."

Almost every day for two weeks I drove to Ninilchik. Walter got restless a couple of times. Polite, but restless. Really needed to check out the situation at the Fishing Hole. So we'd take a day off and I'd drive to Kenai or Soldotna for mini-reunions of my own instead. The evening of one day off I met Walter and McKibben at the Anchor Point Senior Center, a handsome, rambling log structure about halfway between Ninilchik and Homer, for a turkey dinner honoring another impressive octogenarian. Beulah Poindexter, owner of Anchor Point Farms and Greenhouse, had been named Alaska's "outstanding older worker of the year" for 2003. Several visiting speakers plus the whereases in a resolution by the

Kenai Peninsula Borough Assembly listed upward of a dozen roles she plays in the family business and in her personal life and praised her for her "diligent work ethic and for running a successful business well into her golden years." But the most memorable aspects of the evening were the local community's obvious respect and affection and Beulah Poindexter's own infectious good humor.

During our first week Walter was full of mysterious plans for a different outing. "I have to make a phone call," he'd say, and come back anxious or beaming, depending on whether he'd gotten an answer. On a sunny, chill Sunday, we met in the Anchor River Inn parking lot, Walter and his brother Ed and McKibben and I, and set out in Walter's forest green GMC Envoy, license plate CO-MODR, with McKibben at the wheel. Ed's friend Faith Hays had intended to come but was called in that morning to work at her hospital job.

This was my first meeting with Edward Jackinsky, and I was smitten. "No tape recorders," he said sternly, making a show of zipping his mouth as I settled myself beside him in the back seat. Obediently I left my little black machine in the Farmers Market bag, which meant that I enjoyed his wry rejoinders to Walter's hearty observations from the front seat but have not a one to report. It was clear, however, that the brotherly camaraderie as well as the competition was still in flower. Ed's vision and hearing had faded considerably in recent years, but we three simply adjusted our volume accordingly.

Our destination was the Old Believer community of Niko-laevsk, some nine miles inland from Anchor Point, and specifically the Samovar Café of Nina Fefelova, entrepreneur and chef and hostess extraordinaire, or however one would indicate remarkableness in Russian. Indeed, having met her one finds it impossible to say "Nina" without some sort of extra inflection. Nina! Or NINA! Or Niiina! By whatever spelling, Walter had arranged for Nina to receive and feed us in her bright little café/treasure shop, although on Sunday it would normally be closed in accordance with community belief and practice. Nina treated the transaction as tithe rather than commerce: The day's proceeds were destined for an orphanage in Khabarovsk, in the Russian Far East. Nina went to high school and college in Khabarovsk but also has a master's degree in Russian Language Arts from Norwich University in Vermont. Before emigrating in 1991 she was an army engineer, a tourist guide, president of her church sisterhood and college lecturer. For the past 10 years she has been a bilingual instructor in the Nikolaevsk combined elementary and high school, and now she is a doting grandmother as well.

Borscht? Pirozhki? Pel'meni? Those dishes and others would be forthcoming. But first we must be appropriately garbed. McKibben's and my demure calf-length skirts and dark stockings were not sufficient, or too sufficient. Nina flew about the room exclaiming in Russian and charmingly accented English, dark eyes alight, megawatt smile flashing, bestowing a poet-sleeved *rubakha* here, tying a bright woven *poyas* around a waist there, settling huge, ear-flapped fur caps suitable for the bleakest Siberian winter above the abashed grins of the two brothers—and then rearranging people and costumes for what seemed dozens of photos, somehow taken with our cameras even as she posed us. Sit here! Do you love my tea set? Pretend to drink. Don't drop! My son is very good Realtor—here is his card. You look beautiful! You are too handsome! Here, I sit on the floor in front of you. Be sure my shoes are in the picture, my pretty shoes! See? Stand in front of my *matryoshka*. No, not in front. Beside. Here, like this. OK, now you take our picture for my brochure. . . .

We laughed helplessly, telling each other we were exhausted by all this Slavic sunshine. But we managed to clean the plates for every course. By dessert time we'd been in the Samovar for three hours, and McKibben was beginning to worry about the organic farmers she had promised we'd visit before leaving Nikolaevsk.

After "Samovar Special cream puffs" and a separate, ceremonial serving of fragrant fireweed-raspberry-black currant *chai*, Nina fastened long taffeta skirts on McKibben and me—fastened them on the fronts of McKibben and me, with an extra *poyas* tied tight to secure them—and was posing the four of us outside the café in the knife-edged wind when a couple of young tourists approached with

Dressing up at the Samovar Café in Nikolaevsk, Alaska, September 2003: Edward Jackinsky, above; McKibben Jackinsky buttoning a rubakha *for her father, Walter Jackinsky; Walter with Nina Fefelova. Photos by J.R.B. Pels.*

hopeful smiles. Except for Nina and our foursome, who must have looked for all the world like some Kamchatkan portrait from a century ago, the village was Sunday quiet, seemingly deserted. "Are you *open?*" they asked with tentative delight. Seizing the opportunity, McKibben and I backed into the café and hung our half-skirts on a carved wooden hook, and the four of us fled, leaving the young couple—from a Russian émigré family in the Midwest, it quickly developed—to the warmth of Nina. Nina the gracious, Nina the force of nature. Niiina!

Walter and Ed spoke Russian with Nina. With the organic farmers they talked potatoes.

One tries not to generalize, but Alaskans do love their gardens. And potatoes—white, russet, Yukon Gold (developed in Canada but big in Alaska)—are the universal crop. Ed mentioned harvesting his own spud plot soon, and the dedicated young gardeners, Charlotte Deerborn-Crampton and Charles Crampton-Deerborn, were keenly interested in the brothers' near-century of local potato wisdom.

Walter for his part was eying the composting trench on the small farm, filled with glistening red-orange salmon scraps. "I'm curious as to where they got all that, this time of the year," he said the next day. "There is a spot—I had to figure it out this morning—there's a spot, an area in Homer, where you can clean your fish, and then there's a big disposable container where you throw all your garbage in. It's very possible that that could be the only place where he could have gotten it. Everybody that fishes at the Fishing Hole, whatever salmon they catch, they go in and clean it at those tables, and all the scraps go in there. . . .

"I cleaned this one [the one he had cooked a couple of steaks from that morning and offered for breakfast when I arrived] right here. I'd rather clean mine here. I've got a table out back. . . . And then the scraps go to the garbage dump at Deep Creek. You have to seal them in plastic bags and take them there. I don't want the birds or animals to get to them around here, because then they are a nuisance. So I collect all of that stuff and take it down and throw it in there. There's a sign when you're driving to the garbage area that says, 'Toot your horn.' There could be bear around, you know. . . .

"That's why you see moose around here. Those that have calves will hang around an area like this, for protection. They know the bears won't bother them much."

So does he still hunt moose?

"No. There's no need. I wouldn't mind, but there's so much regular meat here—meat from the store. And we don't even eat that much meat anymore."

I'm guessing that not all the salmon "scraps" go to Deep Creek to tantalize the bears, because on another day I was offered fishhead chowder for lunch. Noticing that Walter had brought the soup pot in from the sunlit porch, not the refrigerator, I was cautious. At about age 12 I saw my mother carried off on a stretcher to the chartered plane that would transport her to Seward Hospital with severe food poisoning.

"Nothing to worry about," Walter said. "It's fresh. I made it just last night."

I christened it the Soup of Death but in a devil-may-care mood spooned some up anyway. Granted, Walter had apparently already supped on "the choice parts," but I must say it was delicious. And I'm here to tell the tale.

Shortly after I left Alaska Walter got his Yukon Golds dug as planned but intentionally left the cabbage in the ground for the time being. "It keeps good under a layer of snow," he said in a phone conversation in October. Nature's own root cellar. In the next call: "The doggone moose got my cabbage! Cabbage and the rest of the carrots. Must've smelled 'em, I guess, and they just dug 'em up and ate 'em right there in the snow."

In my high school years on the western Kenai Peninsula I used a simple mnemonic to keep track of the volcanoes across the Inlet, probably not my invention although I thought it was. A I R S. From south to north, Augustine, Iliamna, Redoubt, Spur. At that time we lived just outside Kenai, where Redoubt is most prominent. But on the two-week commute between Homer and

The river meets the sea: Ninilchik village and the mouth of the Ninilchik River, 2003. Photos by J.R.B. Pels.

Ninilchik I came under the spell of Iliamna. Over my left shoulder on the way up, over the right on the way back. I was mesmerized. (Thank goodness the peak of summer traffic was past.) How many times did I give in, glancing at my watch but still pulling over and reaching for my camera to line up some landmark, or on one magical morning the pale daytime full moon, with that looming, luminous presence over the water.

Just try to get a picture of the impressive new Ninilchik High School with Iliamna showing. I did. Try, I mean. Several times I swung impulsively into the parking area across the highway, got out of the car, and backed slowly up the gravel driveway on foot, determined to capture not only Iliamna—"only" Iliamna!—behind the school, but the Alaska and U.S. flags stretched wide in the wind out front. On another couple of occasions I hiked through Ninilchik village to the mouth of the river—strictly obeying the "No Vehicles" sign although Walter scoffed when I told him—because it seemed that Iliamna was pronounced enough in that hour's light to be more than a ghostly silhouette in the camera's eye. Two weeks of Iliamna are not enough. I thought of the generations that have grown up with that vista as their birthright. Consciously or not, it certainly must help shape a person.

"Scoffed" is perhaps overstating Walter's reaction. "That doesn't mean you," he said, in what seems to be one of his personal credos.

The word tenacious occurred to me on first meeting Walter, in comparing him with my late stepfather. These several months later I'm certain that tenacious—strong-minded, strong-willed, persistent, and thank you, *Synonym Finder*—is indeed a good word for both men, as evidenced by their accomplishments, far beyond what their first years might have indicated or the outside world would expect. Sometimes being tenacious also means appearing self-absorbed. (There's a polite Norwegian daughter speaking. Sometimes it means *being* self-absorbed.) But my conversations with Walter have been anything but one-sided. Thanks to his innate curiosity and what seems to be genuine interest in others, we too often wandered off the track of his story, and the transcribers have had to muddle through those digressions as best they could: "Two people talking, can't make it out." "Long discussion here of candy." "Trading songs—do you want this?" He is unfailingly courtly in manner, occasionally a bit flirtatious—and then will come some offhand bit of misogyny in the telling of an anecdote to remind the listener that like Saul of Tarsus and the rest of us mortals, Walter of Ninilchik is still a product of his generation.

We agreed to disagree about party politics, although not before he listened to some oratory from me about how the reasons he is so unhappy with the current administration in Juneau, for which he voted, are magnified a thousandfold in the current administration in Washington, D.C. Now I mostly just bite my tongue/bide my time, and he mostly looks relieved, and we both laugh at the other's forbearance.

On the way back from Nikolaevsk I was invited to come for tea the next week at Ed's homestead, across the highway and in a few miles from Walter's place. Walter assumed he would come along, but I thought I'd like the time with Ed alone, and Walter went fishing instead. I had my recorder along, as had become habit, but I didn't take it out. Later I wished I had persisted with it. My sketchy notes tell a straightforward if spare story, but I wish I had Ed's own words, and his voice.

He was sure I had heard enough about the early days in Ninilchik, although of course I would love to have had his version of some of the stories. So we began farther along the timeline. He enlisted in the Army on Dec. 10, 1941, he said, right after Pearl Harbor, and spent time in the Aleutians—Attu, Adak, Shemya— on a PT boat, a rescue craft. Walter had told me with younger-brother pride about an emergency near Valdez for which Ed, then on military ski patrol, was awarded a hero's medal, and his subsequent duty as a ski instructor, but Ed didn't dwell on either topic. He was in Washington, D.C., he said, when Japan surrendered. From D.C. he traveled to San Antonio, was stationed there for about three months, then on to Camp Baker, Calif., and discharge in Sacramento. He was as eager as Walter to get back to fishing after the war but said he was content now to "let the kids run the fish sites."

*Edward Jackinsky on his homestead north of Ninilchik village, September 2003.
Photos by J.R.B. Pels.*

Ed and his late wife, Wade, were married in 1950 at a Presbyterian church in Fairbanks, with sister Cora and her husband as the only witnesses. After offering that bit of history he went into his bedroom and came out with two photos, one of himself and Wade on their wedding day, one of the two of them some 40 years later at the old Jackinsky fish site cabin. The Alzheimer's that took Wade's life in 2000 was beginning then to manifest itself. It is a beautiful snapshot.

Wade taught school in Ninilchik before and after statehood. She also served as president of the Kenai Peninsula Borough School Board and the Alaska State School Board.

Ed talked with affectionate reserve about his and Wade's six children—daughters Sara, Joann and Mary Sue, sons Timothy, Gary and Benjamin—who among them have produced 12 grandchildren and two great-grands. Grandson Eero Okkonen, daughter Joann's handsome young musician son, was in the kitchen visiting with Ed when I arrived. He and his younger sister Kaija and McKibben's Emily are the only ones I've met of that generation of Jackinskys, but I saw the light in their grandfathers' eyes.

He and Wade enjoyed trips to China and Spain, Ed said, and he had the trip to Russia with Joann and Sara, as well as one to Siberia with a niece, Cheryl Cline.

Ed introduced me to Kostye ("bones," in Russian), his gentle black-and-white husky mix, and told me about his collection of flags from all over the world. Several flew that day from staffs above the porch. My notebook has other jottings: "Bro. George's story from *Agrafena's Children*." "Already Read—[son] Benjamin's bookstore in Kenai." "Redoubt 10,200 feet, Iliamna smaller." "2 days, ±20 miles/day to walk beach to Homer or Kenai—pay attn to tides." Finally, "Ed not much interested in Native org's."

Of that last point I am not certain. Ed had a way of warding off a topic or a question with a wave of his hand and a self-deprecating smile, maybe one dry phrase. Walter also seems ambivalent at times on his participation in the Native community. In any event, it's the next generation, not the Jackinsky patriarchs, who are working to preserve family history, particularly the Alutiiq strand. Ed's daughter Joann and Walter's daughter McKibben are the publishers of *Chainik Keepeet*, the four-seasons series of oral histories gleaned from interviews with Ninilchik elders, including their own fathers. They work under the auspices of the nonprofit Ninilchik Native Descendants, one of several local groups devoted to honoring an uncommon heritage.

McKibben traveled to a conference of Alutiiq elders and young people in Kodiak in 1998 with Ninilchik elder Margaret Steik Rucker (daughter of Julia Crawford Steik, who harbored Walter and Ed and their sisters on many a wintry school day) and 15-year-old Tiffany Stonecipher, from the current Ninilchik generation. Again, I didn't get the text of her stirring speech to that assemblage from McKibben; I happened upon it via the Internet. With her permission it is excerpted here as not only a look at Ninilchik today but an insider's capsule history of the village and a hint of what's to come.

> *Dobrah'eh d'ehn.* Good afternoon from Ninilchik Village. . . .
>
> Being part of this gathering is a big step for us. Ninilchik villagers are a very independent people. This was a vital characteristic built into the foundation of our village.
>
> During the early 1800s employees of the Russian America Company began to reach pension age. Not wanting to return to Russia, desiring to remain in Alaska, they posed an interesting challenge to their employer. And so, over a several year period of time, a plan was put together to develop a pensioner settlement.
>
> First, specific criteria were established to find a location where, along with other things, no other settlement already existed. It took several years to find the perfect spot, but eventually the area that is now Ninilchik was selected.
>
> Secondly, criteria were developed for who could come to this location. They had to be Russian America Company employees of pensioner age who had Native or Creole wives and their children. They were outfitted with enough supplies to get them through the first year.
>
> So you can see how the founding of our village was built on independence from other neighboring communities. . . .
>
> These were hearty, strong, tough, creative, inventive, determined

and independent people. They had to be. To survive gave them no choice. Together, the Russian men and Native women created a village at the mouth of what is now Ninilchik River. The circling of the earth around the sun and the moon around the earth was the clock they set their lives by. There were clams to be dug, fish to be caught, logs to hew into homes, cattle to be fed, chickens to be tended. They planted gardens, picked berries, hunted moose, gathered coal to ward off the biting north winds that blew down the Inlet. The ill were treated, the dead buried, and babies birthed. There was church to attend and school to be taught.

And then others came. From the north and from the south. From Kenai, from Nanwalek.

When Alaska was sold, a whole new wave of people came. Suddenly the language the villagers spoke was no longer acceptable. Confused children found themselves being punished for speaking it when they went to school. Their parents and grandparents, able to look into the future and see the coming changes, no longer allowed it even to be spoken at home. Familiar church holidays were superseded by new holidays. A familiar calendar was replaced by a new one. Boundaries were drawn between homes where boundaries had never existed.

The characteristics that made the villagers who they were became suspect and the cause of ridicule. Being "Native" took on a shameful meaning. Being "Russian" didn't fare so well either.

The strength that had allowed villagers to survive now pulled quietly inside and became a fierce, driving determination to fit—to belong. The brilliant flames of independence burned down to hot coals that fueled a need to measure oneself against imposed values.

Independence, determination, survival took on whole new meanings. Having mastered survival of the natural elements, the villagers were now faced with fitting into a much larger world. The zeal that had allowed them to not only survive, but to thrive, now became a driving force to meet the new challenges. Not only would these proud individuals find a way to blend in, they would excel.

And so it has happened. We've become educators and sat on the state Board of Education. We're active in directing the laws of our state from positions in Alaska's Legislature and a variety of boards and commissions. We're preachers and missionaries. We're interpreters of the English language and foreign languages, opening doors to understanding. We are in the medical profession, tending to the sick. We are lawyers, presenting cases before judges and juries. We are counselors, helping others find smoother paths in their lives. We own businesses. We live on the southern coast of France. We work in South America and Austria. We work in Malaysia and send our children to boarding schools in the Philippines. We ride trains across Russia and openly speak a language once forbidden. We helped build the TransAlaska Pipeline and work in temperatures that dip down to minus 100. We captain ships and we pilot airplanes. We coach award-winning athletes. We are musicians, artists and writers. We are mechanics and fishermen. We have established homes across the United States from Washington to Florida. Our young adults attend colleges and universities and our little children attend preschool. We communicate with e-mail and have satellite dishes in our yards.

And still we are villagers. Connected by an invisible cord. Stumbling across one another at the most unexpected times. Building stronger ties with each meeting.

During the Vietnam war, David Cooper Jr., son of David Cooper Sr. and Wanda McClellan, was on a ship that stopped at a tiny island in the middle of the Pacific Ocean. While in port, he went down the lists of names of others on the island, hungry to see a familiar name in this foreign environment. He could hardly believe his eyes when he saw Duffy Jackinsky's name jump out at him. Duffy is the son of Walter Jackinsky and Marie von Scheele. Suddenly the world wasn't nearly so big or so frightening for either David or Duffy.

Several years ago, the man my daughter was dating (and is now married to) was telling his parents about this wonderful woman he was seeing—as well he should! He told his parents her family was from Ninilchik. They asked what her family name was and he said, "Jackinsky." His mom and dad looked at each other in a way that caused him to think, "Oh man, what do they know about this family that I don't know?" And then they told him that his brother was also dating a woman whose family was from Ninilchik and whose family name was Jackinsky. As it turned out, they weren't dating the same woman. But the brother was dating my cousin's daughter. Although my daughter and my cousin's daughter had never met, they are not only second cousins, but now also sisters-in-law. And their children are not only first cousins, but also third cousins. Reminds me of the song "I'm My Own Grandpa"!

We villagers have accomplished what we determined deep in our hearts years ago to do. We have proved ourselves independent and strong. We have found our way to blend in and to excel. We have become not only citizens of a small village at the mouth of Ninilchik River, not only Alaskans, not only citizens of the United States, but citizens of the world. . . .

We've met the challenge we laid out for ourselves. But being so focused on blending in has come at a price. And so now, we've accepted an even bigger and more exciting challenge: to reclaim and honor who we are. Not just as children of Ninilchik's founding families, but to follow the thread back as far as we can in order to truly know ourselves. In some ways, this is the hardest challenge. The bruises of changes forced on us only a few years ago are still fresh. Painful memories make us reluctant. But we meet this challenge as we have met others: with roots deeply entwined in a bedrock of determination and strong commitment.

Several years ago, Wayne Leman, son of Nick Leman and Marian Broady, began a project that has helped us in our task. He began researching the history of Ninilchik's founding families. With the help of people literally all over the world, he traced our history back to Agrafena Petrovna, an Afognak woman born approximately 1780, and her Russian husband Efim Rasturguev. Wayne's book, *Agrafena's Children*, lists more than 3,000 descendants.

Wayne used the Russian Orthodox Church records of Alaska— the same ones BIA uses in Alaska to compute everyone's blood quantum for Native ancestry. These records are available to the public both in an English index and in the original Russian and are located in the archive section of the University of Alaska's Anchorage library. The records include more than just vital statistics; they also have information on the church and communities.

Wayne also used the U.S. census records for Alaska in 1900, 1910, and 1920, which are available through the federal records building in Anchorage and are also rentable from various genealogy places around the U.S. He scouted the Internet for people's phone numbers and started calling them. And once the word got out, he started receiving phone calls. People with stories, photos and clippings. People who knew other people. Bits and pieces coming together. There were things people were glad to share and other things they didn't want known.

He constantly worked with the "confidentiality" issue, sensitive to everyone's concerns. At first some people were reluctant to even read his finished product. And then, slowly, more and more people have turned to it for information.

It wasn't long before the first edition was completely sold out. Wayne then started in on the second edition. And it has become an even bigger project, including more history. Births and deaths since the first copy. More stories and pictures. Our copies are well worn, margins written in, sentences highlighted, bookmarks frequently moved from one section to another. Pages photocopied and taped to walls provide a quick and easy reference of "who's who." The combined effort of everyone involved in putting together *Agrafena's Children* was a big step toward discovering and reclaiming who we were, who we are, and who we are becoming. . . .

We are discovering that we are not alone in what we're doing. Each discovery, each piece of information provides more links. Like expanding ripples on a still pool, we see our Ninilchik family spreading out, overlapping with other families in other communities. Our discoveries are also their discoveries. Our journey is their journey.

Being at this Alutiiq gathering is part of our journey. Meeting people with names we've only heard of. Listening to Alutiiq being spoken. Wondering if this was the language Grandmother Agrafena spoke so many years ago. And then Maggie, Tiffany and I taking our experience here back to our village. . . .

Thank you for letting us be a part of your journey. Thank you for being part of ours. Your journey and ours are the same.

Spahseeba. Bahlshoeh spahseeba. Thank you. Thank you very much.

At the September 2003 birthday gathering: Judah and Anna Aley in McKibben Jackinsky's "tree house"; Ron Arnold and Edward Jackinsky in suspender animation.
Photos by J.R.B. Pels.

Ages of the September birthday people gathered at the bonfire outside McKibben's cabin ranged from almost-89—that's
Ed—to just-turned-5—little Judah Aley, who is part of the family
tapestry McKibben describes in her speech at the Kodiak conference. The other birthday folk on hand were Judah's grandmother
Carol Aley and Brian Johansen of the Kenai Johansens, whose
mother was a close friend of Alice Jackinsky and whose grandmother nursed Walter in addition to her own child when Mary
Oskolkoff Jackinsky was ill after Walter's birth.

Helping them celebrate were Carol's husband, Lee Aley, and
Judah's younger sister, Anna; family friends Ron Arnold and Nyla
Simmons; Mike Dryden, an associate of McKibben's from her days
working on the North Slope; writer-photographer Jay Barrett, a
mutual friend of McKibben's and mine; Captain Walter Jackinsky
Jr.; and me. In photos I am the one looking woebegone because I
was about to *be* gone.

Carol and Lee Aley are the couple mentioned in the Kodiak
speech. McKibben's daughter Emily is married to the Aleys' son
Joe, whose brother, Jeff, is Judah and Anna's dad, married to Molly
Davis. On their mother's side the girls are great-granddaughters of
George Jackinsky, which—let's see—makes them great-grand-
nieces of Walter and Ed? So grand-nieces of McKibben.

I would like to have met more of the Jackinsky generations on
my September trip, but the birthday party was a good start. Until
there is another opportunity—perhaps Walter's 88th birthday in
May 2004—I have been getting acquainted via *Agrafena's Children*
and long-distance questions to Walter and others. Here is something of what I have learned:

Walter's oldest daughter, Vonnie Jackinsky, from his marriage
to Marie von Scheele, had eight children, Thomas, Judy, Joseph,
Archie, Jonathan, Teresa, Emery and Nicolas; 16 grandchildren;
and as of the 1993 printing of *Agrafena's Children*, one great-grandson, Walter's first great-great-grandchild. With Risa, Shawn and
McKibben, Walter flew to Santa Cruz, Calif., in 1995 for Vonnie's
memorial gathering and encountered many of them for the first
time. He had met Vonnie's son Tom on the *Bartlett*, and Tom's
younger brother Archie when Archie was working on the Kenai.

Their sister Judy has visited Walter in Ninilchik, most recently in fall 2003 when she stopped by with a friend during a stay in Homer.

A 1987 article from the *Santa Cruz Sentinel*, reproduced in *Agrafena's Children*, tells of a documentary film that Judy Peterson produced at the University of California, Santa Cruz. "Our Aleut History: Alaska Natives in Progress" was part of her senior thesis in community studies. In the article Judy expresses concerns shared by her generation in Ninilchik:

". . . The picture that stays in her mind is of two native Alaskan gatherings she attended.

"When Aleutians [the reporter means Aleuts] staged a gathering in Anchorage, the all-Aleutian band played rock 'n' roll while the men and women dressed 'like they were in Hollywood.'

"'The musicians didn't know how to play traditional music,' she said.

"In contrast, the CircumPolar Conference, which is for Eskimos from the northern Arctic Circle, was a showcase for traditional Eskimo ways.

"The Canadian Eskimos practiced the dying folk art of *katajat*, or throat games, where two people stand close together and sing into each other's throats.

"'A lot of younger people don't want to know about their heritage. They want to make money.

"'Maybe when they get to be my age and their kids start asking them questions, well, maybe my film will be in their archives.'"

Agrafena's Children says Tom Peterson is a songwriter and singer whose song "Wild Birds" was part of the soundtrack for Judy's film. Another song he wrote took a first place award from the Northern California Songwriters Guild one year.

About Vonnie Jackinsky, his mother, Tom wrote in a recent letter, "Mom had eight children and was a ceramic doll maker—originals. She sculpted the dolls and made casts and fired them in kilns and made sawdust-filled bodies and beautiful clothing and adorned them with human hair. Hand-crafted the entire doll and painted the faces with subtle beauty and grace. She and her creations were featured in the *San Jose* [Calif.] *Mercury* along with recognition from the mayor. She also painted and played guitar and piano and accordion and sang. She had a good sense of humor and loved people."

Tom has been a teacher, like his mother's mother. In the same letter he remembered Marie von Scheele thus: "My grandma was a schoolteacher in Afognak, Alaska, and loved to garden and cook. She always had a smile on her face, and she spoke seven languages. Sang me to sleep with German lullabies. . . . I lived with Nana and Grandpa Scotty a lot when I was young. (Grandpa Scotty actually fished salmon with Grandpa Walter in Bristol Bay when they were both in their 20s.) . . . I crawled into the attic and found bags of old letters and lessons. I was amazed to read Nana's papers on Mesopotamia, Sumeria and the ancient Near East. They were very erudite for a teenage girl in Alaska, and I wondered where she could possibly have gained such knowledge. . . ."

Duffy (Adolph Wallace) Jackinsky, Walter and Marie von Scheele's son, lives in Anchorage. He served as a radioman in the field in Vietnam and according to his nephew has also worked as a police officer in New York City. The two of them, Duffy and nephew Tom, fished commercially in Bristol Bay for some years on the *Jay D*, a 32-foot salmon gillnetter. Duffy is a "fun-loving, happy, outgoing guy," Tom says. "Mom really loved her little brother." A poem Duffy wrote that appeared in the *Pacific Northwest Fisherman* is quoted in *Agrafena's Children.*

McKibben Autumn Diane (Russian name Tatiana) Jackinsky, daughter of Walter and Alice McKibben Jackinsky, is currently a staff reporter and photographer for the *Homer Tribune* and a free-lancer for any number of other publications. She has worked in sub-zero weather on Alaska's North Slope and in 120-plus temperatures at Lake Havasu City, Arizona, and writes of "the fierce beauty of both places, the arctic desert and the southwest desert." In early 2004 she completed a Coast Guard class in seamanship (proud Walter reports an exemplary final exam grade of 93), and she has applied to the Coast Guard Auxiliary. "I want to spend more time on the water," says this daughter of Ninilchik.

McKibben's Emily and family—husband Joe Aley and children Colby, 7, and Sophia, 2—have recently moved from the Kenai

Peninsula to Portland, Ore., where Emily is employed as an insurance adjuster. Before the move she worked for a time on the Prudhoe Bay oilfield. Emily's older sister, Jennifer, author of *The Inappropriate Baby Book*, now in third printing, will graduate from the California School of Professional Psychology in June 2004 with a Ph.D. in clinical psychology. Walter and McKibben have already planned their trip to Los Angeles, where Jennifer lives with her husband, Craig Stinson.

Artist Risa Ann (Russian name Raisa) Jackinsky, Walter and Alice's younger daughter, is living near Kellogg, Idaho, in a forested area she chose because it seemed to her the nearest to Alaskan surroundings she could get and still make a living from her work as a lifestyle wellness coach. Besides her bachelor of science degree in exercise and wellness, she is certified in almost as many different categories as her mariner father—therapeutic massage and Reiki and reflexology among them. An injury has kept her out of recent marathons, but she is getting back to hiking and says she is enjoying what feels like a respite for mulling her next professional and personal moves.

Walter and Alice's son, Shawn, and his wife Naomi live in Anchorage but maintain their house on the homestead as well. By his father's description, Shawn is a computer whiz. He works with medical computers at the Alaska Native Medical Center, sometimes monitoring activity in the operating room. Naomi and Shawn have a combined family of five sons—Jason, two Joshuas, Ryan and Shawn Jr.—and a daughter, Mercy Autumn. Plus, as of January 2004, four grandchildren, Sam, Simon, Sarah and Zion.

Shawn is passionate about the work of the Alaska Native Tribal Health Consortium, which along with the Southcentral Foundation owns and manages the Alaska Native Medical Center in Anchorage but also does outreach in rural communities. In 2003 ANMC was awarded Magnet Status for Nursing Excellence from the nation's largest nurses group, the first tribal facility and the first in Alaska to earn that honor, and only the 71st nationwide.

Jackie Pearl, the sister Walter still calls Margaret, is now widowed and living in Reno. "I guess I too am a homesick Alaskan," she wrote recently. "There is something about Alaska that keeps

From left, Edward, Shawn and Walter Jackinsky. Jackinsky family photo.

*Family dancers at the double 80th birthday celebration in Ninilchik village:
From left, Margaret (Jackie) Pearl and nephew Gary Jackinsky; Walter Jackinsky
and daughter McKibben. Jackinsky family photo.*

me forever returning! I get up there as often as I can . . . I always bring along a daughter or a grandchild. I even brought a dear friend a few years ago." Jackie's daughter Carroll has two children, David and Wendy, and five grandchildren. Daughter Patty's children are Morgan, Tasha and Patrick.

Jackie Pearl tells a quiet story of family ties: When she and her husband, Al, were ranching in Michigan in the 1980s, Al developed a serious illness that required hospitalization and lengthy therapy. Her brother Walter didn't hesitate, she says. He took six weeks' leave from the *Bartlett* and helped her run the ranch, caring for the stock in harsh midwinter conditions but also driving with her three times a week to the Veterans Administration hospital in Battle Creek, 50 miles away, to visit Al until he was able to come home. Jackie and Al started married life in Fairbanks, where Al taught military science at the University of Alaska and eventually was second in command at Eielsen Air Force Base. He retired as an Air Force brigadier general after a post-World War II assignment in Germany.

In *Looking Both Ways: Heritage and Identity of the Alutiiq People*, McKibben describes an outdoor gathering at Ninilchik for the 80th birthdays of Jackie Jackinsky Pearl and Fedora Kvasnikoff Encelewski. The lifelong friends, bedecked with purple feather boas and silver paper birthday crowns, sat trading stories, younger people at their feet listening closely and laughing with them at the earthier recollections—until, McKibben says, the two women would suddenly be speaking animated Russian, leaving their listeners behind, openmouthed. The highlight of the day was a ceremonial presentation to the guests of honor of a fine king salmon destined for the grill. Jackie and Fedora stood to admire the fish but then exclaimed in unison: "Where's the head?"

Sister Cora and her husband, Don Cook, are another University of Alaska Fairbanks couple. Don has retired as dean of the UAF School of Mineral Engineering. Their sons Galen and Don Jr. are both Alaskans; Don Jr. has two sons, Daniel and Michael. Walter reported recently by long-distance telephone that Cora and Don Sr. were chosen King and Queen Regents for the year 2004 by the Pioneers of Alaska Igloo 4 and Auxiliary 8 (the men's and women's

Clockwise from top left: Siblings Barbara Jaklin Redmond, Cora Jackinsky Cook, George Jackinsky, Clara Linstrang Robinson, Margaret (Jackie) Jackinsky Pearl. Photos courtesy of Ninilchik Native Descendants except Margaret and Cora, Jackinsky family photos.

groups) in Fairbanks. Regents are chosen for their civic-minded-ness each year in communities throughout Alaska; Cora and Don were crowned at the Fairbanks Winter Carnival in March, and their reign extends through the year. Although Cora was somewhat shy about the honor, Walter says, he knows she will be a regal queen.

George Jackinsky served in the Army Air Corps in Europe and Africa during World War II. After he and wife Jeanne settled in Kasilof, he worked for 33 years as a lineman for utilities through-out Alaska and as a commercial fisherman as well. In retirement he has served on the Homer Electric Association board of directors, and Jeanne says they both enjoy their many grandchildren and great-grandchildren. George received a hero's medal from the gov-ernor of Alaska in 1977 after he twice crawled into a crashed and burning airplane to rescue the pilot and co-pilot. And he also is a writer. One of his short stories appears in *Agrafena's Children*.

Barbara Jaklin Redmond is now living in Wasilla. She has three daughters, Judith, Penny and Kim, and two sons, Dennis and Patrick. We exchanged fond grandmother stories on the telephone as she studied a photo of her children's children for naming pur-poses: granddaughters Christine, Kellie, Katrina, Taila, Casey and Andrea; grandsons Brendon, Bradley, Mikie and Jeffrey Scott, who before he entered Harvard Medical School took the name Otter Quaking Aspen in homage to nature and the family's rural roots. And two great-grands, Maverick and Kaylee. Barbara remembers traveling from her foster home as a young teenager to a get-ac-quainted lunch with Walter Jackinsky Sr. in Anchorage, and en-joying subsequent teatimes with Cora Jackinsky Cook, then a young married woman.

Clara Linstrang Robinson of Anchorage, the youngest of Wal-ter's generation, has three daughters, Melody, Winifred and Cindy. Her daughter Janette died shortly after the publication of *Agrafena's Children*. There are six grandchildren, Tiffany, William, Jedidiah, Amy, Marie and Joanie, and eight great-grandchildren. Clara grew up in nearby Homer under the care of her father's sister after her father died, 10 years after Mary Oskolkoff's death when Clara was an infant. But to her sorrow, as she says in *Agrafena's Children*, she knew little about her mother and nothing of her

Ninilchik relatives until she was "well along in life" and somehow had word from siblings Barbara Redmond and George Jackinsky. Now she enjoys acquaintance with various Ninilchik cousins as well ("a cousin under every spruce tree," as Edward Jackinsky joked in welcoming her to the family). Another section of the tapestry in place.

Three weeks after the birthday gathering at McKibben's, two weeks after his 89th birthday, Edward Jackinsky died suddenly on his homestead. His children assembled and made arrangements for his funeral, including a boat-shaped coffin constructed by a Ninilchik craftswoman. He had always insisted he wanted to be "buried in a boat," his brother said. The children lined the coffin with carefully chosen flags from Ed's collection.

To everyone's surprise, since with few exceptions Walter has been known as someone who barely tolerates dogs, he adopted Ed's Kostye, renaming her Tanya in the process. They are boon companions, or were until Walter began to notice possible allergic reactions to his new housemate. Tanya/Kostye is boarding with McKibben for the time being. Perhaps big brother Edward is having the last word.

Edward Jackinsky, Ninilchik

Longtime Ninilchik resident Edward Jackinsky died Wednesday, Oct. 15, 2003, at his home. He was 89.

Funeral services were held at Mr. Jackinsky's home and at the Transfiguration of Our Lord Russian Orthodox Church in Ninilchik on Saturday. Archpriest Simeon Oskolkoff officiated. Mr. Jackinsky was buried in the American Legion Post No. 18 Cemetery next to his wife of 50 years, Wade. His grandchildren were the pallbearers.

Mr. Jackinsky was a descendant of the original settlers of Ninilchik. He was born in Ninilchik on Sept. 28, 1914. As was the cultural custom, he had his right ear pierced when still a babe. He grew up speaking Russian in the home and, when he began school, he learned the English language. He attended school through the eighth grade.

He was involved in fox farming with his family during the 1920s and '30s. He was an avid trapper. He trapped mink on the Ninilchik River until 1965. He hunted yearly until the mid-1970s. At the age of 16, he and his friend John Matson shot their first bear. For years he gold-mined Deep Creek and the beaches of Cook Inlet. He split wood the day he died, a lifetime daily activity for home heat.

A decorated veteran, Mr. Jackinsky won the Soldier's Medal on Feb. 5, 1943, for heroism in World War II for skiing several miles and rescuing two men trapped in a snow cave at a glacier near Valdez. He was in the U.S. Army as an able seaman and hoistman from 1941 to 1945. Some friends from the military became lifelong buddies, many of them settling in the area.

Mr. Jackinsky also was a commercial fisher in Alaska waters. He commercial fished with "batwing sailboats" in Bristol Bay from 1946 to 1949 and operated a commercial set-net site on Kalifonsky Beach from the mid-1940s until his death. He was fond of telling stories of his early years of fishing for Bristol Bay reds and Harriet Point kings. He spent some of his working years traveling to work as an electrician at various canneries around the state.

Mr. Jackinsky built wooden dories that he used to commercial fish on the set-net sites in the Inlet. He wore out many crosscut and chain saws cutting natural roots from spruce trees in which to fashion knees for his boats.

He was the lighthouse keeper in Ninilchik until 1958. He was responsible for keeping the fire burning in the lighthouses on the hill above the village and on the spit across from the village. The lighthouses were to guide freight ships bringing supplies to Ninilchik.

Mr. Jackinsky was a 32nd degree Mason, active in the Methodist Church with his wife, attended the Russian Orthodox Church and was a Ninilchik tribal member and a member of American Legion Post No. 18. He was on the original organizing body for the Ninilchik Native Assocation Inc. (NNAI) and an original shareholder in both NNAI and Cook Inlet Region Inc.

Mr. Jackinsky was preceded in death by his wife, Wade; his brother, Adolph; and his parents, Walter Jackinsky and Mary Oskolkoff.

List of veterans in the adjoining Russian Orthodox and American Legion cemeteries above Ninilchik village. The gravesites of Wade and Edward Jackinsky in the American Legion cemetery overlook the Ninilchik River where it begins its course through the village. May 2004 photos by J.R.B. Pels.

He is survived by his sisters, Margaret, Cora, Barbara and Clara; brothers, Walter and George; his children, Timothy, Gary, Sara, Joann, Benjamin and Mary Sue; 12 grandchildren; and two great-grandchildren.

From the Peninsula Clarion.

This book and I came full circle in May 2004. I arrived at Ninilchik on a bright Saturday evening in time for the advance celebration of Walter's 88th birthday. He and other "spring babies," as the frosting on the communal cake called them, were already gathered around a driftwood bonfire near McKibben's cabin, with sharpened green alder sticks and hotdogs at the ready. Several hours later the sun finally met the snow-covered peaks across the inlet in a band of burnt coral sky that silhouetted Alice's house on our side of the water and drew exclamations from the spring babies and their friends. (One more generalization: Alaskans never seem to become jaded by their surroundings. Count this expatriate among them.) The color lingered till a light rain began to fall and the night turned as dark as May nights ever do at my favorite latitude.

After the other guests left I wanted to put on rain gear and dream by the midnight fire, but my bespoke bed at Kennedy's Lookout B&B a few miles north of the homestead called just a bit more insistently. And so began four full, final book-days.

Walter studied the typescript and made notes, I studied his notes and typed some more, he read again, I typed, until a glance at the clock would tell me that I was as befuddled as any cheechako—greenhorn, in Alaskan—by the light night sky and we were hours past a sensible bedtime. Walter insisted I borrow a watch he had bought on his last trip to Hawaii. Mine had disappeared somewhere on a previous trip, and he thought our tight schedule demanded a dependable timekeeper. "I can wear my Rolex," he said. By then he had read two people's reminiscences about the Rolex and hadn't commented directly. But he said as he watched me buckle the big black band of the Hawaii watch, "I called Alice from Seattle when I bought the Rolex. I was so excited. She wasn't too sure, but I'd always wanted one. I made payments for a year on

McKibben Jackinsky's cabin on the old fox farm property, with Edward Jackinsky's Kostye, far left (J.R.B. Pels photo, May 2004); Kostye on the beach near Deep Creek (photo by McKibben Jackinsky, June 2004).

that watch. I don't remember the name of the shop, but if we were in Seattle I could show you. On Fourth Avenue, around Virginia, I think." He brought out the Rolex and his other prize piece of jewelry, a Masonic ring. He's a 32nd degree Mason, as was his brother Edward—"as high as any of us can go." The only higher degree is earned by doing something "worthy of the lodge," he said. His and Edward's lodge is in Soldotna.

Walter drove twice to the Fishing Hole while I was there, I think just to look longingly at the scene of his summer triumphs. In April he had reported one lone sea lion lazing through the otherwise empty pond. In early May the fish were starting to congregate at the entrance, he said, not quite ready to leave the bay. I said, only half joking, that I should go along to photograph him there, "pretend-fishing," but he recalled that a man who visited the Fishing Hole the previous summer had sent him some photos of himself with a catch. Unfortunately, he, Walter, had immediately sent the pictures on to a friend, but he had the man's address—had, in fact, sent him a couple of cans of salmon as a thank-you—so I boldly phoned. Sam Moore of Sutherlin, Ore., who has written a dramatic story of his own that may soon see publication, was pleased to send extra copies of the photos (see "The Salmon Tsar"). He had been impressed, he said, with Walter's skill over other fishers that day.

The empty Fishing Hole notwithstanding, we did eat succulent "first king salmon of the spring!" during my stay. Erling Kvasnikoff, who lives on the hill above Ninilchik village, netted three fish under his Ninilchik Native Descendants educational fishery permit, issued by Alaska Fish & Game, and shared them in the village tradition. Walter is accustomed to being donor, but this time he was recipient, he and several other elders. McKibben noted that he was honored with "a head half." There was talk of fishhead chowder in addition to our two meals of fillets, but it hadn't happened by the time I left. Erling Kvasnikoff had also dug what Walter believed to be the first razor clams of the season. When the ice was just beginning to break up, Erling crossed the river in his four-wheel-drive truck to dig on the beach and announced afterward that there were two buckets of clams on his porch, available for the taking.

Ninilchik is more famous now than ever for its razor clams, and the inlet no less hazardous. The old village site is bracketed by notices: "STOP," says an imposing Alaska State Parks sign rising from the beach. "CLAM DIGGERS BEWARE! Each clam tide, clam diggers may be stranded when digging clams on the sand bars offshore. Incoming tides flood the area between the beach and the sand bar before the sand bar itself is flooded, stranding unwary diggers. DO NOT get stranded. Watch the tide levels carefully and return before the rapidly rising tides return. Rescue assistance is not always available or possible, and stranded diggers risk hypothermia or drowning in the cold waters of Cook Inlet. STAY ALERT TO TIDE LEVELS. COME IN EARLY AND PLEASE BE SAFE!" And an enterprising notice at a private driveway where the road through the village meets the highway: "CLAMS CLEANED HERE. BUCKETS AND SHOVELS," with two phone numbers for reaching the entrepreneurs.

At last I got to meet McKibben's cousin Joann, Edward Jackinsky's second daughter. The two women are a study in contrasts and a study in teamwork, as witness *Chainik Keepeet*. They are also formidable advocates for Native rights and culture. I enjoyed seeing them relax one evening at the old Jackinsky fish site cabin built by Walter Sr. on the bluff above Kalifonsky Beach, near the present home of Joann and husband Steve Okkonen. Then I realized that even at leisure the cousins were quietly mulling their approach to a current "situation." I would not want to be the perpetrator of the "situation."

Throughout my last day Walter entertained guests. Visitors usually come to the "back door" of his place—actually the north door, as both doors face the inlet. But for two special occasions these two sets of visitors came to the rarely used original cabin door, which somehow seemed more ceremonious.

First were Virgil and Dawn Campbell of *Bartlett* days, who had driven over from Moose Pass not just for the superlative clam-digging promised by a minus spring tide but also for a reunion with the captain. I was delighted to be present but ruing whatever had made me travel without my tape recorder—Walter and both Campbells were full of merriment and ferry tales, most of which were printable. Virgil wondered whether Walter's filleting knife might need sharpening; Walter fetched it from the car, and both looked pleased when his maintenance of the blade met with Virgil's approval. For good measure Walter got out another knife Virgil had given him—"one of the first 20 knives I ever made," Virgil said, which led him to reminisce about a knife a fellow crewman had bought years before, exactly the second one produced in Virgil's knife-making career, and recently gave back to him. Virgil said, "I told him, 'But you *bought* this!' The guy said, 'I only bought it to save you embarrassment. It's the ugliest knife I ever saw.'"

"And you know what?" Virgil said, not at all abashed. "It is!"

Walter's knives are beautiful. The filleting knife has a handle of water buffalo horn, carved with orca heads by Soldotna artist Lyle Johnson. It's housed in a leather sheath made and signed by Dawn Campbell. The handle of the other knife, a fleshing knife, is formed of an *oosik*, or walrus penis bone, and has the look of old ivory. The sheath for the fleshing knife was crafted by Virgil's mother. I'd often wondered about the name of the family business. A traveler on the highway between Moose Pass and Seward can't miss the giant knife pointing heavenward. I.R.B.I., says the sign. Seems Virgil's father, Irvin, and Irvin's brother-in-law, Bill, founded and named the business; the I and R are for Irvin, of course, and the B and I for Bill. Except that Bill soon decided to go back Outside, leaving Irvin with the sign and business cards already printed. According to Virgil, his father decided the initials could as easily stand for I'd Rather Be Independent, so I.R.B.I. it has remained.

On display in Walter's cabin was a photograph of him taken on the beach just north of Ninilchik village, the spot where Virgil and Dawn had filled their clam buckets that day. We all admired it, and the salmon in the photo inspired more fish stories than I could keep track of. Virgil remembered catching a tomcod ("not good eating") with Bugsy Giachino's pole one day. In a move he's sure he could never replicate he rocked the line till it swung into the open porthole of the room below, shared by stewards Ruby Dwyer and Mark Sawyer (later AB). "I called, 'Hey, Mark!' and then I heard the tomcod hit the desk. That was once in a million." Another day, another

Dawn and Virgil Campbell of Moose Pass on a visit to Ninilchik, May 2004. Photo by J.R.B. Pels.

rejected tomcod was stealthily left in the toilet in chief engineer Jim Renfro's room, "and Jim never said a thing. Finally one day I asked him, 'Do you like to fish?' and he said, 'You S.O.B., I knew it was you!'"

The Campbells hosted an end-of-summer-run party at their place one year, Dawn said, for the crews of the *Bartlett* and the *Tustumena*. *Bartlett* cook Homer Herndon prepared pizzas and crab, and it was such a good day that the captain of the *Tustumena* didn't want to leave when it was time to sail from Seward, 30 miles away. According to Dawn, somebody said, "But, Captain—they've already sounded the 10-minute whistle," and the captain sighed, "Oh, darn." Another fine food occasion was a joint effort by Homer Herndon and chief steward John Lam for a Christmas party aboard the *Bartlett* to which the crew of the Coast Guard's *Sweetbriar* had been invited. "Homer and John Lam made everything look so beautiful," Dawn said, "that nobody would touch it. They had to order us to start eating."

(Those spectacular spreads seem to be a Marine Highway System tradition. Soon after meeting the Campbells I made e-mail contact with former head cook Dan Gagnon, who has been with AMHS since 1983 and went to work on the *Bartlett* shortly before Walter retired. He is now chief steward on the *Aurora*, under Captain John Klabo. Dan Gagnon was noted for his gala holiday buffets, and he takes pride in that. But his own principal Walter memory, he said, is of drifting up to the bridge on an exploration of the ship, his first day on the *Bartlett*, and being invited by Captain Jackinsky to steer for a while. "'OK,' I said, and there I was, first time ever on the ship, crossing Prince William Sound and steering the ship right past Bligh Reef, of the *Exxon Valdez* fame. I thought that was sure a moment that few would ever experience!" Walter has a "huge past and heritage," Gagnon said. "It's not hard to come across someone who knows him, even these years later. ... Those were good old sailor days—it's nothing like that out here anymore, for better or for worse.")

Not long after the Campbells set out for home in Moose Pass, Jay Barrett arrived from Kenai for a quick visit and was persuaded to stay for the evening to help greet the Very Rev. Father Simeon Oskolkoff, Walter's cousin, who was traveling with a young couple

From left, the Very Rev. Father Simeon Oskolkoff, Walter Jackinsky, the Rev. Father Daniel Andrejuk, and Matushka *Vera (Andrejuk), May 2004. Photo by J.R.B. Pels.*

from Moscow, the Rev. Father Daniel Andrejuk and his wife, *Matushka* Vera. *Matushka* is the affectionate Russian honorific for the wife of a priest (*Batushka*). Several years before, Walter and Father Simeon had talked about a house-blessing ceremony for the Jackinsky cabin; that much-postponed plan—and the minus tide—had drawn the three down from Anchorage, where Father Daniel is rector for the burgeoning congregation of Saint Tikhon of Moscow Russian Orthodox Mission.

"It's the custom to have cake and *chai*," Walter had said, and he and I made those arrangements early in the day, with fresh strawberries to garnish the cakes and water for the tea fetched from an artesian spring near the grounds of the Kenai Peninsula State Fair, four miles south of the homestead. The old family spring is now part of someone else's property. Walter decided to add apple juice and sparkling cider to the menu, and McKibben arrived after work with a platter of three varieties of smoked salmon from Deep Creek Custom Packing, where Walter has his salmon canned, as well as a tray of cheeses and other savories. Ed's daughter Joann brought the year's first tulips from her father's yard to crown the table. Ed particularly loved his tulips, she said.

Father Simeon stopped by at midday to advise on preparations for the ceremony. Walter had moved his exercise equipment, so the space in that room was ample for the service and the half-dozen observers, but the icons and candles and flowers he had arranged on a table should be on the east side of the cabin, Father Simeon said, not the west. We moved them to an east-facing window ledge and in the process saw in the birches toward the highway a mother moose and two calves. Perhaps even the mother moose and two calves from September; these were not this spring's babies.

Walter dressed for the evening in slacks and long-sleeved white shirt with tie. Throughout, holding the lighted candle Father Simeon had handed him, he looked as earnest as any 7-year-old first communicant.

The two priests donned their liturgical garments and began an unhurried, bilingual service that seemed at once ancient and spontaneous. ("In English?" Father Daniel asked several times, sotto voce, and then followed Father Simeon's lead in either direction with apparent ease.) Father Simeon interrupted himself at the beginning of one Gospel reading and chose the story of the conscience-stricken tax collector Zaccheus instead, which for me harked back to the missionary church I attended with a friend in Kenai when we both were young teenagers. ("Zaccheus was a wee little man, and a wee little man was he," our Sunday School charges would pipe. "He climbed into a sycamore tree, his true Lord for to see. . . .") Joann's brother Gary Jackinsky was given charge of the incense burner on its gleaming chain.

Father Simeon announced that *Matushka* Vera would sing the responses, and her lovely, light soprano was braided with her husband's bass in the old Slavic melodies, to great effect. Add Father Simeon's third harmony on some chants, and the occasional choir formed of Joann's and Walter's voices from opposite corners of the room, and for a music-lover this was close to heaven. One final chant I recognized, from the stories of my own cousins who grew up among Russian Orthodox neighbors on Unga Island: "*Mnogaia leta*" ("No-guy-a-letta"), usually translated as "God grant you many happy years." In this case both a supplication and an acknowledgement.

Even before we moved on to the feast in the kitchen, the two handsome, white-haired cousins were busy with reminiscences, spurred by a photo Father Simeon had brought of the student body of Ninilchik school, circa 1922. In my recently blessed state I resisted absconding with it. Walter said he had the barest memory of Father Paul Shadura coming from Kenai "to bless my mother's house when I was 5 or 6 years old." Around the kitchen table we heard more of Father Simeon's adventurous life and something of the stories of Father Daniel and *Matushka* Vera as well. More books, waiting to be written. The older man and the younger talked of their callings to the priesthood, which however divinely inspired do not necessarily come without sacrifice, it seems. I go to Anchorage airport, Father Daniel said quietly, and watch the planes take off and land, and sometimes I think I will weep. I always wanted to fly. *Mnogaia leta*, Father Daniel.

It was late but of course still light when everyone left, and Walter and I went back to tidying up the pages we'd been working on. Then came a knock at the north door and Walter's favorite musician walked in, apologizing for the 10 p.m. visit. Butch Leman had

In separate frames on a shelf in the old fox farm cabin stand these two likenesses, side by side: Walter Jackinsky, as sketched by his granddaughter Jennifer Long Stinson, and Walter's great-grandson Colby Aley, who here represents his generation of the Jackinsky family.

missed the birthday bonfire because he was playing for the May Day celebration at the Inlet View Lodge (the "I.V.," they call it in Ninilchik), and he missed the house blessing because he and his 15-year-old son had seized the sunny day and taken a long-promised canoe trip down the Kenai River. But here he was, bringing good wishes for Walter and three inscribed copies of his new CD for my sister and other friends. I'd been listening to my copy since the CD first came out. McKibben says that everyone has to be quiet in Walter's car when "Fisherman's Prayer" is playing, and I saw that for myself. It's supposed to be a surprise for Walter that Butch has agreed to our using that song and his Ninilchik verses in the book. We'll see.

Butch was jovial but sunburned and tired from the all-day canoe trip, so I didn't ask him to sing one of his originals from the *North Country Fare* CD, let alone any of the blues or old country-western songs he's also known for. But he gave Walter's guitar a "Russian tuning" and coaxed a minor-key melody from it that was a perfect cap to an extraordinary day. "My Uncle Nick Leman used to play this," he said to Walter as the melody emerged. "Remember?"

Walter announced recently that when this book is ready he's going to have the title and his phone number painted on the side of his car, "and my boy wants to do the same." Recalling his campaign to convince McKibben and me that we should accompany him to Hawaii in January 2004, I feel some empathy for Shawn. Walter: "McKibben thinks it would be a good idea if we went to Hawaii and worked on the book there." Jackie: "Walter says you think it would be a good idea if . . ." McKibben: "He what? I don't even like Hawaii!" Walter, laughing: "OK. But Jackie says we can *celebrate* the book there."

So if you should see *Any Tonnage, Any Ocean* chugging along the Sterling Highway, or parked at the Fishing Hole in Homer, by all means phone the number given and buy a book. Maybe then we'll all go to Hawaii and work on Volume II.

TONY KNOWLES
GOVERNOR

STATE OF ALASKA
OFFICE OF THE GOVERNOR
JUNEAU

P.O. Box 110001
Juneau, Alaska 99811-0001
(907) 465-3500
Fax (907) 465-3532

January 30, 1997

Captain Walter W. Jackinsky
P.O. Box 233
Ninilchik, AK 99639

Dear Captain Jackinsky:

On behalf of the State of Alaska, it is a privilege to extend my deepest appreciation to you at the conclusion of your 34 years of loyal and dedicated service to the Alaska Marine Highway System. Your record of service, performance, and devotion are exemplary.

Beginning with your work on the first crew of the M/V Malaspina, you have dedicated yourself to excellence. Not only have you given extra effort to advance your own education and skill, you have worked to help make our ferry system more efficient. Your dedication and achievements set a high standard and exemplify the Alaska spirit.

In addition to your great work for the State of Alaska, you have been a tremendous asset to the Native community. I admire your work with the Pioneers of Alaska, Veterans of Foreign Wars, Alaska Native Brotherhood, and Sealaska Corporation.

You have a sterling reputation as a professional with high integrity, and you've been a good role model for other employees. I know I join with many in saying you will be missed.

Again, thank you for your years of service, and good luck in the future. May you continue to find rewarding challenges in the years ahead.

Sincerely,

Tony Knowles
Governor

The Captain and Crew
of the
M/V E.L. Bartlett

Cordially Invite You
To A
Community Open House...
and Farewell to its Homeport of Cordova

Monday, September 29, 2003

2:45pm
M/V Bartlett arrival

4:00pm — 8:00pm
Community Open House/Ship's Tour
Cake & Refreshments served

Speeches...Memories...Farewells
Beginning at 5:30pm
Bring your families...your friends...your memories!

EPILOG

THE M/V E.L. BARTLETT MAKES WAVES ON EBAY

"Even when I was there, [the run] between Valdez and Whittier was just getting bigger and bigger and the Bartlett *couldn't handle it anymore. Summertime, when traffic was heavy, lots of tourists, they just couldn't take all that wanted to travel on it.*

"I asked for a bigger ship. I said, 'Why don't you send the LeConte *or Aurora up here, and then we can handle the traffic?' And they said, 'What will we do with the* Bartlett?*' It's made so they were able to use it just on that run and nowhere else. It has a bow that opens up, and you could load on from the bow, but that thing wouldn't fit any of the docks there in Southeast. For a while they thought they could lengthen it. I asked about that. They said, 'It's too late. We'd spend maybe a million dollars or so to lengthen it and she's too old anyhow.' The Coast Guard does inspections every year, and I guess it got to the point where the engineers and the state couldn't keep up with some of the standards that they needed to. The opening doors by then were getting to the point where they weren't safe. . . ."*

October 12, 2003

Longtime Alaskan is ferry's new owner

All Alaskan Seafoods president doesn't know yet what he's going to do with it

By MARY PEMBERTON
The Associated Press

ANCHORAGE — The Bartlett was transferred Friday to its new owner, a longtime Alaskan and Seattle businessman who bought the 34-year-old state ferry in the last 10 minutes of bidding on eBay.

The buyer, who went by the username of Salmon Man 1953 during the online auction that ended Aug. 10, is Lloyd Cannon, the 73-year-old CEO and

president of All Alaskan Seafoods, a company he founded in 1975.

Even though Cannon now lives in Washington, he grew up in Kodiak and fished Alaska waters for decades. He recently sold his home on the island but keeps an eye an all things Alaska, including the online bidding for the Bartlett, he said.

Cannon isn't sure what he will do with the 193-foot ferry now that it's his.

"We already have about five people

with ideas. We just got to figure out if they have any money," he said, laughing.

Money and government regulation are what eventually forced the Bartlett from service in Alaska. Even though the ferry was in good shape for her age, new regulations made her obsolete for passenger service, said Phil Grasser, marine engineering manager for the Alaska Marine Highway System. . . .

It would have cost between $5 million and $6 million to outfit the ferry to satisfy new federal safety regulations that took effect Oct. 1. Those requirements included providing evacuation chutes similar to those on airplanes and with motorized rescue boats.

"Hers were operated with oars," Grasser said.

The Bartlett is a good boat, and he got it for the right price, Cannon said. He paid $389,500. The ferry cost $3.25 million new in 1969.

Faced with a limited market to unload the ship, state property managers turned to eBay to find a buyer, figuring the Internet auction site would provide worldwide visibility and they would get more money for the ferry. The bidding began at $100,000, and at least two dozen bids were posted.

Cannon sent one of his representatives, Rollin "Tiny" Crump, to Cordova to take ownership of the 1,500-ton ferry at 8 a.m. Friday. Seven people were helping to bring the Bartlett south, Cannon said.

During the Bartlett's years of service, its primary ports were Valdez, Whittier, Tatitlek and Cordova. The ferry could carry 29 cars and 236 passengers.

Grasser said two new fast ferries, at a combined cost of $68.9 million, are being built at the Derecktor Shipyard in Bridgeport, Conn. The Fairweather, which is expected to operate out of Juneau, is 85 percent complete and due for delivery in January. The Chenega is about 25 percent complete and should be ready for service in Prince William Sound in 2005.

The ferries are 235-foot catamarans with a faster service speed of 35.8 mph. They should last about 30 years, Grasser said.

The marine highway system expects to send the Aurora from Ketchikan next summer to temporarily provide service to the sound.

Cannon said two ideas have risen to the top for the Bartlett. One is for Alaska cruises. The other is to flag it outside the United States and have it provide ferry service for Sakhalin Island in the Russian Far East.

Reprinted with permission of The Associated Press.

Walter's long-time associate Captain Richard Hofstad died on his way to the Alaska Marine Highway System's farewell ceremony for the *Bartlett*. Walter and others didn't learn of his death until several months later. "Dick Hofstad and I were invited to Cordova for the official farewell," he says. "They wanted him and me to come up there. He traveled from Southern California, got as far as Seattle and had to check in to Virginia Mason Hospital with some health problems. That was all any of us heard at the time.

"So neither of us made it. I was kind of tied up. Fishing, I think."

The M/V E.L. Bartlett. *Photo courtesy of the Alaska Marine Highway System.*

APPENDIX

1. Seven Glaciers and a Senator (Chapter 4):

The **M/V** *Malaspina*, commissioned in January 1963, was the first of the "blue canoes," today's sleek, handsome blue-and-white Alaska Marine Highway ferries, all but one named for Alaska glaciers. The *Malaspina* carries 500 passengers and 107 vehicles. Its namesake glacier, which meets the Gulf of Alaska north of Yakutat, was in turn named for the Italian navigator who explored the northwest coast of North America for Spain in 1791. No one seems to know who coined the nickname "blue canoes," but it's still in affectionate use.

The *Taku* (475 passengers, 83 vehicles) and the *Matanuska* (500 passengers, 108 vehicles) joined the *Malaspina* in April and June of 1963. Taku is the name that has persisted for a glacier 15 miles northeast of Juneau. A couple of honorary namings didn't stick: "Schulze Glacier," in 1883, for the president of the Northwest Trading Co., and "Foster Glacier," in 1890, for President William Henry Harrison's treasury secretary. Taku comes from the Tlingit word *T'àkhú*, short for *T'àwákh Gha?akhú* meaning "goose flood," named for the fact that Goose Slough floods when the geese are nesting. The *Matanuska* got its name from a glacier in the Chugach Mountains northeast of Palmer that was christened by Thomas Corwin Mendenhall, superintendent of the U.S. Coast & Geodetic Survey in the early 1890s. Mendenhall has yet another glacier, but not a ferry, named for him. The word Matanuska is of Russian origin.

The *Malaspina*, *Taku* and *Matanuska* all serve Southeast Alaska. The regular route of the *Tustumena* (1964; 210 passengers, 42 vehicles) includes the Kenai Peninsula and Kodiak Island, with summer runs to the Aleutians. Tustumena is the traditional name for a glacier south of Kenai in the Chugach Mountains, from the Dena'ina Athabascan word *Dusdubena* meaning "peninsula lake." (See *A Dena'ina Legacy: The Collected Writings of Peter Kalifornsky*, in Resources.)

The ferry named in honor of Alaska's longtime political figure Senator E.L. Bartlett was built and christened in Indiana in 1969 and towed down the Ohio and Mississippi rivers to New Orleans, where it set out on its own through the Panama Canal and headed north to its home port of Cordova, in Prince William Sound. The *E.L. Bartlett* can carry up to 190 passengers and 41 vehicles. (Bartlett Glacier, north of Moose Pass on the Kenai Peninsula, was named for Capt. Robert A. Bartlett of Newfoundland, noted Arctic navigator and explorer.)

The *LeConte* (1974; 250 passengers, 44 vehicles) visits Petersburg, Skagway and communities between. LeConte Glacier, at the head of LeConte Bay near Petersburg, was named for University of California, Berkeley, geology professor Joseph LeConte, a close associate of naturalist John Muir.

Largest vessel in the fleet is the *Columbia* (1974; 625 passengers, 134 vehicles), which covers the Seattle-Southeast run. Columbia Glacier, southwest of Valdez and a popular camera stop for passengers on the *Bartlett* in Prince William Sound, was named by members of the Harriman expedition in 1899.

The *Aurora* (1977; 250 passengers, 34 vehicles) serves the southern end of the Southeast Panhandle and was named for a glacier northwest of Hoonah in the St. Elias Mountains. (Visitors to Alaska sometimes assume that the aurora borealis, which transforms the night sky with various colors and configurations, is an Alaska phenomenon, but it is common in parts of Canada, Iceland and Scandinavia as well. The aurora australis, the southern version of the "northern lights," is more rarely seen.)

Until the arrival of the first of two "fast ferries" in 2004 [see Epilog], the *Kennicott* (1998; 748 passengers, 120 vehicles) was the newest ship in the Alaska Marine Highway fleet. It is ocean certified and also designed to serve as a command and logistics center in case of natural disaster or oil spill. Kennicott Glacier at the head of McCarthy Creek in the Wrangell Mountains was named for Alaska explorer Robert Kennicott, director of the scientific corps of the 1865 Western Union Telegraph Expedition. The 1906 Kennecott Mines Co., now the Kennecott Copper Corp., is a misspelled Kennicott namesake, which has led to some confusion over the years.

J.B.P.

2. Governors of Alaska during Walter Jackinsky's watch (Chapter 4):

William A. Egan (Democrat, first governor under statehood), 1959-1966; Walter J. Hickel (Republican), 1966-1969; Keith H. Miller (Republican), 1969-1970; William A. Egan (Democrat), 1970-1974; Jay S. Hammond (Republican), 1974-1982; William J. Sheffield (Democrat), 1982-1986; Steve C. Cowper (Democrat), 1986-1990; Walter J. Hickel (Independent), 1990-1994; Tony Knowles (Democrat), 1994-2002. [Frank Murkowski (Republican), 2002-present.]

3. "Cordova Now in Close Touch With Famous Bonanza Mine at Kennicott, a Big Producer of Fabulously Rich Ore" (Chapter 4):

The goal has been reached. 3:30 p.m., Wednesday, March 29, 1911.

At a cost of over twenty million dollars.

The Copper River & Northwestern Railway, from Cordova to Kennecott, 196 miles.

Wednesday afternoon will ever remain a memorable occasion in Alaska. It records an event that will have important significance throughout the United States.

At the time recorded the last rail was driven into place by a copper spike, that marked the completion of track laying on the new railway that runs from the sea port terminus of Cordova to Kennicott, the end of the line as at present projected.

At the interior terminus is located the renowned Bonanza copper mine; 800 feet beyond the big concentrator and ore bins, on the mountain side opposite one of the largest glaciers in the northland, with a beautiful perspective of snow-covered mountain peaks, frozen rivers and timbered valleys, the modest ceremonies were witnessed that record the accomplishment of one of the most gigantic and daring enterprises known to the commercial world.

The day was most propitious. The sun shone brightly and the crisp, invigorating air, with the thermometer registering 38 degrees above zero, had an inspiring effect on the interested spectators. A tense and anxious feeling was evidenced until the last act was performed that declared the practical completion of the building of the railroad to the end of the line. And it was the obliterating of frontierism from a hitherto remote section, bringing rapid communication and making available all the comforts of civilization, in the development of that vast domain tributary to the Copper, Chitina, Nizina and other unnavigable rivers.

All present realized the full import of the advent of steel rails in the awakening of a new empire of hidden wealth that is destined to soon woo thousands of adventurous prospectors and operators, who will produce mineral values in such quantity as will startle the world.

The tide water terminus is at the land-locked town of Cordova, on an inlet of Prince William Sound. Then, as Mr. Swergal describes it, the road effects a sea level passage of one of the coast spurs of the Chugach range at the junction of Eyak Lake and Eyak River, some six miles from Cordova, the only point of easy penetration to the interior from the southern Alaska coast. After leaving this mountain pass the road is laid on a tangent of thirteen miles, passes the old Russian trading post at Alaganik, crossing the rioting delta of the Copper River by means of modern steel bridges at what are known as Flag Point, Round Island and Hot Cake channels.

Fifty miles from Cordova occurred one of the greatest engineering feats of modern times; the second crossing of the main channel of the Copper by the erection of the Miles Glacier cantilever bridge [the "Million Dollar Bridge"], embattled on either side by the mighty Childs and Miles Glaciers, both presenting a defiant wall of ice 300 feet above and 100 feet below the river and three to five miles in length. Here, in summer, thousands of tons of ice fall into the river in single masses almost hourly, accompanied by thundering roars. These masses of ice throw monster waves across the river, leaving the salmon high on the banks to be gathered by prowling bears and passing prospectors and Indians. . . .

By Will Steel, Chitina *[Alaska]* Leader, *March 1911, reproduced in the* Wrangell St. Elias News, *March & April 2003.*

4. The Alaska Legislature honoring Senior Captain Walter Jackinsky, the Alaska Marine Highway System (Chapter 4):

The Alaska Legislature honors Senior Captain Walter Jackinsky for his outstanding and faithful service to the state of Alaska. Captain Jackinsky sailed on the M/V *Malaspina*'s inaugural cruise on May 15, 1963, and has served the Alaska Marine Highway System since that time.

The only AMHS captain of Alaska Native ancestry, Captain Jackinsky was born in Ninilchik on May 19, 1916. He began his sea life as a young boy commercial fishing with traps and nets in Cook Inlet and later in Bristol Bay on an unmotorized sailboat. During World War II he sailed with the U.S. Merchant Marine on liberty ships and tankers until his ship was immobilized by a mine near the end of the war. After receiving an honorable discharge from the U.S. Coast Guard in 1945, he returned to commercial fishing in Alaska until 1963 when the Marine Highway System began.

Starting as an ordinary seaman, he earned the necessary sea time and studied to advance through the ranks from Second Mate to Master—Any Ocean, Any Gross Tonnage. Captain Jackinsky always looked for ways to improve service such as designing a more efficient loading procedure, compiling a handbook for first mates, and researching and recommending the lengthening of the M/V *Malaspina* to increase revenues. His time also includes numerous assists and rescues to vessels in distress.

Captain Jackinsky's record at sea is spotless. Among his colleagues, he is noted with great respect and high esteem. His dedication, hard work and achievements set a high standard and exemplify the Alaskan spirit.

When not at the helm of an Alaska ferry, Captain Jackinsky finds time to contribute to fraternal organizations including the Pioneers of Alaska, Veterans of Foreign Wars, Alaska Native Brotherhood, Sealaska Corporation, Goldbelt Corporation, Masters, Mates and Pilots Association and the Masons. His family includes his wife, Alice; daughter, McKibben; and son, Shawn, all of Ninilchik; and daughter, Risa, of Flagstaff, Arizona.

The Twentieth Alaska Legislature commends Captain Walter Jackinsky for his 34 years of outstanding service and dedication to the Alaska Marine Highway System. His presence will be missed, but the example he set remains for aspiring Alaskan seamen.

[SEAL of the Alaska State Legislature]
s/ Gail Phillips, Speaker of the House
s/ Mike Miller, President of the Senate
s/ Loren D. Leman [Senator], Prime Sponsor
January 29, 1997

Cosponsors: Senators Torgerson, Hoffman, Pearce, Parnell, Lincoln, Duncan, Taylor, Kelly, Donley, Mackie, Green, Sharp. Representatives Phillips, Kubina, Davis, Austerman, Berkowitz, Brice, Croft, Davies, Elton, Hanley, Hudson, James, Joule, Kemplen, Kohring, Kott, Masek, Mulder, Nicholia, Ogan, Porter, Rokeberg, Ryan, Therriault, Vezey, Williams.

5. "Here Comes Cape Horn!" (Chapter 5):

. . . During the first part of this day [Wednesday, Nov. 5, 1834] the wind was light, but after noon it came on fresh, and we furled the royals. We still kept the studding sails out, and the captain said he should go round with them if he could. Just before eight o'clock (then about sundown, in that latitude) the cry of "All hands ahoy!" was sounded down the fore scuttle and the after hatchway, and, hurrying upon deck, we found a large black cloud rolling on toward us from the southwest, and darkening the whole heavens. "Here comes Cape Horn!" said the chief mate, and we had hardly time to haul down and clew up before it was upon us.

In a few minutes a heavier sea was raised than I had ever seen, and as it was directly ahead, the little brig, which was no better than a bathing machine, plunged into it, and all the forward part of her was under water; the sea pouring in through the bow ports and hawseholes and over the knightheads, threatening to wash everything overboard. In the lee scuppers it was up to a man's waist. We sprang aloft and double-reefed the topsails, and furled the other sails, and made all snug.

But this would not do; the brig was laboring and straining against the head sea, and the gale was growing worse and worse. At the same time sleet and hail were driving with all fury against us. We clewed down, and hauled out the reef tackles again, and close-reefed the fore-topsail, and furled the main, and hove her to, on the starboard tack. Here was an end to our fine prospects. We made up our minds to head winds and cold weather; sent down the royal yards, and unrove the gear, but all the rest of the top hamper remained aloft, even to the skysail masts and studding-sail booms.

Throughout the night it stormed violently, rain, hail, snow, and sleet beating upon the vessel, the wind continuing ahead, and the sea running high. At daybreak (about 3 a.m.) the deck was covered with snow. The captain sent up the steward with a glass of grog to each of the watch; and all the time that we were off the Cape, grog was given to the morning watch, and to all hands whenever we reefed topsails. The clouds cleared away at sunrise, and, the wind becoming more fair, we again made sail and stood nearly up to our course. . . .

From Two Years Before the Mast, *by Richard Henry Dana, Jr.*

6. Sign at a Cook Inlet viewpoint on the Sterling Highway near Ninilchik (Chapter 7):

Mt. Iliamna	Mt. Redoubt
Distance: 52 Miles	54 Miles
Eruptions: None	Jan. 66 & Dec. 89
Activity: Freq. Steam	Ash—45,000 ft.
Elevation: 10,016 ft.	10,197

Mt. Augustine (el. 4,025 ft.) lies 83 miles to the south. Mt. Spurr (el. 11,070 ft.) lies 85 miles to the north. Both mountains can be seen on a clear day. All are in the Ring of Fire that encircles the Pacific Ocean and are part of the Alaska Peninsula-Aleutian Range.

Albert Beck's Eagle Project, Troop 357, 1992.

7. Butch Leman's "Russian tuning" (Chapter 7):

(E) G C G B D.

RESOURCES

Books

Agrafena's Children: The Old Families of Ninilchik, Alaska, edited by Wayne Leman, Agrafena Press, Hardin, Montana, 1993.

Alaska A to Z, from the editors of *The Milepost*, Vernon Publications Inc., Bellevue, Wash., 1993.

Alaska Journey 1919-1934: An adventurous young Norwegian's coming-of-age, by Ralph Soberg, Hardscratch Press, Walnut Creek, Calif., 1993.

Alaska's Heroes: A Call to Courage, by Nancy Warren Ferrell. Alaska Northwest Books, Anchorage, Portland. 2002. Nancy Ferrell's book includes an account of George Jackinsky's rescue of two men from a burning airplane.

Alaska's Inside Passage Traveler: See More, Spend Less (by ferry), by Ellen Searby, Windham Bay Press, Occidental, Calif., 2000 (updated annually).

Alaska's Kenai Peninsula: The Road We've Traveled, Kenai Peninsula Historical Society, 2002.

Alaska's Kenai Peninsula Death Records and Cemetery Inscriptions, compiled by Kenai Totem Tracers, 1983 (new edition under way in 2004).

Alaska's No. 1 Guide: The History and Journals of Andrew Berg 1869-1939, by Catherine Cassidy and Gary Titus, Spruce Tree Publishing, Soldotna, Alaska, 2003.

Alaska's Ocean Highways: A Travel Adventure Aboard Northern Ferries, photography by Mark Kelley, text by Sherry Simpson, Epicenter Press, Fairbanks, Seattle, 1995.

Along the Alaska Marine Highway, photography by Alissa Crandall, Greatland Graphics, Anchorage, 1994.

The Associated Press Stylebook for Alaska, compiled and edited by Dean M. Gottehrer, 2nd printing, Epicenter Press, Fairbanks, 1992.

Blue Latitudes, by Tony Horwitz, Henry Holt and Co., New York, 2002. (Chapter 12 opens with a "big weather" trip on the M/V *Tustumena*.)

Captain Farwell's Hansen Handbook (for piloting in the inland waters of the Puget Sound Area, British Columbia, Southeastern Alaska, Southwestern Alaska, Western Alaska), revised and enlarged edition, Lowman & Hanford Co., Seattle, 1951.

Chainik Keepeet: The Teakettle Is Boiling, Volume I, Issues 1-4, Ninilchik Native Descendants' Historical Documentation Project, Ninilchik, Alaska, 2003. (Other historians can empathize with an editorial note in Issue 2: "It was discovered that in addition to '*chainik*' literally meaning 'teakettle,' some Ninilchik villagers used it to refer to certain parts of the male anatomy. Although that discovery originally caused considerable embarrassment among this newsletter's editorial staff, we have since been the subject of some good-natured teasing, proving that this project is doing exactly what was intended: piecing together stories of Ninilchik's history that were unknown by more recent descendants. . . . ")

Cordova, The First 75 Years: A photographic history, by Rose C. Arvidson, Fathom Publishing Co., Cordova, Alaska, 1984.

A Dena'ina Legacy / K'tl'egh'i Sukdi: The Collected Writings of Peter Kalifornsky. Alaska Native Language Center, University of Alaska Fairbanks, 1991.

Derevnia's Daughters: Saga of an Alaskan Village, by Lola Harvey, Sunflower University Press, Manhattan, Kansas, 1991.

Dictionary of Alaskan English, by Russell Tabbert, The Denali Press, Juneau, 1991.

Disappearance: A Map / A Meditation on Death & Loss in the High Latitudes, by Sheila Nickerson, Harcourt Brace & Co., San Diego, New York, 1997.

Discover Alaska First at Cordova: A Guide to the Cordova Area, published by the Cordova Iceworm Festival Committee under the auspices of the Cordova Chamber of Commerce, 1967.

Gágiwádu.àt: Brought Forth to Reconfirm / The Legacy of a Taku River Tlingit Clan, by Elizabeth Nyman and Jeff Leer. Alaska Native Language Center, University of Alaska Fairbanks (joint publication with Yukon Native Language Centre, Whitehorse), 1993.

Highway on the Sea: A Pictorial History of the Alaska Marine Highway System, by Stan Cohen, Pictorial Histories Publishing Co. Inc., Missoula, Montana, 1994.

A Larger History of the Kenai Peninsula, Elsa Pedersen, ed., published by Walt and Elsa Pedersen, Sterling, Alaska, 1983.

Looking Both Ways: Heritage and Identity of the Alutiiq People, Aron L. Crowell, Amy F. Steffian, Gordon L. Pullar, eds., University of Alaska Press, Fairbanks, 2001.

Looking for a Ship, by John McPhee, Farrar Straus Giroux, New York, 1990.

Making History: Alutiiq/Sugpiaq Life on the Alaska Peninsula, by Patricia H. Partnow, University of Alaska Press, Fairbanks, 2001.

Once Upon the Kenai: Stories from the people, compiled by the Kenai Historical Society, Walsworth Publishing Co., Marceline, Mo., 1984.

Science Under Sail: Russia's Great Voyages to America 1728-1867, by Barbara Sweetland Smith, Anchorage Museum of History and Art, Anchorage, 2000.

Seldovia, Alaska: An Historical Portrait of Life in Herring Bay, by Susan Woodward Springer, Blue Willow Inc., Littleton, Colo., 1997.

Two Years Before the Mast, by Richard Henry Dana, Jr., Signet Classic edition, Penguin Putnam Inc., New York, 2000.

United States Coast Guard Navigation Rules / International—Inland, U.S. Department of Transportation, 1982.

United States Coast Pilot 9: Pacific and Arctic Coasts, Alaska, Cape Spencer to Beaufort Sea, Seventh (1964) Edition. U.S. Department of Commerce, Coast and Geodetic Survey.

Who's Who in Alaskan Politics, compiled by Evangeline Atwood and Robert N. De Armond, Binford & Mort, Portland, Ore., 1977.

Periodicals

"Credit due mariners who delivered the goods," by Jack Lessenberry, Toledo Blade, Toledo, Ohio, June 25, 2000. Available at www.usmm.net/creditdue.html

"From Plate to Plaything / Anglers butt heads over the conservation benefits of catch-and-release sport fishing," by Tony Lewis, *Alaska* magazine, Vol. 70, No. 3, April 2004.

"The Insider's Passage," by Matt Villano, Alaska magazine, Vol. 70, No. 6, August 2004.

"Northern Latitude: Cordova," by Les Palmer, Alaska magazine, Vol. 70, No. 6, August 2004.

Miscellaneous

"Recreational Fisheries in the Lower Cook Inlet Management Area 1995-

2000," a report to the Alaska Board of Fisheries, by Nicky Szarzi and Robert Begich, Alaska Department of Fish & Game, Division of Sport Fish, Homer, Alaska, October 2001.

"Salmon Fish Traps in Alaska: An Economic History Perspective," by Steve Colt, 1999. Institute of Social and Economic Research, Anchorage. ISER Working Paper 99.1. Available at http://www.iser.uaa.alaska.edu/publications/fishrep/fishtrap.pdf

Sport Fishing Regulations Summary, Southcentral Alaska, 2003, Alaska Department of Fish & Game, Juneau.

Music

Love Songs of the '20s, Hal Leonard Corporation, Milwaukee, WI, 1995.

North Country Fare (CD), by Butch Leman, Sturdy Music, BMI, 2003. (www.butchleman.com)

Websites

Re Alaska Native Medical Center: www.anmc.org

Re Andrew Gronholdt:
www.ucsd.net/dist_info/Virtual_Museum/pages/andrew_gronholdt.html
www.ankn.uaf.edu/sop/SOPv3i4.html

Re Exxon Valdez:
www.evostc.state.ak.us/facts/details.html

Re the Fleet training airplane: www.eaa231.org/Museum/Fleet/Fleet

Re Liberty ships: www.ssjeremiahobrien.org/links.html

Re Uluru (Ayers Rock) in Australia:
www.traveladdicts.connectfree.co.uk/Australia/Uluru.htm

Re U.S. Merchant Marine:
www.ssjeremiahobrien.org/links.html

www.usmm.net/creditdue.html

www.usmm.org ©1998-2002 U.S. Maritime Service Veterans

Re U.S. Naval Historical Center:
http://www.history.navy.mil/index.html

Re Wrangell Narrows: www.alaskacruise.com

Alaska Journey 1919-1934 / An adventurous young Norwegian's coming-of-age, by Ralph Soberg (three earlier books in one volume: *Captain Hardscratch & Others, Survival on Montague Island, Confessions of an Alaska Bootlegger*). ISBN: 0-9625429-6-2.

Bridging Alaska / From the Big Delta to the Kenai / A personal account of 30 years of pioneer bridge and road construction throughout the 49th state, by Ralph Soberg. ISBN: 0-9625429-2-x.

The Dragline Kid / A gold miner's daughter from Hope, Alaska . . . , by Lisa Augustine. ISBN: 0-9678989-3-5.

Gilbert Said / An oldtimer's tales of the Haida-Tlingit waterways of Alaska, by Marian L. Swain. ISBN: 0-9625429-4-6.

Kachemak Bay Years / An Alaska homesteader's memoir, by Elsa Pedersen. ISBN: 0-9678989-1-9.

Miner, Preacher, Doctor, Teacher / Stories of an odyssey from Ann Arbor, Mich., to Ketchikan, Alaska, to a pioneering medical career in Oakland, Calif., compiled by Lee Sims. ISBN: 0-9625429-9-7.

Umnak: The People Remember / An Aleutian history compiled by Tyler M. Schlung and students of Nikolski School, Umnak Island, Alaska. ISBN: 0-9678989-4-3.

Unga Island Girl [Ruth's Book], by J.R.B. Pels. ISBN: 0-9625429-7-0. [Out of print.]

California:

The Morning Side of Mount Diablo / An illustrated account of the San Francisco Bay Area's historic Morgan Territory Road, by Anne Marshall Homan. ISBN: 0-9678989-2-7.

New England:

Circuses & Sailing Ships / Recollections of a Runaway New England Boy, by Nelson F. Getchell. ISBN: 0-9678989-0-0.

MCML / Mary Cole Mason Lord, 1887-1988 / A sampler of stories from a turn-of-the-century girlhood in Marblehead, Mass., by Martha Mason Lord Getchell. ISBN: 0-9625429-5-4.

For children (in Spanish and English):

Cuando llegabas, nieto mío / La valiente hermana mayor (When you were on your way, grandson / The brave big sister), by J.R.B. Pels. ISBN: 0-9625429-8-9.

ACKNOWLEDGMENTS

This book was hatched and nurtured by good Alaskan happenstance.
Stepping back a couple of years, I'm grateful to Lee Poleske of the Resurrection Bay Historical Society in Seward for offering me the chance to publish Elsa Pedersen's homesteading memoir, and to Peggy Mullen of River City Books in Soldotna for suggesting that I send a copy of the finished work to reviewer McKibben Jackinsky of Ninilchik. "She's the best writer we have," Peggy said, and the bookwoman was right. Aside from McKibben's introducing me to her remarkable father and handing me a title for his story, her tender reminiscences, "Motherland of the Spirit" and "Fishhead Soup," and her eloquent speech to the Alutiiq gathering in Kodiak give this book a depth it would not otherwise have had.

The graceful essays by McKibben's mother, Alice Jackinsky, round out the accounts of life in Ninilchik village in the 1940s and '50s, and I'm grateful to McKibben for lending them.

Thanks also to McKibben and her cousin Joann Jackinsky Okkonen of Ninilchik Native Descendants for permission to use anecdotes and photographs that first appeared in *Chainik Keepeet*, their valuable oral history series. We have the same aim in our work, and I hope to see more of theirs.

Walter Jackinsky's youngest children, son Shawn and daughter Risa, were generous with their recollections, and I'm grateful as well to Walter's oldest grandson, Tom Peterson, who provided glimpses of the von Scheele family that could have come only from a skilled and affectionate observer. Walter's sisters Margaret (Jackie) Pearl and Cora Cook thought this should be "Walter's book," so I didn't pester them further. But I enjoyed telephone conversations with my fellow Jackie and with siblings Barbara Redmond, Clara Robinson and George Jackinsky. Brother Edward Jackinsky figures large in the narrative and is much missed.

Eileen Mullen of beautiful Island Watch B&B on the hillside above Homer has put me up and put up with me a number of times and through a number of projects. As noted, she also initiated an important topic in Walter's story (and cooked and shared the bounty of fresh-caught salmon he sent with me from Ninilchik for two weeks in September 2003). Eileen and Peggy Mullen are members of a longtime Kenai Peninsula homesteading family of the "hardy and harmonious" sort described by Alice Jackinsky.

In May 2004 I had only a few follow-up days to spend working with the captain and decided I should board somewhere close by. The Ninilchik Chamber of Commerce website lists nearly a dozen lodging possibilities, all appealing in one way or another, so it surely was serendipitous that I chose Kennedy's Lookout B&B. Not only are Katie Kennedy and Don Erwin fine hosts, warm and witty, and their Cook Inlet aerie a haven, but Katie put me in touch with AB Virgil Campbell, who put me in touch with Bosun Tom Faulkner and Captain John Klabo and AB Larry Edwards, who put me in touch with Cordova terminal agent Toni Bocci. Thanks to all for their salty tales and to Virgil and Larry and Toni for the use of their photos. Special thanks to family archivist Dawn Campbell.

The work of Barbara Sweetland Smith ("A Mixed Bequest"), Tim Troll ("Work Boats First and Foremost"), Jack Lessenberry ("They Have Delivered the Goods") and Joe Upton ("You'd Better Pull Over and Let Us By") provides context and color for various facets of Walter's life, and all four writers were gracious and encouraging, as was author-publisher Stan Cohen (*Highways on the Sea*). Thanks to Larry Campbell and Norman Goldstein of the Associated Press for permission to include Mary Pemberton's story on the sale of the M/V *E.L. Bartlett*.

I'm doubly grateful to photographer Alissa Crandall, for the use of one of the images from her book, *Along the Alaska Marine Highway*, and for urging me to call her friend Cathy Hart, manager of the Anchorage office of the Alaska Marine Highway System. Cathy in turn introduced me by e-mail to Walter's old friend Fred Lange, who lives now in Cordova and sent books on the area along with his vivid memories of the winter he spent on the Jackinsky fox ranch. Fred and Mae Lange will celebrate their 57th wedding anniversary in August 2004, when this book is due.

The volunteer members of Project Liberty Ship are among the most committed people I've encountered. Thanks to archivist William Hultgren in particular for sending information on the SS *Henry L. Abbott*. We also, through sheer good luck in both cases, have Buddy Ferguson's striking aerial photograph of the M/V *Malaspina* and Earl Simonds' winter 1949 view of Ninilchik village, kindly lent by his daughter-in-law Sue Simonds. Sam Moore sent his photos of Walter at the Fishing Hole and shared the first chapter of his own Alaska adventure. Thanks as well to Norwegians Arve Saastad and Sylvia Strand for translations and to pilot Brad Poling for research.

AMHS' Cathy Brown, Michael Frawley, Sharon Gaiptman and Michael Wilson have also been helpful. M/V *Columbia* Captain Karl Schoeppe and Chief Purser Jim Beedle searched their ship for an historic painting we had heard might be aboard. Frances Mallory of the Cordova Historical Museum answered questions about the Million Dollar Bridge and put me in touch with Dan Gagnon, former head cook on the *Bartlett* and now chief steward on the *Aurora*. Dan has a keen interest in "real people's history," and he and Captain Klabo have been of great help with photo captions. Robert Begich and Nicky Szarzi in the Homer office of Alaska Fish & Game patiently answered questions, and Kay Shelton of the Alaska State Library in Juneau is forever helpful and efficient. It's been said, but I'll say it again: All our books are love letters to librarians. Terri Leman, herself a busy woman, fielded questions for songwriter-fisherman Butch Leman as the hectic Cook Inlet charter season was opening. Two friends from Kenai Territorial School days, Lisa Augustine and Edward Segura, aided in research, and so did Mary Ford, Elsie Seaman and Peggy Petersen Arness of the Kenai Historical Society. Peggy was my first-grade teacher, and I am still learning from her. Former Forest Service interpreter Diane Olthuis of the Kenai Peninsula Historical Society sent *Bartlett* reminiscences and photographs, and Lola Harvey, author of *Derevnia's Daughters*, searched out and sent information regarding the von Scheele family.

Werner Pels greatly eased the photo selection process by offering to scan all the possibilities for pondering. But before that he presented me with the laptop computer that enabled the erstwhile editor to run away for a month and *write*. I'd been resisting both the technology and the discipline. I'm grateful to him and to my fellow runaways, reading/writing women Barbara White and Suzanne Poling, for tolerating my mood swings and feeding me. Betsy Lombard's long-distance writing collective is the very model of discipline.

The production crew for this book is listed on the colophon page but deserves recognition in larger type. Transcribers Peggy McIntyre, Christina Daniels and especially Ted Holmes were as equal as anyone could be to the primitive audiotapes they had to work with. The project might have ended there. Andrea Avni and Bart Arenson, also known as A-to-Z WordWright, are top-notch indexers, devoted to their craft and to all good causes. Sharp-eyed Dorothy Dorsett is the best-natured proof-reader I know. Librarian Rose Schreier Welton, author and publisher of a stirring World War II collection, *We Clear the Way: A tribute to my uncle, Staff Sgt. John L. Schreir, and the 319th Engineer Combat Battalion, 94th Infantry Division, U.S. Army*, first befriended Hardscratch Press almost a decade ago. Thank you, Rose, in memory of the original Ruth.

That our books have been well received over the years is a direct reflection of the work of artist David Johnson, who has designed and produced every one. That our friendship has survived all those deadlines is a direct reflection of his fortitude. (Thanks to Rebekah for the therapeutic checkers games.) The good notices also speak to the standards of typesetters Dickie Magidoff and Scott Perry of Archetype Typography and of our printer, Inkworks Press. Walter Jackinsky is no more proud of his membership in the International Organization of Masters, Mates and Pilots than I am of mine in the Newspaper Guild (CWA). The Graphic Communications International Union (GCIU) logo in Hardscratch Press books is important to everyone.

Two Newspaper Guild colleagues read an early version of *Any Tonnage, Any Ocean* and not only told me where it fell short, which is what I hoped for, but encouraged me to keep at it, which is what I needed. After many a midnight deadline together at the *San Francisco Chronicle* I knew them both as discerning editors, and "Wiper John" Jordan's early tour of duty in the Merchant Marine was a bonus. Gerry Fregoso, a beacon to all who know her, has saved more than one reporter's reputation with her perspicacity.

And then there's the honorary commodore himself. Telling Walter's story was my idea, not his, but after an initial pause to consider the notion his enthusiasm has not flagged, and he has graciously entertained all sorts of questions, some for a second or third or fourth time. He hasn't always *answered* the questions (sorry, Gerry and John), but his dissembling usually comes in the form of some new anecdote that's sufficiently distracting.

"Any tonnage, any ocean" refers of course to Captain Walter Jackinsky's unlimited master mariner's license. Even more it signifies his no-limits approach to life. In attitude, in energy, in character he does remind me of my late stepfather, Ralph Soberg, and of my father, Jack Benson, as well. That's a tribute to all three resolute Alaskans.

—J.B.P.

INDEX

Any Tonnage, Any Ocean
Conversations with a Resolute Alaskan

Project coordinator and editor: Jackie Pels
Book design and production: David R. Johnson

CIP data by Rose Schreier Welton, MLS
Copy editors: Geraldine Fregoso and John Jordan
Index by A-to-Z WordWright, Seattle, Wash.
Proofreader: Dorothy M.L.B. Dorsett
Transcribers: Ted Holmes, Christina Daniels, Peggy McIntyre
Kenai Peninsula map by David R. Johnson

Composition by Archetype Typography, Berkeley, Calif.
Printed and bound at Inkworks Press, Berkeley, Calif. 147 INKWORKS
Alkaline pH recycled paper ☻ (Solutions by Domtar)

If I Had A Talking Picture Of You
from Sunny Side Up

Hardscratch Press
2358 Banbury Place
Walnut Creek, CA 94598-2347
Phone/fax 925/935-3422

[HARDSCRATCH]

www.hardscratchpress.com